GLOBAL SECURITY WATCH

THE CAUCASUS STATES

GLOBAL SECURITY WATCH

THE CAUCASUS STATES

Houman A. Sadri

 PRAEGER

AN IMPRINT OF ABC-CLIO, LLC
Santa Barbara, California • Denver, Colorado • Oxford, England

Library of Congress Cataloging-in-Publication Data

Sadri, Houman A.
  Global security watch—the Caucasus states / Houman A. Sadri.
    p. cm. — (Global security watch)
  Includes bibliographical references and index.
    ISBN: 978–0–313–37980–2 (hard copy : alk. paper) — ISBN: 978–0–313–37981–9 (ebook)
  1. National security—Azerbaijan. 2. National security—Armenia (Republic) 3. National security—
Georgia (Republic) 4. Security, International—Caucasus, South. 5. Azerbaijan—Foreign relations.
6. Armenia (Republic)—Foreign relations. 7. Georgia (Republic)—Foreign relations. 8. Presidents—
Azerbaijan—Biography. 9. Presidents—Armenia (Republic)—Biography. 10. Presidents—Georgia
(Republic)—Biography. I. Title. II. Title: Caucasus states.
  UA853.A97S23   2010
  355′.0330475—dc22   2009053359

ISBN: 978–0–313–37980–2
EISBN: 978–0–313–37981–9

14 13 12 11 10   1 2 3 4 5

This book is also available on the World Wide Web as an eBook.
Visit www.abc-clio.com for details.

Praeger
An Imprint of ABC-CLIO, LLC

ABC-CLIO, LLC
130 Cremona Drive, P.O. Box 1911
Santa Barbara, California 93116-1911

This book is printed on acid-free paper (∞)

Manufactured in the United States of America

This research book is first and foremost dedicated to all my students, whose stimulating questions and quality discussion about the Caucasus region during our seminars was my main motivation to complete this project. Also, I would like to dedicate this work to the hardworking, kind, and devoted people whom I met during my visits to the Caucasus region. I wish them all the best during the current challenging transition era to hopefully better days. They all deserve a free, secure, and prosperous life.

Contents

Preface

In August 2008, the Russian invasion of Georgia shocked the world and captured the headlines for days. Watching the CNN videos, people witnessed the tragedy of war in yet another region. Soon, "the Caucasus," "the Caucasus States," and "Georgia" became household terms. People were caught by surprise, since their attention was originally focused on the Beijing Olympic Games and the swimming phenomenon Michael Phelps. Some criticized President George Bush for not leaving the games immediately to focus on the unfolding crisis, as Prime Minster Vladimir Putin did soon after the invasion began.

The crisis was certainly significant for the region and the globe. Nearly 20 years after establishment, it was the first time that the new Russia had invaded a sovereign state. For those who remembered the earlier days, it was a reminder of the Soviet invasion of Afghanistan in 1979. Still, there were others who even recalled the Soviet invasions of Hungry in 1956 and Czechoslovakia in 1968.

What does the Georgian invasion imply about the new Russia? Is there a difference between the new Russian and the old Soviet policies? Why must Georgia suffer while protecting its territorial integrity? What does the invasion mean for other Caucasus States and former Soviet republics? How would it affect the growth of democracy and Western-style development among the Newly Independent States (NIS)? How would this invasion impact the new trans-Caucasus pipelines that bring fossil fuel to Turkey and Western Europe? Was the invasion the sign of a new Cold War?

The last question is especially important for scholars, policymakers, and even ordinary people. At the end of the Bush administration, the neoconservatives were particularly concerned about the implication of such blunt Russian actions and the inability of the United States to make a difference despite supplying

Tbilisi with equipments, military advisers, and finance. The final Russian-Georgian cease-fire agreement was also a European solution, not an American one. Thus, the American role in the region was seriously challenged and discredited. Is Washington a useful ally for the NIS to deter future Moscow "projection of power"?

Such considerations were confusing for many who were led to believe that the United States was the only superpower, democracy had triumphed over dictatorship, and capitalism had survived the death of socialism. How could such a blunt violation happen in a unipolar world with the United States as the only superpower? There were those who had an explanation for the so-called new Cold War. Their answer came from the "Clash of Civilizations" perspective of Samuel Huntington. The advocates of this view confidently claim that such clashes are rooted in gaps between Moscow and Washington, which in turn are the result of conflicting American and Russian civilizations. One should expect clashes occasionally due to their opposing nature.

The Clash of Civilizations perspective is supposed to explain conflicts at all levels of international interaction, including bilateral, regional, and global. This way, the troubled U.S.-Iran bilateral relations are an example of a clash of civilizations; the long, bloody Arab-Israeli Conflict serves as an example of this view at the regional level; and the tragic 9/11 terrorism is a clash at the global level. Are such assertions accurate? Was the invasion of the (more) democratic Georgia by the (more) authoritarian Russia another example of such a clash? These are some questions that puzzled my students, just as they did experts and ordinary people. Such puzzles were my motivation to look closer at their causes instead of the symptoms. The Caucasus was historically an inspiration for perspectives like the Great Game, the Balance of Powers, and the New Great Game.

This book attempts to explain the following: how do the Caucasus states fit into the international chess game; what are their main sources of threats; how do the Caucasus states interact with each other; and how do they relate to the regional as well as global powers. Moreover, I examine the relevance of the Clash of Civilizations perspective to this vital geographic region that has been the crossroads of many civilizations in history. Nowadays, the Caucasus is even more strategically significant because of the pipelines from the Caspian Sea to Europe via Turkey. The region's vital energy pipelines diversify the fuel imports of Western Europe, which was traditionally dependent on the Middle East and, gradually, on Russia.

The chapters in this book analyze the security environment, sources of threat, and policy options of the Caucasus states in the twenty-first century. I use a comprehensive notion of security, which goes beyond the discussion of military balance and terrorism. The security of Caucasus NIS is not only a function of external threats, international rivalry, and terrorism, but also domestic factors such as ethnic conflict, separatism, demands for democratic initiatives, devastated economies, and internal instability. Therefore, each chapter analyzes the geographic, demographic, historical, political, and economic variables that contribute to security calculations. Chapters 2 to 4 also examine ties between each Caucasus state with neighbors as well as with regional (i.e., Iran and Turkey) and global powers (i.e., the EU, Russia, and the United States).

In this region, Iran and Turkey represent two different models for political development. Since the 1979 Revolution, the Islamic Republic of Iran (IRI) is an example of a theocracy in modern era. On the other hand, Turkey stands as a secular republic since the abolishment of the Ottoman Muslim Empire. How different are the foreign relations as well as policy goals and means of Tehran and Ankara in the Caucasus? Another level of rivalry occurs between the European Union (EU) and the United States on one side and Russia on the other side. How influential has the West been in the Caucasus by providing economic, political, and military aid for two decades? Interestingly enough, the other global players (i.e., China and Japan) are not as involved in this region so far, despite their great appetite for hydrocarbons.

This work could have not been completed if it were not for the support that I received for years. At the University of Virginia, I learned plenty from R. K. Ramazani and Inis Claude Jr., who generously mentored me. I can only return their favors by being an honest scholar in my field and a caring teacher for my students. At the University of Central Florida, I fortunately earned the support of Robert Bledsoe and Roger Handberg (as consecutive Department Chair) who provided me with the means and opportunities to conduct research during extensive trips beyond my teaching and service duties. Also at UCF, I sincerely appreciate the support of Trudi Morales and Madelyn Flammia, who have helped without any expectation.

At the International Studies Association, I am indebted to Tom Volgy and Dana Larsen, who have always given excellent advice and encouragement in securing funds for research trips. Their friendship means a great deal to me. Also at ISA, I thank my colleagues at the Post Communist States in International Relations (PCSIR) section. They have been sources of academic stimulation, knowledge, and experience. I especially appreciate the assistance of: Robert Donaldson, Nader Entessar, Gregory Gleason, Gregory Hall, Reuel Hanks, Dmitri Katsy, Andrei Korobkov, Andrei Melville, and Vidya Nadkarni. Moreover, my field trips would have not been possible without the financial supports of the U.S. State Department, Fulbright Program, IREX, Moscow State Institute of International Relations (MGIMO), and Rotary International, to name a few. These organizations, however, are not responsible for the ideas presented here.

Next, I thank all my students, whose stimulating questions and discussions were a major inspiration for completing this book. I acknowledge the contributions and assistance of Albert Citron, Omar Vera Muniz, Donald Plungis and especially Nathan Burns: without their help this project could have not finished on time. Last but not least, I genuinely thank my wife and family who have created a warm environment that I feel free to travel, conduct research, and write. I could have never accomplished anything without their full support.

H.A.S.

Orlando, FL

September 2009

Abbreviations

AD	Anno Domini
ADR	Azerbaijan Democratic Republic
AIOC	Azerbaijan International Operating Company
AKP	Justice and Development Party (Azerbaijan)
AXC	Azerbaijan Popular Front
BAK	Baku-Achalkalaki-Kars railway
bbl	billion barrels (oil)
BC	Before Christ
bcf	billion cubic feet (natural gas)
bcf/y	billion cubic feet per year (natural gas)
BP	British Petroleum
BTC	Baku-Tbilisi-Ceyhan pipeline
BTE	Baku-Tbilisi-Erzurum pipeline
BTK	Baku-Tbilisi-Kars railway
cf	cubic feet
CIS	Commonwealth of Independent States
CSCE	Conference on Security and Cooperation in Europe
CSTO	Collective Security Treaty Organization
EC	European Council
ECHO	European Community Humanitarian Office
ENM	United National Movement (Georgia)
ENP	European Neighborhood Policy
ESDP	European Security and Defense Policy
EU	European Union
EUJUST THEMIS	European Union Rule of Law Mission in Georgia
FDI	Foreign Direct Investment
GDP	Gross Domestic Product
GTEP	Georgia Train and Equip Program

GUAM	Georgia, Ukraine, Azerbaijan, and Moldova
GUUAM	Georgia, Ukraine, Uzbekistan, Azerbaijan, and Moldova
HHK	Armenian Republican Party
HHSh	Armenian Pan-National Movement
HZK	Armenian People's Party
IMF	International Monetary Fund
INF	Intermediate-range Nuclear Forces
IPAP	Individual Partnership Action Plan
IRI	Islamic Republic of Iran
JPKF	Joint Peace Keeping Forces
KGB	Committee for State Security (Soviet Russia)
MAP	Membership Action Plan
MGIMO	Moscow State Institute for International Relations
NATO	North Atlantic Treaty Organization
NGO	Non-Governmental Organization
NIS	Newly Independent States
NKR	Nagorno-Karabakh Republic
OPEC	Organization of Petroleum Exporting Countries
OSCE	Organization for Security and Cooperation in Europe
PCA	Partnership and Cooperation Agreement
PfP	Partnership for Peace
SALT 1	Strategic Arms Limitation Talks 1
SALT 2	Strategic Arms Limitation Talks 2
SOCAR	State Oil Company of the Republic of Azerbaijan
SSR	Soviet Socialist Republic
START 1	Strategic Arms Reduction Treaty 1
START 2	Strategic Arms Reduction Treaty 2
tb/d	thousand barrels per day (oil)
tcf	trillion cubic feet (natural gas)
TDFR	Transcaucasian Democratic Federative Republic
TNC	Trans-National Corporation
TSFSR	Transcaucasian Soviet Federative Socialist Republic
UK	United Kingdom
UN	United Nations
U.S.	United States
USA	United States of America
USSR	Union of Soviet Socialist Republics
WTO	World Trade Organization
WWI	World War I
WWII	World War II
YAP	New Azerbaijan Party
YMP	New Equality Party

CHAPTER 1

Security and the Caucasus States

The South Caucasus region, which is occupied by the Caucasus states of Azerbaijan, Armenia, and Georgia, has historically been central to many significant national, regional, and international security issues, primarily due to its sensitive geopolitical position at the crossroads of regional and global powers. Few other regions in the world straddle as central a geographic position relative to major international security issues. This fact was underscored by the August 2008 war between Russia and Georgia. Georgia is a small Newly Independent State (NIS) that was long under Russian control. Despite Georgia's relative insignificance in size and population, the 2008 war caused great international disturbance.

International attention was focused on the 2008 Olympics when the Georgian military launched a military campaign against the separatist region of South Ossetia. Immediately, Moscow responded to the crisis with overwhelming military force, sending thousands of troops and equipment across the Georgian border, rapidly routing Georgian troops. The weight of the Russian counteroffensive and the duration of the Russian military operations in Georgia caused the West (particularly the United States) to clamor for a halt to the violence. While Washington refrained from direct intervention, it dispatched naval ships to the Black Sea and mobilized humanitarian aid for Georgia.

The crisis produced a chill in American-Russian relations that was, according to some experts, reminiscent of the Cold War era. Since the conclusion of the Cold War, there have been repeated efforts to explain the new balance of global power and the new range of security issues confronting the world. In *The End of History*, Francis Fukuyama's optimistic verdict was that democracy had triumphed and would usher an age of peace. That opinion appears to have fallen short of its inspiring view of the future of security issues. On the opposite side of the scale, among scholars with pessimistic visions of the post–Cold War international system, Samuel Huntington is perhaps the most well-known. He still has a significant number of diverse followers in some academic institutes, policy corners, and even among ordinary people who are devoted fans of his book *The Clash of Civilizations*. In this work, Huntington claimed that the world is divided into major civilizations, mainly along religious lines, and argued that differences between these civilizations would be the main driver of insecurity in the post–Cold War world.[1]

Beyond shedding light on the recent developments of the Caucasus region, this book will also demonstrate that neither Huntington's thesis nor the vision of an emerging New Cold War in the Caucasus fit with the patterns of insecurity in the region. Current regional security issues are far more complicated, providing the hope that a major conflict between great powers (i.e., the United States and Russia) can be avoided, while revealing the hard realities of deep, intractable differences that separate neighboring states and nations. In the South Caucasus, the most salient of these security concerns are the separatist conflicts in Abkhazia and South Ossetia (in Georgia) and the territorial dispute of the Nagorno-Karabakh (between Armenia and Azerbaijan). In order to establish a foundation for understanding such complex security problems, this chapter presents a general overview of the geographic setting, historical evolution, and international political conditions in which contemporary security issues faced by the states of the Caucasus (or, more accurately, the South Caucasus region) are rooted.

After this foundation is laid, the three states of the South Caucasus will be closely examined in separate chapters. The term, "South Caucasus," is used here to more specifically capture the non-Russian Caucasus region, because all territory north of the Caucasus Mountains remains a part of the Russian Federation. Each chapter will present a case study of state security issues, beginning with Azerbaijan, then moving on to Armenia, and finally ending with Georgia. This order has been selected, not based on any ranking of importance or to play favorites, but rather to allow a natural flow from the discussion of one state's security to that of another. For instance, in the chapter on Azerbaijan, the war between Azerbaijan and Armenia over the Nagorno-Karabakh is addressed. Then, it is natural that the following chapter be devoted to Armenia, since that discussion has already begun. And while Armenia could have been treated first, in keeping with an alphabetical order, treating Armenia in the middle of the book allows this work to draw out important implications of the Armenia-Georgia relationship. Next follows the chapter on Georgian security challenges, which leads to the most recent security shake-up in the region, the 2008 Russian-Georgian War. Finally, this work ends with a concluding chapter that highlights the three significant, common sources of security threat to the Caucasus States and provides a summary statement about patterns of relations in the region.

GEOGRAPHY AND SECURITY IN THE SOUTH CAUCASUS

A predominant factor that influences security considerations in the Caucasus is the geography of the region. Despite the technological advances of the twenty-first century, this book demonstrates that geography still remains vital to security of the Caucasus today. There is no doubt that the technological revolution, particularly in transportation and communications, has reduced the importance of geographic distance. Nevertheless, natural barriers, like mountains, are still challenging the mass movement of people and resources. Moreover, even the idea of an increasingly smaller world has a vital spatial component, which is relevant to the increasing number of people sharing critical natural resources. For instance, different kinds of natural resources have historically been vital to the essential interest of both states and empires.[2] The uneven geographic distribution of natural resources around the world, then, means that some regions are more valuable or strategic than others (Maps 1.1 and 1.2).

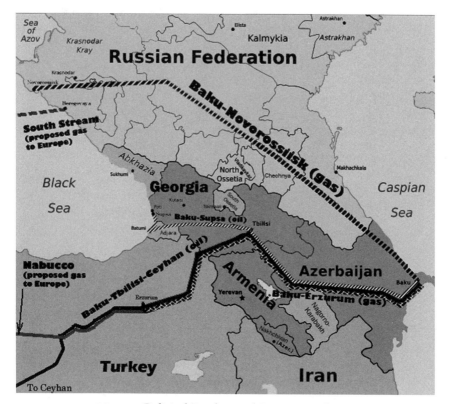

Map 1.1 Political Borders and Energy Pipelines

Note: None of the pipelines illustrated on this map pass through Armenia or the disputed Nagorno-Karabakh region. (Designed by Albert Citron. Used with Permission.)

Today, the means by which states gain access to or control different resources have shifted since the age of imperialism and colonialism. Nowadays, states generally no longer have to conquer territory to gain resources. Instead, they attempt to access resources via the manipulation of political and market forces. In addition, modern states have realized that, in order to derive power from critical resources, it is not necessary to own such resources but only to be able to deny others access to them.[3] Small states, like those in the Caucasus, are particularly vulnerable to this sort of manipulation, as their small territories are less likely to provide them with all natural resources necessary to be self-sufficient economically.[4]

Contemporary energy politics clearly demonstrate this point. Oil and natural gas are vital natural resources that are not evenly distributed around the globe. The scarcity of these resources makes them and the states that claim ownership of them strategic international focal points. This is because oil and natural gas

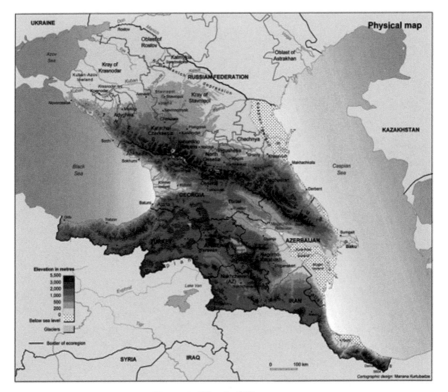

Map 1.2 Physical Features

Modified version of a map designed by Manana Kurtubadze. Used with Permission. (*Source*: UNEP/ GRID-Arendal, The Caucasus ecoregion, topographic map, *UNEP/GRID-Arendal Maps and Graphics Library*, http://maps.grida.no/go/graphic/the-caucasus-ecoregion-topographic-map. Accessed August 29, 2009.)

are essential to the current functioning of modern societies and civilizations. A state's ability to provide the means necessary for the functioning of its society is a measure of its independence. When a state must rely on another state for oil imports, this may produce an economic dependency that could inhibit the free exercise of state power.[5]

Another important feature of geography is its relationship to routes of transportation. Highways, airways, and energy pipelines are all vital transportation routes, which facilitate trade, communication, and the deployment of military forces. The size, number, direction, and geographic distribution of such transportation routes are factors closely related to the ability of a state to deny access to strategic areas of the world. For example, focusing on energy resources, Russia's monopolization of gas pipelines to Eastern and Western Europe endowed Moscow with significant political leverage in relationship to many European states, which are often concerned about the repercussion of any move against Russia.[6] In the Caucasus, Armenia and Georgia are dependent on gas and oil imports. The fact is that there are only a limited number of pipelines and routes on which they can rely. Moreover, there are even fewer neighboring states with such resources that can serve as a reliable trade partner.

Physical Geography in the Caucasus

The central, rugged geography of the Caucasus has had a significant influence on the history of the region. At the crossroads of great empires, the location of the Caucasus between Europe and Asia and near the Middle East along with its mountainous terrain are linked to the "late and weak formation of statehood" and the complex ethnic geography of the region.[7] The Caucasus is generally divided into two subregions—the North Caucasus and the South Caucasus. The Caucasus Mountains stretch across this region, dividing it into these two segments as they run from the Black Sea to the Caspian Sea. These mountains are an impressive geographic feature and a natural boundary. The Caucasus Mountains are actually two parallel mountain ranges that run 685 miles, about 6–9 miles apart, forming a barrier that is on average about 100 miles across.[8]

Because the North Caucasus is a more rugged territory, it maintained its independence from advancing empires for longer period than did the South. There are only two main roadways that pass through the Caucasus Mountains. One is the Ossetian Military Road, which passes through the Mamison Pass, and the other is the Georgian Military Road, which passes through the Daryal Gorge and the Kestovy Pass. The North Caucasus has three geographic subareas: (1) the western subarea from the Elbrus River to the Black Sea, (2) the eastern subarea from the Terek River to the Caspian Sea, (3) and the central subarea high in the mountains. Each of these regions has its own distinct ethnic groups, as

discussed in the following demography section. While the mountains historically protected the diverse local population, they also kept them divided and
fragmented—making it difficult to establish political unity and central rule.
Eventually, the North Caucasus was conquered by the expansionist Russian
Tsars, and it has remained a part of Russia since then. Moscow maintained control of the region despite rebellions, the most recent of which were the bloody
Chechen wars for independence.

Since the last Chechen war, Russia has managed to crush hopes of Chechen
independence. In the South, the security situation is still in greater flux. Separatist conflicts in the South remain unsolved, and the future of the three states of
the South Caucasus is volatile. The states of the South Caucasus are the Republics of Armenia, Azerbaijan, and Georgia. This book focuses on the security of
these three former Soviet states. These states lie below the line of the Caucasus
Mountains and are geographically more open. In particular, Azerbaijan's territory
has large swaths of lowland along the Caspian Sea. Due to their geographic openness, all three states have had various armies and empires sweep across their
territory throughout history. Today, the South Caucasus still remains highly
influenced by the local and distanced greater powers as well as regional powers,
all of which have an interest in the region's energy and other resources.

Regarding regional energy sources, Azerbaijan is the key state, sitting directly
on the shore of the Caspian Sea with access to its rich fossil fuels. According to
the U.S. Energy Information Administration, the Caspian Sea Region is estimated to hold between 17 and 44 billion barrels (bbl) of oil and 232 trillion
cubic feet (TCF) of natural gas. That means it holds oil reserves comparable to
Qatar on the low end and the United States on the high end. Its natural gas
reserves are close to those of Saudi Arabia. Azerbaijan holds between 7 and
12.5 bbl of these oil reserves and around 30 TCF of the Caspian Sea Region's
natural gas.[9]

Demography in the Caucasus

Technological advances have brought the world closer together and promoted
globalization, but the reaction to the globalization revolution has produced
localization and fragmentation, often along ethnic, cultural, and linguistic
lines.[10] Demographic factors have historically played a role in the Caucasus conflicts, and they remain relevant today.[11] Indeed, demographic factors like ethnicity have proven central to the separatist movements in the Caucasus. Though the
South Caucasus is a relatively small geographic region, it has a startlingly heterogeneous demography. The region is a mix of various ethnic and linguistic groups.
Also, there is a split between allegiances to the Muslim and Christian faiths. This
diverse mix of local population is the result of the historic collision of various
empires and the movement of varied national groups in the area. It is also due to

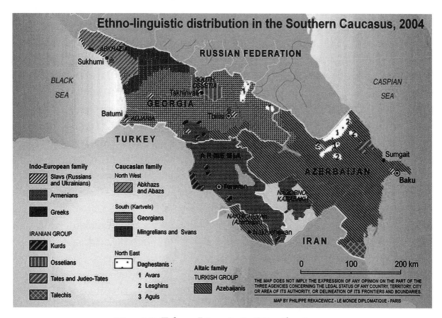

Map 1.3 Ethno-Linguistic Distributions

Modified version of a map designed by Philippe Rekacewicz, Le Monde Diplomatique. Used with Permission. (*Source*: UNEP/GRID-Arendal, Ethno-linguistic distribution in the Southern Caucasus, UNEP/GRID-Arendal Maps and Graphics Library, http://maps.grida.no/go/graphic/ethno_linguistic_distribution _in_the_southern_caucasus. Accessed August 29, 2009.)

the rugged and mountainous geographic features that have kept groups of people isolated from one another for long periods of time.

The North Caucasus is a mix of Russians, Dagestanis, Chechens, Ingushians, Ossetians, Kabaradins, and Balkars. The Ethno-Linguistic Distributions Map 1.3 clearly illustrates the demographic distributions among the South Caucasus states. The most ethnically homogenous of these states is Armenia, where Armenians are 97.9 percent of the population. In this republic, the Kurds (1.3%), Russians (0.5%), and others (0.3%) make up the rest of the population.[12] Azerbaijan has slightly more minorities, as Azeris are 90.6 percent of the population, Dagestanis 2.2 percent, Russians 1.8 percent, Armenians 1.5 percent, and others 3.9 percent.[13] Almost all of the Armenians recorded as living in Azerbaijan, however, reside in Nagorno-Karabakh. Georgia is the most heterogeneous Caucasus state, as Georgians comprise only 83.8 percent of the total population even after the separation of South Ossetia and Abkhazia. The Azeris (6.5%), Armenians (5.7%), Russians (1.5%), and others (2.5%) make up the rest of the population of Georgia.[14]

Historically, the populations of Georgia and Armenia have been predominantly Christian, while Azerbaijan has been mainly Muslim, most of whom are

Shia. These religious differences have become intertwined with ethnic differences in the conflicts of the Caucasus. Nevertheless, it should be emphasized that the demographic differences (e.g. ethnicity and religion) are the necessary conditions for the emergence of conflicts, but they alone are not sufficient conditions to provide an explanation for ethnic, nationalist, or religious clashes. Yet, some research indicates that when one ethnic group is close to gaining majority status in a population, there is a correlated increase in the probability of conflict. At the same time, in societies that are either highly homogeneous or highly heterogeneous, ethnic differences are found to be less correlated with violent conflict.[15]

Once violence has begun, demographic cleavages have also been demonstrated to influence the pattern of conflicts.[16] The borders of separatist conflicts have been defined by the distributions of ethnic groups.[17] All three South Caucasus states have been involved in separatist conflicts since their independence in the early 1990s. And in each instance, separatist groups were defined based on their ethnicity and/or religion.

HISTORY OF CONFLICT IN THE SOUTH CAUCASUS

As explained in the previous section, the geographic location of the South Caucasus has led the region to serve as the crossroads for advancing armies and empires as well as great and regional powers. A review of the shared history of the region also emphasizes the role that both geography and demography have historically played in regional conflicts. Nevertheless, the geography and demography are not the only factors influencing the nature, frequency, and intensity of conflicts in this region. Therefore, we turn to a discussion of trends in regional tensions that are induced by external powers, empires and states, as they have attempted to exert their own will on the region and carry out their political and/or economic interests.

Pre-Soviet History

The discovery of Achaemenid and Sassanid coins, art crafts, and ruins in the Caucasus are all indications of the cultural, economic, and political interactions of the Caucasus people with the ancient Persian empires before the age of Islam. In the mid-seventh century, the first Arab armies reached the Caucasus but found it impossible to hold onto. The Islamic faith that the Arabs brought, however, eventually took root. The South Caucasus was more readily conquered than the mountainous North, and also more completely embraced Islam. In the thirteenth century, Mongol invasions further spread Islam. By the seventeenth century, the entire Caucasus was at least superficially Islamized.[18]

At that time, the primary powers in the region were the Islamic empires of the Turkish Ottomans and Persian Safavids. The Turkic Seljuk Empire had preceded both of these empires, but Mongol invasions had weakened it.[19] This weakness allowed the Ottoman Turks to establish themselves in the Anatolian peninsula. As Seljuk power waned in comparison to Ottoman might, opportunity also became available for the Safavid Empire to establish itself in Persia. The Safavids too were originally a Turkic dynasty, but after making Persia their home, they adopted Persian culture. The Safavids also distinguished themselves from the Ottoman Turks in their adoption of the Shia sect of Islamic faith. This way, there were two Islamic empires, Shia Safavid and Sunni Ottoman.

In the seventeenth century, however, both the Safavid and Ottoman empires began to weaken internally. The Safavid dynasty fell first, leaving a political vacuum in the South Caucasus, which was ultimately filled by the Tsarist Russian Empire. Russian expansion into the Caucasus had begun in the second half of the sixteenth century, following Tsar Ivan IV's capture of the Khanate of Astrakhan in 1556. Various Russian advances and retreats followed from that date forward, including the Persian Campaign of Peter the Great in 1722–1723. A series of repeated wars between Russia and the Persians and Russia and the Turks followed.

The first two Russo-Turkish Wars (1768–1774 and 1787–1792) established Russia in the North Caucasus, preparing it to further push into the South Caucasus.[20] In 1801, Georgia was officially annexed to Russia, and that was followed by annexation of Mingrelia in 1803. This positioned Moscow for the first Russo-Persian War (1804–1813) and the third, overlapping Russo-Persian War (1806–1812). In that time span, Russian Tsars conquered Imeretia and Guria in 1804 and the Khanates of Shirvan, Sheka, Shuragel, and Karabakh in 1805. Then, they captured Ossetia, the Khanates of Kuba, Derbet, and Baku in 1806. Next, Russia controlled Abkhazia in 1810 and the Khanate of Talysh in 1813.

Between wars with the Ottomans and Qajars (of Persia), Moscow consolidated its control of south Dagestan in 1819. When the Second Russo-Persian War took place (1826–1828), it was yet another crippling defeat for the Qajar Dynasty, forcing them to surrender control of eastern Armenia. Under the Treaty of Turkmenchay in 1828, the Qajars also completely surrendered their holdings in the South Caucasus and the Aras River was established as the new border between Russia and Iran. War continued to be the dominant feature of the region thought the rest of the nineteenth century. The Fourth Russo-Turkish War (1828–1829) immediately followed the last Russo-Persian war. Then, in 1834, a local hero, Shamil, was made an imam in Dagestan. He led a stubborn indigenous rebellion against Russians until he was finally forced to surrender in 1859. During that time, the Crimean War was also fought (1853–1856), and a Fifth Russo-Turkish War (1877–1878) occurred again before the nineteenth century ended.

Soon, the Caucasus territories that Russia conquered during these campaigns began a process of steady integration into the rest of the Tsarist Russian Empire—a process that included settlement by Russians and the "Christianization" of the region.[21] Christian Armenians and the Russians established a close relationship in this time that heightened ethnic and religious tensions. Armenians were settled by the Russians in territory inhabited by Azeri populations, leading to conflicts between Christian Armenians and Muslim Azeri Turks. These tensions laid the foundation for territorial conflict that would simmer until bursting forth in the 1990s when Armenia and Azerbaijan formed their own independent states.[22]

Until World War I (WWI), however, Moscow ruled the region with a very heavy hand, preventing ethnic, religious, and territorial disputes from gaining any momentum. When WWI broke out, Russia joined the Allies and prepared for yet another war with the Ottoman Empire, which had allied itself with the Central Powers. During this time, the Armenian people still within the Ottoman Empire suffered ethnic violence for their perception as a potential fifth column for Russia. In 1915, the relocation of Armenians from the borders of the Ottoman Empire resulted in what has been called the Armenian Genocide. In the war, Tsar's forces fared well against the Turks, but internal political turmoil soon began to upset the Russian war effort. In 1917, the Communist Bolshevik Revolution splintered Russia and divided its army, forcing Moscow to officially withdraw from the war in 1918. As the Bolsheviks brought down the Tsar, Russian rule of the Caucasus collapsed. Azerbaijan, Armenia, and Georgia were hastily incorporated into the Transcaucasian Democratic Federative Republic (TDFR), but that institution dissolved in only a matter of months as each nation sought their own independent state.[23]

Soviet History

For a time, the future of the Caucasus was in a great state of flux, with each South Caucasus nation fighting the others and Ottoman forces advancing to claim the region for themselves. As soon as the Bolshevik Communists had consolidated their power, however, they quickly turned to restoring Russia's former empire. In 1920, the Russian Red Army recaptured the South Caucasus, and in 1922, Azerbaijan, Armenia, and Georgia were all reintegrated as the Transcaucasian Soviet Federated Socialist Republic (TSFSR).[24] Eventually, however, the Caucasus was divided based on nationalities.[25] Separate Soviet Republics were created for each of the current South Caucasus states as, like the Tsars, the Soviet Union reengineered borders and demographics in the region. This meant the Azeris, Armenians, and Georgians received some of the political autonomy for which they had longed.

Yet, the Soviets also created a great deal of social turmoil at the same time. After being incorporated into the Soviet Union, Georgia was joined with three different ethno/religious/political entities created by the Soviets: Abkhazia, South Ossetia, and Adjaria. Abkhazians are not Georgian by ethnicity and traditionally were Muslims, as Abkhazia had been Ottoman territory that was only captured by Russia in 1864. South of Abkhazia, another Muslim region, Adjaria, was also incorporated with Georgia as an autonomous region. Despite their Muslim faith,

Adjarians are actually Georgian by ethnicity. The final region to be granted autonomy within the greater Georgian political entity was South Ossetia. Of Persian descent, the Ossetian people intermarried with Georgians, Chechens, Russians, and Circassians. The Ossetians not only intermarried but also settled on both sides of the Caucasus Mountains. In fact, that is why there is a North Ossetia on the Russian side of the Caucasus Mountains today. Ossetians in Georgia were granted an autonomous district within Georgia, while North Ossetia was made an autonomous republic.[26]

In Azerbaijan, the large Armenian population in the Nagorno-Karabakh region was not politically integrated with Armenia, but was granted autonomous status within Azerbaijan. This arrangement left both Azeris and Armenians dissatisfied, as the Armenians wished for total unification and the Azeris viewed the land of Nagorno-Karabakh as Azeri territory. Conversely, in Armenia, Azeris were moved from their homes and relocated to Azerbaijan. Christianization was replaced with Russification, causing additional dislocation, as religion was repressed and the inhabitants of the Caucasus were forced to learn Russian.[27]

When World War II (WWII) erupted in 1939, Turkey stayed out of the war, and did not challenge Russia's grip on the Caucasus. Iran's position during WWII, however, was more complex. Declaring neutrality, Tehran (under the new Pahlavi Dynasty) aimed to work with both Allied and Axis Powers, as Switzerland had done. Some rumors, however, suggested that the new Iranian monarch (i.e., Reza Shah Pahlavi) collaborated with Germany in hopes of regaining power in the Caucasus, just as the Ottoman Empire had allied with Germany against Britain and Russia in WWI. In reality, Reza Shah was an opportunistic leader who hoped to gain from great powers by setting one against another. He had some modernization projects with the Allies, while he had invited German technicians to build the North-South Trans-Iranian Railway. Nevertheless, such political moves in a strategic country were totally unacceptable to the Allies, especially when the German eastern front was coming close to the Caucasus. Thus, the Allies decided to invade neutral Iran, depose Reza Shah, and replace his son (Mohammad Reza Shah). In September 1942, while the British Navy attacked Iran from the South, the Soviet forces advanced into northern Iran, occupying Iranian Azerbaijan and urging Azeris in the area to break away. But the British would not allow Russia to occupy the rest of Iran because of its valuable oil resources, so in 1942, all the Allied Powers (including Russia) agreed to respect Iran's territorial integrity.

After the war, in March of 1946, Soviet troops were supposed to withdraw from Iran. The Soviets, however, attempted to expand their occupation of Iran. The resulting international crisis over the status of Iran, in many ways, was the beginning of the Cold War.[28] It was in the midst of this crisis that Churchill proclaimed that an "iron curtain" had fallen across the portions of the globe that had been occupied by the Soviets. Great Britain and the United States led international opposition to the extended Soviet occupation, utilizing the newly created UN Security Council to eventually convince the Soviets to withdraw in return for assurances that they could maintain a stake in Iranian oil. Following the withdrawal, the Soviet-encouraged uprisings of Azeris in northern Iran were quickly crushed by Iranian troops. The Aras River was reestablished as the border between Iran and Soviet Azerbaijan, perpetuating the continued division of ethnic Azeris from then until today.[29]

While Azerbaijan hope for national unity was crushed after the Soviet retreat, Armenian national feeling was growing. The desire of Armenians can be understood in light of their sense of territorial loss and mistreatment at the hands of Turks. Some estimate that the territory once occupied by Armenians was once six times larger than the territory of Soviet Armenia, the smallest of all Soviet Republics.[30] Though the Soviets granted the large Armenian population in Nagorno-Karabakh an autonomous political entity within Azerbaijan, the desire for unification only continued to gain steam.

Early Independence

When the Soviet Union collapsed in 1991, the nationalist feelings of Georgians, Azeris, and Armenians rose as they moved to establish themselves as independent states. Nevertheless, the manner in which the Soviets pressed different nationalities together, while simultaneously granting them recognition, complicated this move to independence. In short, the Russian general policy can be defined based on the principle of divide-and-conquer, the method their British rivals had successfully used to control their overseas possessions for centuries. Thus, with the demise of the USSR, the violence between Armenians (in Nagorno-Karabakh) and Azeris soon moved into an open war that pitted the new states of Azerbaijan and Armenia against each other until 1994.

In Georgia, the rise of Georgian nationalism alarmed the Ossetians, Abkhazians, and Adjarians, who feared they would completely lose their political autonomy. Between 1991 and 1992, Georgia fought the Ossetians to prevent them from succeeding. In 1992, fighting began between the Georgians and Abkhazians that would last until 1993. These wars produced turmoil in the South Caucasus that compounded the economic and political collapse in the former Soviet Republics. At the same time, the turmoil in the South also spread into the Russian Federation, as the Chechens attempted to gain their own independence in the First Chechen War (1994–1996) in the North Caucasus. That desperate, bloody war gave hope that the peoples of the Caucasus might separate themselves from Moscow once and for all. However, in 1999, the war resumed after Chechen incursions into Dagestan. That began the Second Chechen War, which practically concluded in 2000, although sporadic fighting and terrorism have continued since then.[31]

MODERN CAUCASUS STATES AND INTERNATIONAL AFFAIRS

The collapse of the Soviet economic structure, combined with separatist conflict, created instability and destruction that societies in the Caucasus are still recovering from today. All three Caucasus states have responded to the insecurity of their region by investing in military personnel and armaments. The combined military expenditures of these states has increased "by more than 500 percent in real terms over the 10-year period 1998–2007 and by 285 percent over the five years 2003–2007." In 2006, all three of these states spent more than the world average (2.5%) of their GDPs on their militaries. These expenditures serve several national goals including: gaining advantage in separatist conflicts, modernizing to meet standards for membership in the North Atlantic Treaty Organization (NATO), defending themselves from each other, deterring the influence of neighboring powers, and protecting their energy resources and transportation routes.[32] One major factor influencing all such issues is the role of external powers, to which we turn in the following sections.

Global Powers and Security Organizations

After the collapse of the USSR, the South Caucasus rose from its isolation, allowing Western states to develop political and economic ties in a region that had been almost solely Russian-dominated space since the Tsarist Russian Empire forced Persia to sign the Treaty of Turkmenchay. As the Russian economy imploded in the early 1990s, its influence waned and the influence of the Europeans and Americans grew. Thus, nowadays, a significant factor in the security of the South Caucasus is the new competition evolving between Russia and the West (the European Union and the United States). This recent rivalry owes its very existence to the importance of the region's oil and natural gas deposits, the energy pipelines in the area, and its newly gained strategic value since the start of the U.S.-led War on Terror.

United States

Energy, security, and democracy briefly constitute the three major American foreign policy priorities in the U.S. relationships with the South Caucasus states. Upon the independence of the three South Caucasus states, Washington officially recognized their sovereignty and included them in the Freedom Support Act of 1992. This bill is designed to support the development of free markets and democratic systems in the NIS. Generally sympathetic to the desires of others to gain independence, the United States also initially took a supportive stance on the Armenian independence movement in Nagorno-Karabakh. Many Armenians immigrated to the United States in the years of Ottoman brutality and after the conclusion of WWI. Today, Armenian-Americans- constitute a powerful political lobby. In fact, the strong Armenian lobby in the state of Massachusetts actually prompted Senator John Kerry to propose the sanctioning of Azerbaijan under Section 907 of the Freedom Support Act, in support of the Armenians fighting for independence in Nagorno-Karabakh.[33] (See text of Section 907 in Appendix G.)

In the mid-1990s, however, American foreign policy began to reflect an interest in the Caucasus' energy resources, in addition to encouraging democracy and general stability. Although the United States does not really have a need for the Azeri oil and gas (mostly located in their Caspian Sea shore), Washington has an interest in preventing Moscow from developing a monopoly on energy resources in the region. Like the Soviet pattern, the new Russia Federation have controlled most of the regional energy resources, and the old Soviet pipeline networks have perpetuated its dominance of the energy market. In addition to facing possible Russian domination of all Caucasus energy resources, the United States has also involved itself to keep the Islamic Republic of Iran from economically benefiting from building an energy export relationship with Azerbaijan.

Both Presidents George H. W. Bush and Bill Clinton realized the negative consequences that Section 907 had for the future of American-Azeri relations, and the complications that such tensions created for the advancement of U.S. interests regarding the region's energy politics. Yet neither president was able to convince the U.S. Congress to repeal that legislation.[34] Only after the shocking and tragic events of the September 11 (9/11) terrorist attacks did the U.S. Congress move to waive Section 907 at the request of President George W. Bush. (See text of the Waiver of Section 907 in Appendix G.) Securing over-flight permission from the Caucasus states was essential for the United States and NATO to carry out the invasion of Taliban-controlled Afghanistan as Washington initiated its War on Terror.[35]

North Atlantic Trade Organization

NATO is a collective security alliance that originated in April of 1949 when 10 Western European states, the United States, and Canada signed the Washington Treaty. The primary purpose of NATO was specified in Article 5 as a collective agreement that an armed attack against one or more of the member states would be considered an attack against all members. The first secretary general of the organization, Lord Ismay, personally described NATO's original mission as having three functions: (1) to keep the Americans in, (2) to keep the Russians out, and (3) to keep the Germans down.[36]

Today, despite the collapse of the Soviet Union and the integration of unified Germany into NATO, the organization continues to be central to security in the Western Hemisphere. It also continues to be perceived as an anti-Russian organization. NATO's Partnership for Peace (PfP) program is an example of NATO's continued attempts to expand international participation in its security network, and is a mechanism for expansion that Russia clearly distrusts.[37]

All three South Caucasus states are members of the PfP program, and while this does not make them NATO members, it does further military and political co-operation with the West and the modernization of defensive forces in the region.[38] NATO is a significant international security organization (i.e., military pact) with important ties to the Caucasus states, which require attention in any comprehensive analysis of the South Caucasus affairs. In fact, it is due to NATO's role that it is possible to speak of a semi-cohesive Western security orientation that seems anti-Russian in the Caucasus and elsewhere.

European Union

Like the United States, the member states of the European Union (EU) share an interest in Georgia because of energy, security, and democracy. Upon the independence of the three South Caucasus states, European states were quick to officially recognize their sovereignty and supported international efforts to build regional stability and promote democracy. Since the EU structure did not offi-cially exist until 1993, one of the primary mechanisms for initial European involvement in the South Caucasus was the Conference on Security and Cooperation in Europe (CSCE) or what is now known as the Organization for Security and Cooperation in Europe (OSCE). Using the Berlin Mechanism, the OSCE facilitated negotiations in the Nagorno-Karabakh conflict between Armenia and Azerbaijan.[39]

In the mid-1990s, energy politics in the Caucasus also became an important issue for Europe, since the EU states have long been major energy importers. Before even the end of the Cold War, Russian energy was a large source of Euro-pean imports, and the EU energy dependency on Russian Federation has only increased since the admission of former Soviet Republics. In 2006, 33 percent of the EU's oil and 40 percent of its gas came from Russia.[40] Thus, unlike the United States, the EU states have a direct strategic interest in limiting Moscow's ability to monopolize energy originating from the Caspian Sea basin. In 2007, the EU produced 2,394 barrels per day (tb/d) of oil and 18.6 billion cubic feet (BCF) of gas but consumed 14,861 tb/d of oil and 47 BCF of gas.[41] In order to diversify its source of fossil fuel imports, the European Union has encouraged (with U.S. support) the construction of new pipelines in the Caucasus. This pre-cipitated European participation in energy projects such as Azerbaijan's Deal of the Century, the Baku-Tbilisi-Ceyhan (BTC) oil pipeline, the Baku-Tbilisi-Erzurum (BTE) gas pipeline, and the Baku-Achalkalaki-Kars (BAK) railway. The BTC provided an opportunity for imports diversification with Azeri oil. There are also plans for the known Nabucco pipeline project, which promises even greater potential. The Nabucco project proposes a gas pipeline along the Caspian seabed from Turkmenistan to Baku that would attach to the BTE pipe-line to feed Turkey and Europe.[42]

In 1999, the EU demonstrated its growing foreign policy role when it implemented Partnership and Cooperation Agreements with all three Caucasus states, inviting them into closer political and economic relationships.[43] In 2004, the EU opened the door for further cooperation with the South Caucasus states when it unveiled its European Neighborhood Policy and made it clear that Azerbaijan, Armenia, and Georgia had a place as future members.[44] This step was indicative of even further unification of the foreign policies of European states through the EU structure, including the development of a comprehensive security policy. One of the primary goals of the EU in this respect is to minimize instability in neighboring states. For instance, "the European Security Strategy, adopted in December 2003, emphasizes the need for the EU to seek to build a belt of well-governed countries on its periphery."[45] On the frontier of Europe, the South Caucasus states, geographically located between Europe and the Middle East, appear to be a major part of this periphery.

Organization for Security and Cooperation in Europe

The OSCE is the world's largest regional security organization, with 56 member states.[46] Having originated from the CSCE, the OSCE received its name change in 1995. The OSCE plays an important role in the EU's efforts to create a belt of stable states along its periphery, and its efforts to encourage the settlement of separatist conflicts in the Caucasus may be seen in this light. The OSCE has also been central to European-Georgian relations since Georgian independence. In 1992, the OSCE created a specific Mission to Georgia, which was has remained focused on a resolution to the separatist conflicts with Abkhazia and South Ossetia. Since 1993, the OSCE has also had a role in monitoring the Georgia-Abkhaz border through the UN-led peace process. The OSCE Mission to Georgia also monitors Joint Peace Keeping Forces (JPKF) deployed in the Georgian-Ossetian conflict zone.[47] Moreover, the OSCE was also the primary forum for peace negotiations between Armenia and Azerbaijan during the war for Nagorno-Karabakh.[48]

Yet the OSCE has had little success in resolving all Caucasus conflicts. In fact, this organization has developed a strain in its relationship with Armenia because of its criticism of Nagorno-Karabakh's calls for international recognition. Furthermore, the OSCE appears to have little influence over Russia, which has been the decisive external factor in all of the conflicts in the greater Caucasus region. One particular political analyst asserted that the OSCE "can either function as a 'community' in consensus with Russia and remain irrelevant, or give up on the consensus with Russia and risk ceasing to function at all."[49] Thus, one may conclude that the organization has difficult policy choices in this region, considering the local and international conditions.

Russia

Of the three major global political powers influencing the Caucasus, Russia is the closest geographically and has the longest history of involvement with the region. Its interests in the region include security and energy, which simultaneously overlap. Due to its imperial and Soviet-era domination of the region, the Russian Federation remains tied to the politics, security, and economies of the Caucasus states. It controls energy import and export routes, maintains military bases in the region, and mediates territorial disputes. Moreover, significant numbers of Russians still reside in the population of these former Soviet Republics. Throughout history, the very presence of one nation's members in another nation's territory has been used as an excuse to justify military and political interventions. Russia has certainly used such opportunities to its own benefit in the Caucasus. Time after time, Moscow has claimed that it was protecting Russian citizens when it countered Georgian troops in South Ossetia during or before the 2008 campaign.[50] Thus, Moscow is likely to use similar arguments in the future to justify its moves.

The collapse of the Soviet Union left Russia struggling to pull itself back together socially, politically, and economically. Today, as Russia recovers some of its former economic strength, Moscow is once again asserting itself in the Caucasus, simply because it never intended to completely surrender its influence in the region. When the Soviet Union came unglued, Russia created the Commonwealth of Independent States (CIS) to provide an international institution through which it could maintain a special relationship with its former republics, just as the British had done by establishing the British Commonwealth to maintain some form of influence over their former colonies.

Russian leaders, particularly since former President Putin, consider the former Soviet Republics as a natural part of their "sphere of influence." Thus, they view the expansion of NATO into such republics as a security threat. The Caucasus is considered to be a part of Russia's Near Abroad, which constitutes a security buffer that is perceived to encompass the first line of Russian security defense.[51] Considering that the Caucasus used to be the front lines in the old Cold War, it is understandable that this region still has much of Russian security infrastructure beyond Russia's official borders in the post-Soviet era. For example, the Russian Federation has attempted to maintain its old military bases in Armenia and Georgia and continues to operate the Gabala radar station in Azerbaijan.[52]

In addition to Moscow's interest in preserving the old security network, the turmoil in the Caucasus region also threatens the integrity of Russian borders, its own internal stability, and Russia's economic recovery. For instance, the fighting between South Ossetia and Georgia has often threatened to involve the whole Ossetian nation, including even the population of the North Ossetia, inside Russia. The separatist conflicts in both South Ossetia and Abkhazia created a training ground for foreign fighters, particularly Chechen fighters who would return to Chechnya to wage war against Moscow.[53]

Energy is another reason for Russia to have a security interest in maintaining the stability of the Caucasus. Russian resurgence on the international stage is rooted in Moscow's domestic politics. The economic recovery that former President Vladimir Putin presided over bolstered his popularity with the Russian people and allowed Russians to focus outward once again. Under Putin, the Russian economy experienced great growth that was largely due to new oil revenues. In 2003, the profits of Lukoil (a major oil exporting firm) rose 38 percent. Within first four months of 2003, the Central Bank's currency level increased 10 percent ($4.8 billion).[54] This new economic muscle made Putin's dreams of a New Russia a possibility.

As a major energy producer, Russia does not necessarily need the fossil fuels from the Caspian Sea basin to meet domestic demands. In fact, Russian gas reserves are the largest in the world, and Russia possesses the world's eighth largest oil reserves. Oil production in 2007 was about 9,876 tbl/d while domestic consumption was only 2,858 tbl/d. This allowed the export of 7,018 tbl/d. Russian gas production also allows room for exports, as it consumed only 16,598 bcf of the 23,167 bcf produced in 2006.[55] Yet, Russia's gas and oil fields are aging and production is gradually slowing. Tapping additional reserves will take both time and money.[56] If Moscow can dominate the sale of energy from the Caspian Sea basin, it will benefit from transit fees and may maintain its lucrative exports to Europe.[57] Simultaneously, Russia stands to lose political and economic ground if foreign companies continue to undermine Russia's hold on the energy sector of the Caucasus. In the Caspian Sea basin, Western companies already account for roughly 70 percent of oil production.[58] Thus, the threat to Russian economic leverage in the region is real.

For the New Russia, energy is a vital security interest, because it is the main component of positioning the country as an Energy Superpower. The current energy sector is critical for the Russian economy, but it is also a potential source of political power. In 2006, Putin ordered a reworking of the old Soviet energy system. At the time, former Soviet Republics were still receiving gas at lower prices than European consumers. For example, Austria was paying around $221 for roughly every 35,315 cubic feet (cf) of gas per year, Germany $217, and Turkey $243. Former Soviet Republics, alternately, were paying in the range of $50–80 for roughly the same amount. Therefore, when Putin hiked prices to former Republics, it was not necessarily unreasonable or an exercise in heavy-handed politics. However, the timing of Russia's price hikes provides reason to suspect that they were designed as a warning to former Republics about the cost of ignoring Russia. Gazprom announced the new prices just before the onset of the cold Caucasus winter, placing states in a position between budgetary crises or leaving their citizens to freeze.[59]

Now, Azerbaijan, Georgia, and Turkey form an energy corridor for the West, by which Western companies access the Caucasus and break Russian energy dominance in the region. The BTC and BTE pipelines are the most vital lines in this corridor. They may be extended (via Nabucco line) in the future by a trans-Caspian pipeline that could tap the energy resources of the Central Asian side of the Caspian Sea.[60] In order to secure its interest, Moscow has begun to reassert itself in the Caucasus. In that region, Georgia occupies a critical, strategic location. If Georgia can be persuaded (or forced) into complying with Russian interests, then Moscow could control NATO's air corridor into Central Asia, its efforts in Afghanistan, and the Western energy corridor provided by the BTC and BTE lines. The problem has been that Georgia has consistently challenged Russian interests, particularly since President Mikheil Saakashvili's election in 2003 (see Appendix C for biography). The latest phase of the Georgia-Russia struggle led to the Russia-Georgia War in 2008.

Commonwealth of Independent States

On December 8, 1991, Russia created the Commonwealth of Independent States (CIS) in an attempt to maintain a special relationship with its former Republics. The CIS is a rather loose confederation of Russia and its former Republics that resembles some aspects of the British Commonwealth, which eventually lost its status. Similarly, the future integrative growth of the CIS is also in doubt. Nevertheless, CIS membership is important to Russia because it sees its former Republics as its Near Abroad or a natural "sphere of influence." Cooperation through the CIS was to offer protection of the national sovereignty for all its member states, which are supposedly equal. But there is a clear power distribution asymmetry in this organization, as Russia is the dominant state at the center of the CIS.

Membership in the CIS has been a contentious issue from the beginning. In the early 1990s, Azerbaijan and Georgia, both initially governed by nationalist presidents, did not join the CIS. Soon, their strength was sapped by their losses in respective separatist conflicts, and new presidents with new priorities came to office. In 2006, the continued fractiousness of the CIS was evidenced when plans for a CIS anniversary meeting were canceled by Russia and Kazakhstan. There was speculation that this was the result of the Kremlin's "inability to garner support from other members for a plan to revamp the organization."[61] As Russians' assertiveness in their foreign policy increased under Putin's presidency, some CIS member states expressed the ideas that a "dignified divorce" from the CIS might be necessary in order to maintain their independence.[62]

Collective Security Treaty Organization

While the CIS incorporates some security mechanisms, it is not the only security organization engineered by Moscow. In 2002, on the heels of the U.S.-led

War on Terror following 9/11, Russia led the way by the establishment of the Collective Security Treaty Organization (CSTO), which originated from the CIS Collective Security Treaty. More than the CIS structure, the CSTO consti- tutes a real alternative security organization to NATO. Not all CIS member states, however, aimed to join this additional institution and umbrella international security organization. In fact, Georgia and Azerbaijan have both avoided membership so far. On the other hand, Armenia has joined the organiza- tion, reflecting its consistent willingness to get in line with Russia.

Thus far, the CSTO has held several military exercises, which have sometimes served as opportunities to foster ties with the Shanghai Cooperation Organiza- tion (SCO).[63] It also now possesses a small, rapid deployment security force of 4,000 troops. The 2003 Iraq War served as another catalyst to urge Moscow's development of the CSTO as an alternative to NATO, especially since the American-Russian relations were really falling apart at the time.[64] Now, after the Russia-Georgia War, Russian President Dmitri Medvedev has called for a new, stronger rapid deployment force.[65] At the Moscow summit of the CSTO members in February 2009, CSTO government delegations agreed to a plan, which called for 16,000 troops, including 8,000 from Russia, 4,000 from Kazakhstan, and the other 4,000 from the other member states.[66]

Regional Powers

As the brief review of the history of conflicts in the South Caucasus revealed, Turkey and Iran are two regional powers that have long played significant roles in the security of the Caucasus. Both states are the remnants of past empires that dominated the region at various times, and they still continue to possess religious and ethnic ties to the Caucasus people, as well as political and security interests. With the end of the Cold War and the relative retreat of Russian influence, the regional rivalry between these two states has returned. Their natural rivalry has contributed to regional tensions that are important to understanding Caucasus states security considerations in the contemporary era.

Turkey

The modern state of Turkey is the inheritor of the Ottoman Empire's legacy in the Caucasus, as the bordering Anatolian peninsula served as the heart of that great power. At its height in the 1500s, the Ottoman Empire stretched from the Balkans to the Caspian Sea, across the Middle East, and over North Africa. The history continues to connect modern Turkey with the Caucasus states, for good and for bad. While shared ethnic ties with Azeris have been a positive develop- ment for Ankara in promoting strong ties with Azerbaijan, Turkey's relationship with Armenia is a different story. Ankara-Erevan ties are still influenced by the memories of violence perpetrated by Ottoman Turks against Armenians during the WWI era: this experience has engrained animosity between these two states.

In the wake of WWI, the Ottoman Empire was dismembered, and the Anatolian Peninsula was occupied by the Allies. At this time, Mustafa Kemal Ataturk emerged as the hero of Turkish nationalism and cemented his legacy as the father of the Turkish state when he successfully expelled the foreign forces and established what is now the secular Republic of Turkey. Under Ataturk leadership, Turkey began pursuing modernization and westernization by secularizing its government. This included dramatic reforms that produced significant social dislocation. The enduring nature of Ataturk's secularization, however, was demonstrated in 1937, when secularism was adopted as a provision in the modern Turkish constitution.[67]

Turkey's commitment to secularism and western-style democracy contrasts with that of its regional rival, Iran, which established a theocratic form of government. Since the Caucasus states' reappearance in the world stage from their forced isolation, Turkey has had a dynamic role to play in the region, as a modern state role model. This has been particularly true for Azerbaijan, which emulates Turkey—with which it has both ethnic and religious affinity. In the Caucasus, Ankara's regime serves as a role model not only for its domestic political features, but also for its mainly accommodating foreign policy posture toward the West. In the eyes of many people in the Caucasus, Turkey has developed economically and politically as a result of its general strategy of working with the West, as opposed to struggling against it. Thus, it is not a coincidence that Turkey is repeatedly referred to as a bridge between the East and the West, between Europe and the Middle East, and between Christianity and Islam.

Iran

Like Turkey, Iran has had a rich culture, glorious history, and impressive civilization. In fact, Iran has experienced its own greatness as an empire (under different names) in the Caucasus from the ancient times to the nineteenth century. The influence of the Shia Safavids (1501–1736) has permanently impacted the religion of Azerbaijan. Moreover, Iranian culture, customs, and language overlap with those of many diverse ethnic groups of both Indo-European (e.g., Ossetians) and Turkic origin (e.g., Azeris). Therefore, Tehran still continues to have political ties to the Caucasus.[68]

In comparison to the Ottoman Empire, the less modernized Persian Empire faded more rapidly in the face of rapid Russian expansion, and it struggled to avoid loss of political sovereignty to Russia.[69] In 1927, the first monarch of the Pahlavi Dynasty (Reza Shah) began an ambitious modernization process in Iran, hoping to catch up to the strength of European nations. Iranian economic, social, and political reforms were far-reaching and somehow similar in their style and social dislocation impact to those implemented under Ataturk. Contrary to the Turkish experience, however, Reza Shah's reforms were for the most part implemented in a more dictatorial manner, which provoked popular resentment and opposition.[70] As explained earlier, there was a major foreign policy difference between Reza Shah and his contemporary Ataturk during WWII. While Turkey declared neutrality and stayed away from the world stage, Iran chose active neutrality aimed at using the international opportunities to secure benefits from the opposing camps. Reza Shah's decision to keep a working relationship with the Axis Powers backfired and led to the occupation of the country by the British and Soviets. Allies eventually called Iran the "bridge of victory," by which they provided Soviets with supplies to slow-down the German advances near Stalingrad.

Under the leadership of Reza Shah's successor, Mohammed Reza Pahlavi, Iran established closer ties to the West and relatively moved to a more open and democratic system.[71] This allowed Iranian nationalists to gain power, and led by Prime Minister Mohammad Mosaddegh, nationalist forces sought the expulsion of Mohammed Reza Shah. The international conditions, however, were not suitable for the moves of Iranian nationalists in a country with a significant strategic value connecting the Persian Gulf to the Caspian Sea Region. The British and the Americans were not willing to allow their close ally, the Shah, to be deposed. The American CIA, in association with British MI6, supported a coup to oust Mosaddegh. The coup permanently marred the perception of the Iranian masses of the United States and set the stage for the Iranian 1979 Revolution, as the Shah forcefully cracked down on all dissents within Iran after his return.

The 1979 Islamic Revolution, led by the Ayatollah Ruhollah Khomeini, removed the Shah and set Iran on its course toward theocracy and autocracy. Since the revolution, Turkey and Iran have provided two contrasting state role models for their Muslim neighbors, including Azerbaijan. The bitterness of U.S.-Iran relations following the Iranian Hostage Crisis (November 1979–January 1981) permanently strained relations between Tehran and Washington, eventually leading Iran to turn to Russia for support. Mainly due to the regional and international conditions that we discussed, Turkey and Iran also provide two contrasting political and security orientations in the Caspian Sea Region: one Westward and the other toward Russia.[72]

With the preceding discussion of the general political and security environment in the Caucasus region, we are now ready to examine the particular security features, opportunities, and challenges of each South Caucasus state. Our discussion begins with Azerbaijan in the next chapter. In Chapter 3, the Armenian security case study will be fully explained. Next, we investigate the special characteristics of the Georgian security, which has led some to hypothesize that maybe a new Cold War is on its way to the international stage. Finally, we conclude this book with a chapter which summarizes the main findings, identifies special foreign security behavioral patterns, and makes suggestions about the application of a "Clash of Civilizations" perspective in explaining and predicting the Caucasus affairs.

NOTES

1. Francis Fukuyama, *The End of History and the Last Man* (New York: Simon and Schuster, 2006); Samuel P. Huntington, *The Clash of Civilizations and the Remaking of World Order* (New York: Simon and Schuster, 1997).

2. Niccolò Machiavelli, *Discourses on Livy*, trans. Julia Conaway Bondanella and Peter Bondanella (Oxford: Oxford University Press, 2003), 60, 384; Raymond Aron, Daniel J. Mahoney, and Brian C. Anderson, *Peace & War: A Theory of International Relations* (Brunswick, NJ: Transaction Publishers, 2003), 54; Hans Joachim Morgenthau, *Politics Among Nations: The Struggle for Power and Peace* (New York, NY: Knopf, 1967), 109–114.

3. Gilpin, 138; Peter Liberman, "The Spoils of Conquest," *International Security* 18, no. 2 (Fall 1993): 125–153; Peter Liberman, *Does Conquest Pay?: The Exploitation of Occupied Industrial Societies* (Princeton, NJ: Princeton University Press, 1996).

4. Commonwealth Secretariat, *Small States: Economic Review and Basic Statistics* (Commonwealth Secretariat, 2008), 33.

5. Morgenthau, 109.

6. Elaine M. Holoboff, "Bad Boys or Good Business?: Russia's Use of Oil as a Mechanism of Coercive Diplomacy," in *Strategic Coercion: Concepts and Cases*, Lawrence Freedman, ed. (Oxford: Oxford University Press, 1998), 179–211.

7. Christoph Zürcher, *The Post-Soviet Wars: Rebellion, Ethnic Conflict, and Nationhood in the Caucasus* (New York, NY: New York University Press, 2007), 11.

8. Ibid., 12.

9. EIA, "Caspian Sea Region: Survey of Key Oil and Gas Statistics and Forecasts," Energy Information Administration, July 2005, http://www.eia.doe.gov/emeu/cabs/caspian _balances.htm (accessed September 2, 2009).

10. Moshe Gammer, ed., *Ethno-Nationalism, Islam and the State in the Caucasus: Post-Soviet Disorder* (New York, NY: Routledge, 2008), 2; Benjamin R. Barber, *Jihad vs. McWorld* (New York, NY: Times Books, 1995).

11. Paul Collier and Anke Hoeffler, "Greed and Grievance in Civil War," *Oxford Economic Papers* 56, no. 4 (2004): 563–595; Gammer, 1–2.

12. CIA, "Armenia," *The World Factbook* (Washington, D.C.: Central Intelligence Agency, 2009), https://www.cia.gov/library/publications/the-world-factbook/geos/am.html (accessed May 18, 2009).

13. CIA, "Azerbaijan," *The World Factbook* (Washington, D.C.: Central Intelligence Agency, 2009), https://www.cia.gov/library/publications/the-world-factbook/geos/aj.html (accessed May 18, 2009).

14. CIA, "Georgia," *The World Factbook* (Washington, D.C.: Central Intelligence Agency, 2009), https://www.cia.gov/library/publications/the-world-factbook/geos/gg.html (accessed May 18, 2009).

15. Paul Collier and Anke Hoeffler, "Greed and Grievance in Civil War," *Oxford Economic Papers* 56, no. 4 (2004): 563–595.

16. James D. Fearon and David Laitin, "Ethnicity, Insurgency, and Civil War," *American Political Science Review* 97, no. 1 (February 2003), 75–90.

17. Zürcher, 7; Gammer, 1–2.

18. Zürcher, 16.

19. Tamara Sonn, *A Brief History of Islam* (Oxford: Blackwell Publishing, 2004), 78.

20. Ole Høiris and Sefa Martin Yurukel, *Contrasts and Solutions in the Caucasus* (Aarhus: Aarhus University Press, 1998), 36–37.

21. Johannes Rau, *The Nagorno-Karabakh Conflict Between Armenia and Azerbaijan: A Brief Historical Outline* (Berlin: Verlag Dr. Köster, 2008), 21.

22. Zürcher, 20.

23. Tadeusz Swietochowski, *Russia and Azerbaijan: A Borderland in Transition* (New York, NY: Columbia University Press, 1995), 68–69.

24. Swietochowski, 68–69, 103, and 105; Glenn E. Curtis, ed. *Azerbaijan: A Country Study.* Washington, DC: GPO for the Library of Congress, 1995, http://countrystudies.us/azerbaijan/10.htm (accessed May 22, 2009).

25. Ole Høiris and Sefa Martin Yurukel, *Contrasts and Solutions in the Caucasus* (Aarhus: Aarhus University Press, 1998), 39–40.

26. Thomas Goltz, *Georgia Diary: A Chronicle of War and Political Chaos in the Post-Soviet Caucasus* (London: M. E. Sharpe, 2006), 26, 51–52.

27. Rau, 32.

28. Jamil Hasanlı, *The Soviet-American Crisis Over Iranian Azerbaijan, 1941–1946* (Lanham, MD: Rowman & Littlefield Publishers, Inc., 2006), 225–228.

29. Ibid., ix–xii, 225–228, 252, and 255.

30. Khachig Tölölyan, "The Armenian Diaspora as a Transnational Actor and as a Potential Contributor to Conflict Resolution," *Diaspora: Journal of Transnational Studies* (2006): 1; Razmik Panossian, *The Armenians: From Kings and Priests to Merchants and Commissars* (New York, NY: Columbia University Press, 2006), 277.

31. Olga Oliker, *Russia's Chechen Wars 1994–2000: Lessons Learned from Urban Combat* (Santa Monica, CA: Rand, 2001).

32. SIPRI. *SIPRI Yearbook 2008: Armaments, Disarmament and International Security* (Oxford University Press, 2008), 185.

33. Svante E. Cornell, "The Politicization of Islam in Azerbaijan," *CA-CI SR Paper* (October 2006): 30.

34. Ibid., 9.

35. Farian Sabahi and Daniel Warner, eds., *The OSCE and the Multiple Challenges of Transition* (Burlington, VT: Ashgate Publishing Co., 2004), 132.

36. Josef Joffe, "Nato: Soldiering On," *Time Magazine*, March 19, 2009. http://www.time.com/time/magazine/article/0,9171,1886470,00.html (accessed August 8, 2009).

37. Georgeta Pourchot, *Eurasia Rising: Democracy and Independence in the Post-Soviet Space* (Westport, CT: Praeger Security International, 2008), 119.

38. Ministry of Foreign Affairs (Azerbaijan), "Information on Azerbaijan-NATO Relationship," Ministry of Foreign Affairs, http://www.mfa.gov.az/eng/index.php?option=com_content&task=view&id=263&Itemid=1 (accessed September 2, 2009).

39. OSCE, *OSCE Handbook* (Organization for Security and Cooperation in Europe, 2007), 7, http://www.osce.org/publications/sg/2007/10/22286_952_en.pdf (accessed September 2, 2009).

40. Europe's Engery Portal, "Energy Dependency," European Union, http://www.energy.eu/#dependency (accessed January 21, 2009).

41. British Petroleum, *BP Statistical Review of World Energy June 2008* (British Petroleum, 2008), http://www.bp.com/statisticalreview (accessed January 29, 2009).

42. Alexander Cooley, "Principles in the Pipeline: Managing Transatlantic Values and Interests in Central Asia," *International Affairs* 84, no. 6 (2008): 1181; Andrew E. Kramer, "Putin's Grasp of Energy Drives Russian Agenda," *New York Times*, January 28, 2009, http://www

.nytimes.com/2009/01/29/world/europe/29putin.html?_r=1&scp=2&sq=putin&st=cse (accessed January 28, 2009).

43. EP, "The EU's External Relations," European Parliament, 2008, http://www .europarl.europa.eu/parliament/expert/displayFtu.do?language=en&id=74&ftuId=FTU_6.4 .3.html (accessed September 2, 2009).

44. EC, "European Neighborhood Policy: Strategy Paper," European Commission, May 12, 2004, http://ec.europa.eu/world/enp/pdf/strategy/strategy_paper_en.pdf (September 2, 2009

45. Lynch, 125.

46. OSCE, "Facts and Figures," Organization for Security and Cooperation in Europe, http://www.osce.org/about/19298.html (accessed September 2, 2009).

47. OSCE, "Overview," OSCE Mission to Georgia, http://www.osce.org/georgia/13199. html (accessed May 22, 2009).

48. RFE, "Nagorno-Karabakh: Timeline of the Long Road to Peace," *Radio Free Europe*, February 10, 2006, http://www.rferl.org/content/article/1065626.html (accessed April 10, 2009).

49. Vladimir Socor, "Moscow Pleased with OSCE's Response to Missile Drop on Georgia," *Eurasian Monitor* 4 (September 11, 2007), http://www.jamestown.org/single/?no_cache =1&tx_ttnews%5Btt_news%5D=32986 (accessed January 31, 2010).

50. BBC, "Russian Tanks Enter South Ossetia," *British Broadcasting Corporation*, August 8, 2008. http://news.bbc.co.uk/2/hi/europe/7548715.stm (accessed April 10, 2009).

51. CSIS, "Russia Report," CSIS Files no. 1, Center for Strategic and International Studies, May 2007, 24, http://www.csis.ro/docs/CSIS.ro_Russia_Report.pdf (accessed August 14, 2009).

52. Rovshan Ismayilov, "Azerbaijan Ready to Discuss Russian-US Use of Radar Station," EurasiaNet.org, June 8, 2007, http://www.eurasianet.org/departments/insight/articles/ eav060807.shtml (accessed April 10, 2009).

53. Robert Seely, *Russo-Chechen Conflict, 1800–2000: A Deadly Embrace* (Portland, OR: Frank Cass, 2001), 210.

54. Milton F. Goldman, *Russia, the Eurasian Republics, and Central/Eastern Europe*, 11th ed. (Dubuge: McGraw-Hill, 2008), 35.

55. EIA, "Russia Energy Profile," Energy Information Administration, http://tonto .eia.doe.gov/country/country_energy_data.cfm?fips=RS (accessed May 12, 2009).

56. Boris Rumer, "The Search for Stability in Central Asia," In Boris Rumer, ed., *Central Asia: A Gathering Storm?* (Armonk: M. E. Sharpe, 2002), 56.

57. Houman A. Sadri and Nathan L. Burns, "Geopolitics of Oil and Energy in Central Asia," In Reuel R. Hanks, ed., *Handbook of Central Asian Politics* (forthcoming from Routledge Press, London and New York, 2010).

58. Dmitri Trenin, "Russia and Central Asia: Interests, Policies, and Prospects," in *Central Asia: Views from Washington, Moscow, and Beijing*, Eugene Rumer, Dimitri Trenin, and Huasheng Zhao (New York: M. E. Sharpe 2007), 106–108.

59. Pourchot, 80–81.

60. Alman Mir Ismail, "Is the West Losing the Energy Game in the Caspian?" *CA-CI Analyst* (May 6, 2009), http://www.cacianalyst.org/?q=node/5100 (accessed May 12, 2009).

61. Pourchot, 106.

62. Ibid., 105.

63. Alyson J. K. Bailes et al., "The Shanghai Cooperation Organization," *SIPRI Policy Paper No. 17*, May 2007, 24. http://books.sipri.org/files/PP/SIPRIPP17.pdf (accessed September 2, 2009).

64. John A. Mowchan, "The Militarization of the Collective Security Treaty Organization," *Center for Strategic Leadership* 6-09, July 2009, 1, http://www.csl.army.mil/usacsl/publications/IP_6_09_Militarization_of_the_CSTO.pdf (accessed September 2, 2009).

65. RFE, "Russian-led CSTO Grouping Adds Military Dimension," Radio Free Europe, February 4, 2009, http://www.rferl.org/Content/Rapid_Reaction_Force_Adds_Military_Dimension_To_CSTO/1379324.html (accessed September 2, 2009).

66. Ilya Kramnik, "CSTO: Joining Forces in a Crisis," *RIA Novosti*, May 2, 2009, http://en.rian.ru/analysis/20090205/119991573 (accessed September 2, 2009).

67. Sina Aksin, *Turkey: From Empire to Revolutionary Republic* (New York, NY: New York University Press, 2007), 195.

68. Ali M. Ansari, *Confronting Iran: The Failure of American Foreign Policy and the Next Great Crisis in the Middle East* (New York, NY: Basic Books, 2006), 9.

69. Brenda Shaffer, *Partners in Need: The Strategic Relationship of Russia and Iran* (Washington, DC: The Washington Institute for Near East Policy, 2001).

70. Touraj Atabaki, ed. *The State and the Subaltern: Modernization, Society and the State in Turkey and Iran* (New York, NY: I. B.Tauris & Co. Ltd., 2007), 73.

71. Ali Farazmand, *The State, Bureaucracy, and Revolution in Modern Iran* (New York, NY: Praeger 1989), 15.

72. Nathan L. Burns, "Iran Carrying Out Policy in the Caspian Sea Region," In H. Sadri and D. Katsy, eds., *Trends, Prospects and Challenges of Globalization* (St. Petersburg, Russia: St. Petersburg State University Press, 2009), 32–47.

CHAPTER 2

Azerbaijan

Map 2.1 Azerbaijan and Nagorno-Karabakh

Note: The area around Nagorno-Karabakh is Azeri territory occupied by Armenian forces. (Designed by Albert Citron. Used with Permission.)

Photo 2.1 Azeri President

Ilham Heydar Oglu Aliyev, President of the Republic of Azerbaijan Addressing the United Nations General Assembly, UN Headquarters, New York, USA, September 24, 2004. (# 42871 UN Photo by Michelle Prioré.)

In the South Caucasus, Azerbaijan possesses a central position in the region's energy geopolitics. It is the only one of the three South Caucasus states with significant natural gas and oil reserves, a fact that owes to Azerbaijan's geographic position against the energy-rich Caspian Sea. Azerbaijan is the largest of the South Caucasus states, at about 86,100 square kilometers.[1] This territory and Azerbaijan's offshore holdings have given it control of the world's nineteenth largest oil reserves in the world. In addition to its estimated 7 billion barrels in oil reserves, Azerbaijan also controls roughly 30,000 billion cubic feet of natural gas reserves[2] (Map 2.1).

Due to this central geographic position and its energy reserves, Zbigniew Brzezinski (National Security Advisor to President Carter) stated that Azerbaijan is now a strategic international pivot.[3] The growing strategic importance of energy in the international economy has made Azerbaijan an interest for today's major global powers. In turn, this has attracted international interest to the South Caucasus as a whole. If Azerbaijan did not control such strategic natural resources, it is unlikely that the geographically distant EU states and the United States would have involved themselves as deeply as they have in South Caucasus affairs.

Photo 2.2 Azeri Minister of Foreign Affairs

Elmar Maharram oglu Mammadyarov, Minister for Foreign Affairs of the Republic of Azerbaijan Addressing the general debate of the 63rd United Nations General Assembly United Nations Headquarters, New York, USA, September 27, 2008. (# 198803 Photo by Marco Castro.)

The wealth that oil and gas have brought to Azerbaijan have not only given it a notable international position, but it has facilitated Azerbaijan's economic recovery from its war with Armenians over control of Nagorno-Karabakh in the early years after the Soviet collapse. Though violence has declined in recent years, this conflict has yet to be resolved and continues to influence the course of politics in the region. This fault line of ethnic conflict and other geographic characteristics serve to constrain Azerbaijan's ability to formulate an independent foreign policy orientation. Azerbaijan is landlocked, and therefore depends on export pipelines through Georgia and Russia to get its oil and gas to market. Pipeline politics between Russia and the West, then, play a significant role in influencing the stance that Azerbaijan adopts toward these powers and its own neighbors.

PRE-SOVIET HISTORY

The earliest political entity known to have occupied the geographic space of the modern state of Azerbaijan is Caucasian Albania. "The Albanians' language formed part of the north-eastern group of Caucasus languages," and they "are considered one of the ancestors of the modern Azerbaijani people."[4] The inhabitants of Caucasus Albania included Turkic tribes, providing an ethnic link between Turkey and Azerbaijan today.

Turkic influence in this area increased under the rule of the Seljuks in the tenth and eleventh centuries. Under their reign, large numbers of Turkic peoples migrated to the South Caucasus, forming an ethnic majority across the territory of Azerbaijan and northwestern Iran. So, ethnically, Azerbaijan has been defined as a Turkic country. Yet, Azeri Turks have been separated from their brothers in Turkey by their religious persuasion. While the Seljuks were Sunni Muslims, the Azeri Turks mixed Islam with their pre-Islamic religious beliefs. These shamanistic, Christian, and Zoroastrian traditions combined to create a syncretistic heritage that embraced mysticism. This bent toward the mystic contributed to the Azeri adoption of Shia Islam, a sect that is more tolerant of mysticism than Sunni Islam.[5]

From the mystic Sufi sects among the Turkic tribes, one particularly strong sect emerged in the fifteenth century. The Safavids, a "military brotherhood of Turkish nomads," established a dynasty in the region based in the city of Tabriz. Under the Safavids, the Azeri Turks came into conflict with the expanding Ottoman Turks from whom the modern state of Turkey emerged later. This shared ethnic heritage proved less important than religious orientation during these power struggles. Though the Sufism of the Safavids was originally a branch of Sunni Islam, their mysticism was more compatible with Shia Islam and tied the Azeri Turks closer to the Shia Persians. In the ensuing battles between the Ottoman and Safavid armies, very few Safavid Turks deserted to the Ottoman-Turkish enemy. Only in the north did much of the Azeri Turkic population remain Sunni, opposing the Shia-Persian orientation of the Safavids. The Safavid embrace of Persian culture and the Shia faith led to the eventual relocation of the Safavid court to the Persian city of Isfahan, transforming the Safavids into more a Persian dynasty than a Turkish one, laying the foundation for the modern Iranian state.[6]

As the Persian Safavid dynasty and the Ottoman Empire began to weaken in the seventeenth century, the Azeri Khanates had an opportunity to develop a more independent political identity of their own. But the weakening of Islamic empires in the South Caucasus also opened the door for the expansion of the Tsarist Russian Empire. As the Tsar's forces advanced into the region, they fought two wars with Persia. Both Russo-Persian wars (1804–1813 and 1826–1828) went badly for Persia. After its defeat in 1828, Persia abandoned the whole South Caucasus to Russia in the Treaty of Turkmenchay. The Russia-Iran border was then set at the Aras River, a natural boundary, but one that split the geographic space inhabited by Azeri-Turkic people in two. This border left the majority of ethnic Azeris on the Iranian side.[7] That border now divides the states of

Azerbaijan and Iran, continuing the separation of these Azeri-Turkic people and complicating any conception of a cohesive and united Azeri nation.

For the Azeris north of the Aras River, the Treaty of Turkmenchay meant steady integration into the Russian Empire. The Christianization of the Caucasus was a major component of this integration.[8] The Christian ties between Russians, Georgians, and Armenians excited tensions with the Muslim populations in the region. Under the Russian Empire, Armenians began to settle in Azerbaijan, leading to further conflicts with the indigenous Muslim Turks. These tensions laid the historical foundation for the territorial conflict that would emerge between Azeris and Armenians when they gained independence from the Soviet Union.[9]

SOVIET HISTORY

The turmoil of WWI and the subsequent Bolshevik Revolution in Russia (1917) offered the first real opportunity for Azerbaijan to break away Russia. With WWI, fighting erupted once again between Russia and the aging Ottoman Empire. Russia's forces fared well at first, until the Bolshevik Revolution began to tear the Tsarist Empire apart from the inside. The chaos forced Russia to withdraw from WWI in 1918 and to abandon its efforts to control the Caucasus while attempting to suppress the revolutionaries. Azerbaijan, Armenia, and Georgia were incorporated into what was called the Transcaucasian Democratic Federative Republic (TDFR), and tasked with their own political administration and defense. In a foreshadowing of the ethnic conflict that would emerge following independence, the TDFR lasted only a few months as the Georgian, Armenian, and Azeri peoples each moved to create their own separate states.[10]

Azerbaijan declared itself to be an independent democratic republic in May of 1918. Fighting erupted between all three of the newly formed South Caucasus states but was particularly brutal between Azeris and Armenians.[11] Advancing Ottoman and British forces confused fighting in the region even further, but Russia was not yet willing to surrender the Caucasus. Once the Communist Bolsheviks had consolidated their power and defeated the Tsar's "White" Russian loyalists, the Bolshevik "Red" Army turned to restoring the territorial holdings of the Russian Empire. By 1920, the whole of the South Caucasus was once again under Russian control. In 1922, the Communists reintegrated Azerbaijan, Armenia, and Georgia into one political entity, this time called the Transcaucasian Soviet Federative Socialist Republic (TSFSR).[12]

In accordance with Lenin's doctrine of recognizing ethnic identities, however, the Azeri nation was eventually recognized with political autonomy.[13] When the TSFSR was abolished, Georgia, Armenia, and Azerbaijan were each recognized as separate Soviet Republics. Soviet protection of ethnic identities also meant, however, the creation of convoluted boundaries in the region. For Azerbaijan, this meant that the large Armenian population in Nagorno-Karabakh, a region well within the borders of the Azeri Soviet Republic, was granted a degree of political autonomy. As well, Nakhichevan, a region with a large Azeri population, was cut off from Azerbaijan by the territory of Armenia, whose Soviet-determined borders stretched all the way south to the Iranian border. Despite this recognition of their identities, Azeris in Nakhichevan really wished to be joined with Azerbaijan and Armenians in Nagorno-Karabakh wished to be joined to Armenia. The Soviet refusal to do so meant that the Azeris and Armenians would go to war to redraw their boundaries as soon as they gained independence.

In addition, Soviet manipulation of ethno-national identities laid a foundation for relations between the Azeri state and Iran. When Iran declared neutrality during WWII, the Soviets (with the blessing of their Allies) invaded Iran. By crossing the Aras River and occupying the Azeri-populated north, the Soviets offered a chance for a united Azeri nation. Iranian Azeris were encouraged to form their own political institutions and secede from Iran. In 1942, however, the Allied Powers agreed that Iranian territorial integrity should be respected. The Soviet refusal to withdraw was viewed by the West as an attempt to further expand Soviet territory. This resulted in Soviet-American crisis over Iran, which marked (in many ways) the beginning of the Cold War.[14]

As the Soviets moved to occupy greater parts of Iran in March of 1946, Winston Churchill famously proclaimed that an "iron curtain" had fallen across Soviet-occupied lands. The British and Americans used the newly created United Nations to counter the Russians. Eventually, this pressure resulted in a Soviet withdrawal based on the condition that it retain a stake in northern Iranian oil resources. For Iranian Azeris, however, this "victory" of the West meant the evaporation of their hope for independence. The Shah's army, unopposed by the Red Army, moved into the northwestern Iran and squashed Azeri separatists. The Aras River was reestablished as the northern Iranian border, perpetuating the division of the Azeri nation into northern and southern segments until today.[15]

Soviet rule also had social and economic repercussions for Azerbaijan. Under the atheist Soviets, policies of Christianization were replaced with policies of Russification. This meant the forced abandonment of Islam in Azerbaijan, and contrary to Leninist encouragement of ethno-national identities, Stalin also implemented policies to force the people of the South Caucasus to learn Russian. Additionally, Soviet economic centralization made the economy of Azerbaijan more dependent upon Russia. Transportation and communication infrastructures were oriented in a core-periphery relationship between Moscow and Baku.[16] The pipeline infrastructure for the export of Azeri energy was also oriented to serve the needs of the Soviet Union. Thus, even after independence, Azerbaijan's energy infrastructure remained largely dominated by Russia because its main export pipelines passed through Russian territory.

INDEPENDENCE AND DEVELOPING SECURITY OF THE STATE

As the Soviet Union began to come unglued, nationalist feeling peaked in the South Caucasus, and Azerbaijan was no exception. On August 30, 1991, Azerbaijan declared its independence. Ayaz Mutalibov, who had been appointed Communist Party leader under Gorbachev (see Appendix A for biography), was elected president thereafter. That election, however, was boycotted by the nationalist Azerbaijan Popular Front (AXC), which opposed the grip the old Soviets still held on the government. Their boycott contributed to Mutalibov's ability to maintain the presidency, but the delegitimization of his election heightened political disunity in the young Azeri state. To this internal political strife was added the economic turmoil created by the Union's collapse, which weakened the Azeri state and its ability to counter Armenian separatism in Nagorno-Karabakh. The resulting war with Armenia proved to be such a disaster that it forced Mutalibov to resign before he had even served a full year as the first elected president of Azerbaijan.

War for Nagorno-Karabakh

The conflict that erupted in Nagorno-Karabakh was a long time in the making. Religious conflict between Armenians and the Azeri Turks had persisted since Islam was brought to the Caucasus. With religious differences defined along ethnic lines, Christian Armenians versus Muslim Turks, this conflict assumed all aspects of ethnic violence. When Russian control of the Caucasus slipped during WWI, fighting between Armenians and Azeris in the Zangezur and Karabakh regions was characterized by ethnic cleansing.[17]

When Russian control of the Caucasus was restored by the Soviets, it delayed this inevitable conflict. However, the Soviets also exacerbated the ethnic situation through the drawing of convoluted borders. For example, Azeri-Armenian tensions were only somewhat mitigated when Soviets designated Nagorno-Karabakh as an autonomous region. Ultimately, however, Nagorno-Karabakh was still politically subordinate to Azerbaijan, a situation that the Armenians in the region repeatedly appealed to the Communist Party to change. As the Soviet Union was unraveling in 1988, Karabakh Armenians twice attempted to separate from Azerbaijan. Armenians and Azeris realized that this conflict was inevitable. Between November and December of 1989, nearly 160,000 Azeris and 180,000 Armenians abandoned their homes in disputed areas and moved deeper into their respective states.[18]

In 1989, Armenia made it clear that it was going to involve itself in the controversial status of Nagorno-Karabakh when the Armenian government called for the annexation of Nagorno-Karabakh. Across Azerbaijan, this excited ethnic violence and led to anti-Armenian riots in Baku. Soviet troops were deployed to crush that riot in what became known as Black January.[19] All Soviet military intervention in the growing dispute, however, came to an end after the Moscow *putsch* in August of 1991.[20]

Both Armenia and Azerbaijan officially accepted their Soviet-demarked borders in 1992 as a condition of their membership in the OSCE. But by that time, Karabakh Armenians were already fighting for their independence with the unofficial support of the Armenian state. In February of 1992, Armenian forces accompanied by the old Soviet 366th Motorized Rifle Regiment attacked and captured the Azeri town of Khojali, perpetrating what Human Rights Watch has called "the conflict's largest massacre."[21]

Armenian forces were united and resolved in their commitment to separate Nagorno-Karabakh from Azerbaijan, while domestic politics in Azerbaijan were torn by internal power struggles. By May of 1992 the towns of Shusha and Lachin were in the possession of Armenian forces, opening a strategic roadway into Armenia through which arms and supplies could flow. With that route open, Armenian support for the Karabakh separatists was becoming undeniable. Mutalibov's inability to defeat the Armenians led to his eventual ousting by Azeri nationalists, who elected Abulfaz Elchibey (see Appendix A for biography) as the next Azeri president. Yet Elchibey's popularity began to fade quickly as he too could not bring about Azeri victories. Armenian forces, after establishing the connection between Armenia and Nagorno-Karabakh, began to expand beyond the borders of Nagorno-Karabakh. As Armenian forces continued to advance, it became increasingly clear that external intervention would be required to bring an end to the conflict before more Azeri territory was lost.[22] The United States and Europe attempted to use the OSCE to facilitate peace talks, but generally adopted the position that the South Caucasus was the responsibility of Moscow. Russia, then, was the best hope for Azerbaijan but Azeri nationalism translated into anti-Russian feeling, which Elchibey embraced himself. During his short, 13-month term in office, Elchibey refused to take a pragmatic approach toward Moscow and even succeeded in alarming Tehran with discussions of unification with Azeris in northwestern Iran.[23]

Elchibey's idealistic embrace of nationalism proved to be shortsighted because it left Azerbaijan with no allies among its immediate neighbors. While Turkey supported Azerbaijan in its dispute with Armenia, Turkey only shares a border with Azerbaijan's isolated Nakhichevan region, and it stopped short of direct military support for Azerbaijan. Under these conditions, Armenian forces soon occupied roughly 20 percent of Azerbaijan's territory.[24] This was devastating for Baku and Elchibey's popularity and perpetuated the internal political chaos in Azerbaijan. From this chaos a military insurrection emerged, led by a Colonel named Suret Husseinov. Seeking to keep Azerbaijan from being torn apart, Elchibey turned to the powerful old Soviet leader of Azerbaijan, Heydar Aliyev (see Appendix A for biography). On June 18, 1993, Elchibey fled from Baku and Aliyev assumed the presidency soon after.[25]

A former Soviet party boss, Aliyev demonstrated willingness to pragmatically defer to Moscow to bring an end to war. He made a personal visit to Moscow in 1993 and agreed to join the CIS, a move that both Mutalibov and Elchibey had rejected.[26] In return for Aliyev's recognition of Russia's special role in the Caucasus, Moscow applied pressure on Yerevan to halt its advance. Instead of relying on nationalistic rhetoric, Aliyev based his opposition to Armenian separatism on arguments for the respect of territorial integrity and internationally recognized borders. By assuming this rhetorical stance, Aliyev created a viable legal argument against the legitimacy of Nagorno-Karabakh's succession. By championing territorial integrity over the determination of borders based on nationalities, Aliyev also abandoned the logic that Elchibey had employed when he discussed the possibility of unification with Iranian Azeris.[27]

The Moscow-devised Bishkek Protocol officially brought an end to the war over Nagorno-Karabakh in 1993. (See text of the cease-fire agreement in Appendix G.) By then, Azerbaijan had suffered an estimated $60 billion in damage, roughly 30,000 killed, 1.3 million displaced, and the loss of 16 percent of its territory.[28] Armenian forces maintained a buffer zone around Nagorno-Karabakh, which they have refused to surrender. And though the conflict has largely remained frozen since then, a final peace agreement has remained elusive because neither side has been willing to surrender their territorial claims.

Heydar Aliyev's son, Ilham Aliyev (see Appendix A for biography), replaced his father in 2003 and has maintained the presidency despite accusations of electoral fraud and media intimidation.[29] Ilham Aliyev has repeated his father's pragmatic rhetorical stance on the Nagorno-Karabakh conflict and maintained largely positive ties with Russia and Iran. Thus far, no state has officially recognized Nagorno-Karabakh's independence, and when the region adopted its first constitution in 2006, it was widely condemned.[30] Still, Nagorno-Karabakh has maintained de facto independence for nearly two decades, and time appears to be on the side of the Armenians.

Status of Azerbaijan's Military

Military growth is a major priority for Baku, as it strengthens its position in regards to Nagorno-Karabakh dispute. In 2006, Azerbaijan spent 3.6 percent of its GDP on military expenditures. That translates into US$625 million (almost a doubling of its 2005 expenditures).[31] Baku justified this expenditure as a response to Moscow's transfer of military equipment from a military base in Batumi, Georgia to its 102nd Military Base in Gyumri (Armenia). Azerbaijan viewed this development as a backhanded way to supply arms to Armenia.[32] Since 1998, Azerbaijan has led the South Caucasus states in total dollars spent on the military. Between 1998 and 2007, Azerbaijan's military expenditures increased by 554 percent in real terms.[33] In 2008, the reported total expenditures (in constant U.S. 2005 dollars) were 697 million. This may show an increase through 2009 as Azerbaijan attempts to create a military that could drive Armenian forces from Nagorno-Karabakh.[34] Azerbaijan has made a commitment to outspending Armenia, which is maybe motivated by a desire to produce an arms race that Yerevan cannot win. This way, Baku hopes to bring Armenia back to the negotiating table, when Azerbaijan enjoys a favorable military balance.[35]

Between 2004 and 2006, Azerbaijan has reportedly acquired several significant weapons. The list includes: 12 "Smerch" multi-launch rocket systems, 85 120mm PM-38 artillery systems, 72 100mm MT-12 anti-tank guns, and 105 T-72 tanks.[36] Since 2004, Baku has also invested significant funds to upgrade its air force. It has purchased 6 SU-25 fighter-bombers, 1 SU-25UB fighter aircraft, and 14 MIG-29 fighter aircraft.[37] Additionally, seven aerodromes have been undergoing modernization, and there are reports that Azerbaijan has tried to purchase U.S. aircraft (like the F-15) from other developing countries.[38]

While it is difficult to get precise quantitative measurements of the military strength of Azerbaijan (and other South Caucasus states, for that matter), most estimates appear to give Baku the edge in heavy armaments if fresh fighting breaks out with Yerevan.[39] As Azerbaijan has acquired its new military equipments, Armenia has repeatedly claimed that Baku is in violation of the Conventional Armed Forces in Europe Treaty. Yerevan has alleged that Azerbaijan is in possession of 1.5–2 times the amount of allowable tanks as well as armored vehicles, and it owns 2–2.5 times more than the allowed amount of artillery.[40]

Azerbaijan's Energy Resources

Similar to the former Soviet Republics, the first few years of independence in Azerbaijan brought major economic dislocation. The war with Armenia further crippled the Azeri economy as the war effort gobbled up scarce resources and human lives while the Armenian advance captured territory and destroyed infrastructure. The destruction that the Nagorno-Karabakh war brought could have entirely crippled Azerbaijan, if it was not for the positive contribution of its large energy deposits.

Onshore and offshore deposits of oil and natural gas along the Caspian Sea have been critical for the Azeri economic recovery—allowing Azerbaijan to make the greatest economic gains among the South Caucasus states since its independence. In Azerbaijan's GDP totals, oil and gas account for around 60 percent. Driven primarily by oil exports, the GDP of Azerbaijan has grown by an average of 21 percent over the past five years. And in 2006, it reached an astounding 34.5 percent growth, the world's largest GDP growth rate in that year.[41]

Energy resources provide an economic advantage that Azerbaijan maintains over Georgia and Armenia. In 2007, Azeri exports reached 733 tb/d. This means that Azerbaijan is capable of exporting most of the energy that it is producing, as the total oil production came to roughly 848 tb/d that year. Both Georgia and Armenia are dependent on energy imports. But Azerbaijan has the potential to expand its oil exports in the years to come. Baku possesses an estimated 7 bbl of oil reserves, and its refining capacity currently stands at 399 tb/d. Relative to its huge oil deposits. Azerbaijan's natural gas reserves are smaller at an estimated 30,000 bcf. In 2006, gas production came to 241 bcf, which failed to meet all of Azerbaijan's domestic needs of 399 billion cubic feet per year (bcf/y).[42] In order to supply this consistent shortfall, Azerbaijan imports gas from both Russia and Iran. However, Baku could increase its gas production with foreign direct investment (FDI), and it has the potential to become a net exporter of natural gas as well as oil.[43]

Initially, the energy sector sagged like the rest of Azerbaijan's economy. In fact, oil production declined every year after independence until 1997. Heydar Aliyev realized not only the economic potential of Azerbaijan's energy, but also its political implications. Once he became president, he temporarily suspended negotiations with foreign companies in order to focus on patching up relations with Russia. Once a partnership was established with Russia's Lukoil, he then focused on creating a large consortium of foreign energy companies in what was termed "the Deal of the Century."[44] With Western companies, Azerbaijan also constructed a western-flowing pipeline, the Baku-Tbilisi-Ceyhan (BTC), to diversify its export route options. Completed in 2005, the BTC is a 1,040-mile pipeline that travels from the Azeri capital of Baku to the Georgian capital of Tbilisi and then terminates at the Turkish port of Ceyhan. These moves heralded a revival in Azerbaijan's energy industry that has been followed by incredible production growth in the major Chirag Guneshli oil fields. In both 2006 and 2007, Azerbaijan had the largest oil production growth outside of the Oil Producing and Exporting Countries (OPEC).[45] Azerbaijan now has "over 20 major field agreements with approximately 30 companies from fifteen different countries."[46] The major consumers of Azeri oil are Russia, Italy, Turkey, and Germany.[47]

Despite Aliyev's efforts to develop mutually beneficial oil business relationships with the international community, Azerbaijan's energy resources are simply too significant to escape the energy politics that evolved between global and regional powers in the Caspian Sea Region. Baku's deal with Western companies for the BTC pipeline in 1999 was concluded without Moscow's participation, because Russian negotiators had left the discussions to demonstrate their opposition to any pipeline projects that did not transit through Russian territory. Before the BTC, Azerbaijan exported oil to Europe via a Russian pipeline that ran to the Black Sea port of Novorossiysk.[48] The BTC diverted oil from this route, reducing Russian income from transit fees, and reducing Moscow's ability to gain political leverage through the control of Europe's critical energy supplies. The BTC not only allows Azerbaijan to export outside of the old Russian energy infrastructure, but it has also allows Kazakhstan to export its oil by using barges to make deliveries to Baku across the Caspian Sea. The BTC could also serve as the Western leg of a trans-Caspian pipeline, which would allow both Kazakhstan and Turkmenistan to export significant amounts of energy without any assistance from Russia or Iran.

With its Caspian neighbors Turkmenistan and Iran, Azerbaijan has also had energy disputes. Turkmenistan and Azerbaijan have been unable to agree on the ownership of fields in the middle of the Caspian.[49] The legal division of the Caspian Sea is an issue that has yet to be resolved. Azerbaijan, Russia, and Kazakhstan have agreed to classify the Caspian as a sea and divide it as such in accordance with international law. On the other hand, Turkmenistan and Iran prefer to treat the Caspian as a lake. In this dispute, each state has adopted the legal stance that would provide it with the greatest ownership of Caspian energy resources.[50] As long as this ambiguity persists, a trans-Caspian pipeline is a distant possibility.

In regard to natural gas, similar energy politics apply. Baku's electrical production facilities almost completely operate on gas, a good portion of which must be supplied by Russia. In recent years, Russia has been raising gas prices to its former Soviet Republics. When Azerbaijan gained independence, Gazprom was charging $110 for 35.3 bcf. In late 2006, Gazprom hiked the price to $235. Like other former Soviet Republics, Baku condemned the hike as "commercial blackmail." It was not the only time that Russia was accused of using its gas resources as a coercive political tool. Azerbaijan has negotiated with Iran for an alternative gas partnership, but a pricing agreement has not yet been reached. Instead, Baku is now refining oil as a substitute in electrical production.[51]

Status of Azerbaijan's Economy

Azerbaijan's economy continues to be the strongest economy among the three Caucasus states, even through the recent global recession. The annual percentage change in Real GDP growth declined between 2007 and 2008; and the International Monetary Fund (IMF) predicted that this trend will continue through at least the end of 2009. Nevertheless, this decline is expected to rapidly reverse itself (relative to the other Caucasus states), and Azerbaijan's current account balance is projected to continue to improve.[52] All of these indicators point to a relatively stable economy in Azerbaijan for the near future (Tables 2.1–2.4, Graphs 2.1–2.4).

However, there are some security concerns related to Azerbaijan's economy. For instance, the rebounding Azeri economy, particularly its oil wealth, has facilitated the government's ability to increase its spending on the military, possibly in preparation for future hostilities in Nagorno-Karabakh.[53] Moreover, while oil revenues have proven to be an economic blessing, the primary focus on oil exports is a weakness. Large revenues from a single natural resource may undermine a country's economy through a process known as "Dutch Disease."[54]

Table 2.1 Azerbaijani Export Volume

	1998	1999	2000	2001	2002	2003	2004	2005	2006	2007	2008
US	13.857	29.83	8.005	13.662	51.975	63.865	25.992	43.202	98.191	289.17	4080.55
EU	141.175	438.525	1101.12	1624.38	1507.04	1745.57	1841.03	2029.11	3556.93	1583.03	14253
Japan	0.022	0.404	0.119	0.188	0.263	19.799	0.347	0.018	0.045	0	45.9972
China (m)	0.901	0.167	4.879	2.439	1.312	19.286	31.718	99.238	6.39	10.104	111.333
Russia	105.787	83.071	98.302	77.558	95.688	147.881	209.76	285.416	344.259	527.121	509.016
CIS (8)	49.472	56.334	62.276	42.081	67.204	74.352	215.66	411.538	300.182	231.533	267.3395
Iran	44.469	22.668	7.68	9.144	29.885	49.129	153.561	166.468	295.902	434.731	549.151
Turkey	135.838	69.081	104.981	67.382	83.397	107.036	182.593	275.959	388.145	1056.32	844.019
Armenia	0	0	0	0	0	0	0	0	0	0	0
Georgia	76.915	71.723	74.64	103.236	80.828	110.06	188.784	208.436	285.276	343.82	392.527
Azeri Subtotal	**568.436**	**771.803**	**1462.002**	**1940.07**	**1917.592**	**2336.978**	**2849.445**	**3519.385**	**5275.32**	**4475.829**	**21052.93**
World Subtotal	**607.051**	**929.228**	**1745.36**	**2315.76**	**2166.72**	**2590.1**	**3615.42**	**4347.15**	**6372.16**	**6058.33**	**24064.8**

(m) = mainland; CIS (8) = Belarus, Kazakhstan, Kyrgyzstan, Moldova, Tajikistan, Turkmenistan, Ukraine, Uzbekistan.
Source: IMF's Direction of Trade Statistics.

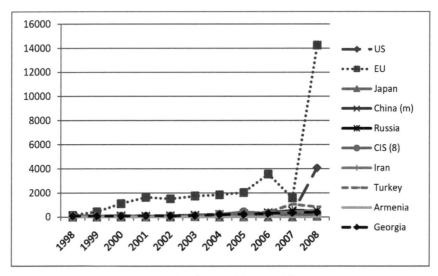

Graph 2.1 Azerbaijani Export Volume

As increasing oil profits drive up the value of Azerbaijan's currency, the price of Azeri exports also increase, which can drive down export sales and lead to the economic slowdown of non-oil industries. This is a dangerous situation, because the oil industry in Azerbaijan is still developing and this industry employs only a small percentage of the population.[55] Furthermore, when oil is the primary revenue source, the volatile price of oil dictates national wealth, as is the case for many developing countries.

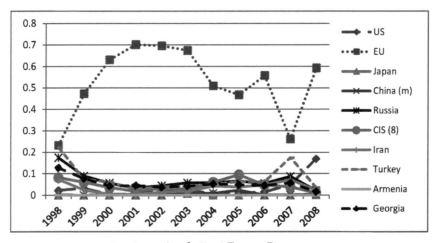

Graph 2.2 Azerbaijani Export Percentage

Table 2.2 Azerbaijani Export Percentage

	1998	1999	2000	2001	2002	2003	2004	2005	2006	2007	2008
US	2.28%	3.21%	0.46%	0.59%	2.40%	2.47%	0.72%	0.99%	1.54%	4.77%	16.96%
EU	23.26%	47.19%	63.09%	70.14%	69.55%	67.39%	50.92%	46.68%	55.82%	26.13%	59.23%
Japan	0.00%	0.04%	0.01%	0.01%	0.01%	0.76%	0.01%	0.00%	0.00%	0.00%	0.19%
China (m)	0.15%	0.02%	0.28%	0.11%	0.06%	0.74%	0.88%	2.28%	0.10%	0.17%	0.46%
Russia	17.43%	8.94%	5.63%	3.35%	4.42%	5.71%	5.80%	6.57%	5.40%	8.70%	2.12%
CIS (8)	8.15%	6.06%	3.57%	1.82%	3.10%	2.87%	5.97%	9.47%	4.71%	3.82%	1.11%
Iran	7.33%	2.44%	0.44%	0.39%	1.38%	1.90%	4.25%	3.83%	4.64%	7.18%	2.28%
Turkey	22.38%	7.43%	6.01%	2.91%	3.85%	4.13%	5.05%	6.35%	6.09%	17.44%	3.51%
Armenia	0.00%	0.00%	0.00%	0.00%	0.00%	0.00%	0.00%	0.00%	0.00%	0.00%	0.00%
Georgia	12.67%	7.72%	4.28%	4.46%	3.73%	4.25%	5.22%	4.79%	4.48%	5.68%	1.63%
Azeri Subtotal	93.64%	83.06%	83.77%	83.78%	88.50%	90.23%	78.81%	80.96%	82.79%	73.88%	87.48%

(m) = mainland; CIS (8) = Belarus, Kazakhstan, Kyrgyzstan, Moldova, Tajikistan, Turkmenistan, Ukraine, Uzbekistan.
Source: IMF's Direction of Trade Statistics.

Table 2.3 Azerbaijani Import Volume

	1998	1999	2000	2001	2002	2003	2004	2005	2006	2007	2008
US	39.841	82.957	117.71	230.933	98.695	132.621	131.887	141.409	197.986	268.906	262.79
EU	249.349	210.77	261.381	294.778	407.239	867.158	1190.81	1248.12	1569.65	1661.02	3290.11
Japan	0.375	55.504	16.391	66.656	48.444	101.489	127.123	70.611	188.294	295.09	84.4132
China (m)	6.135	13.72	23.091	41.986	51.024	92.393	145.497	173.812	222.493	278.794	634.391
Russia	193.83	226.499	249.329	152.994	280.943	383.901	569.461	717.223	1181.58	1003.89	1236.32
CIS (8)	185.651	89.2	115.894	287.306	356.871	457.07	616.638	686.807	867.381	835.484	981.944
Iran	42.571	47.433	56.83	55.425	57.933	50.608	45.324	76.318	85.917	105.236	138.327
Turkey	219.689	142.979	128.503	148.167	156.219	195.252	224.995	313.002	385.04	624.692	1832.97
Armenia	0	0	0	0	0	0	0	0	0	0	0
Georgia	25.2	9.486	10.317	4.935	12.742	10.232	14.493	45.499	49.202	62.931	71.846
Azeri Subtotal	**962.641**	**878.548**	**979.446**	**1283.18**	**1470.11**	**2290.724**	**3066.228**	**3472.801**	**4747.543**	**5136.043**	**8533.111**
World Subtotal	**1076.5**	**1035.67**	**1171.87**	**1431.11**	**1665.48**	**2625.71**	**3516.02**	**4211.35**	**5266.76**	**5712.2**	**9318.14**

(m) = mainland; CIS (8) = Belarus, Kazakhstan, Kyrgyzstan, Moldova, Tajikistan, Turkmenistan, Ukraine, Uzbekistan.
Source: IMF's Direction of Trade Statistics.

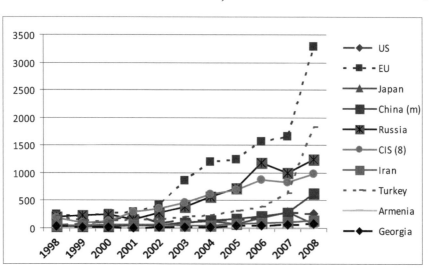

Graph 2.3 Azerbaijani Import Volume

With Western encouragement, Baku has created a state oil fund designed to preserve "macroeconomic stability," decrease "dependence on oil revenues," stimulate "development of the non-oil sector," and finance "major national scale projects to support socio-economic progress."[56] Still, the IMF indicated that Azerbaijan is not doing enough. In mid-2007 assessment, the IMF noted a "continued lack of improvement in corporate governance of some state-owned enterprises, and strongly advised the government to rapidly reduce a non-oil fiscal deficit that is estimated to be about 40 percent of GDP."[57]

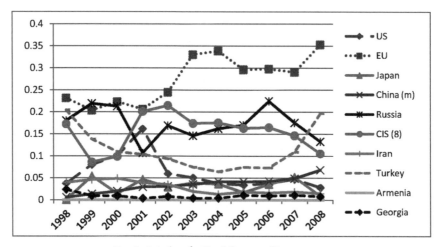

Graph 2.4 Azerbaijani Import Percentage

Table 2.4 Azerbaijani Import Percentage

	1998	1999	2000	2001	2002	2003	2004	2005	2006	2007	2008
US	3.70%	8.01%	10.04%	16.14%	5.93%	5.05%	3.75%	3.36%	3.76%	4.71%	2.82%
EU	23.16%	20.35%	22.30%	20.60%	24.45%	33.03%	33.87%	29.64%	29.80%	29.08%	35.31%
Japan	0.03%	5.36%	1.40%	4.66%	2.91%	3.87%	3.62%	1.68%	3.58%	5.17%	0.91%
China (m)	0.57%	1.32%	1.97%	2.93%	3.06%	3.52%	4.14%	4.13%	4.22%	4.88%	6.81%
Russia	18.01%	21.87%	21.28%	10.69%	16.87%	14.62%	16.20%	17.03%	22.43%	17.57%	13.27%
CIS (8)	17.25%	8.61%	9.89%	20.08%	21.43%	17.41%	17.54%	16.31%	16.47%	14.63%	10.54%
Iran	3.95%	4.58%	4.85%	3.87%	3.48%	1.93%	1.29%	1.81%	1.63%	1.84%	1.48%
Turkey	20.41%	13.81%	10.97%	10.35%	9.38%	7.44%	6.40%	7.43%	7.31%	10.94%	19.67%
Armenia	0.00%	0.00%	0.00%	0.00%	0.00%	0.00%	0.00%	0.00%	0.00%	0.00%	0.00%
Georgia	2.34%	0.92%	0.88%	0.34%	0.77%	0.39%	0.41%	1.08%	0.93%	1.10%	0.77%
Azeri Subtotal	**89.42%**	**84.83%**	**83.58%**	**89.66%**	**88.27%**	**87.24%**	**87.21%**	**82.46%**	**90.14%**	**89.91%**	**91.58%**

(m) = mainland; CIS (8) = Belarus, Kazakhstan, Kyrgyzstan, Moldova, Tajikistan, Turkmenistan, Ukraine, Uzbekistan.
Source: IMF's Direction of Trade Statistics.

Quantitative research studies have also revealed that high levels of internal social violence are correlated with great natural resource wealth.[58] Perhaps more threatening to the long-term social stability of Azerbaijan is the correlation between oil wealth and a democracy deficit.[59] The leaders of oil-wealthy states do not have to rely on their populations for revenue via taxation. This removes the state from accountability to its people, decreasing its need to respond to public dissatisfaction and setting the stage for political unrest. Since Azerbaijan's political status as a democracy is suspect at best, such political deficit is a very real security issue for a young state.

Beyond the discussion of political and security ties of Baku with global and regional powers, it is also important to observe the trade patterns of Azerbaijan to completely understand the big picture of its foreign relations. In order to illustrate the most recent trade trends of this Former Soviet republic, Azerbaijan export and import data were collected from the IMF Direction of Trade Statistics for the period of 1998 to 2008. The first table indicates the volume of Azeri exports to major global and regional powers in addition to Azerbaijan's neighboring states. The result of this table is more clearly illustrated in a graph, which may serve as evidence for politicians who speak diplomatically about the supposedly growing trends of their country's trade with others. Both the export volume table and graph support such claims, with the exception of Azeri exports to Armenia, which are simply zero.

However, a rather different picture of Azeri export patterns shows when we calculate the percentages (out of the subtotal of trade with selected strategic partners) of Azeri exports. While both volume and percentage graphs of Azeri exports indicate that the EU has been the main destination of Azeri goods, the percentage graph illustrates more variation in export percentage for the other destinations of Azeri goods (most of which are fossil fuels). Without the doubt, the EU is the main beneficiary of Azeri exports; and it took this position from the traditional destinations of such goods—Russia and other CIS states. Interestingly enough, the trends of Baku exports to key states such as the United States, Russia, Turkey, and Iran are not simple escalating or decreasing lines. They all vary depending on the politics of Azeri bilateral, regional, and global relations as discussed earlier. It is also significant to emphasize that despite their hunger for fossil fuels, neither China nor Japan is a major destination of Azeri exports yet. Finally, the export trends with neighboring countries are very one-sided. While Georgia is a significant Azeri trade destination (even in comparison to the United States, Russia, Iran, and Turkey), there is simply no economic connection with Yerevan.

In terms of the Azeri import volume and percentages, there are interesting patterns in relation to foreign relations. First of all, the volume of imports again shows a steadily growing Azeri trade with the same groups of regional and great powers, with the exception of Armenia. Secondly, the EU again takes the first place in both volume and percentage graphs. Thirdly, there is more diversity among the sources of imports for Baku, despite the fact that the EU takes the first place. In comparison to the export percentage graph, the second, third, fourth, and subsequent positions of Azeri import sources are not as far behind the EU as they were for the exports. Fourthly, Russia, Turkey, and the CIS are respectively the second, third, and fourth most important sources of Azeri imports. In the next cluster of the import percentage graph, China, the United States, Iran, and Georgia respectively take the next ranked positions. Thus, Baku has succeeded more in diversifying its sources of imports, as opposed to the destination of its exports.

Islamic Resurgence in Azerbaijan

Years of atheism under the Soviets significantly undercut the role of Islam in Azerbaijan. Though 90 percent of the population is officially Muslim, Islam has become largely a cultural heritage. Shia Azeris have much more liberal attitudes toward alcohol, pork, and women than Iranian Shia now living in Azerbaijan. While 65–70 percent of the population is Shia and 30–35 percent Sunni, Svante Cornell argues that the distinction between these two sects has actually become blurred in Azerbaijan, and many Azeris are not knowledgeable about the differences between the two sects.[60]

Following the Nagorno-Karabakh conflict, however, one of the most momentous demographic transitions experienced by Azeris has been the resurgence of Islam in the population. The resurgence of Islam may be a positive occurrence as Azeris return to cultural and religious roots that they were forced to abandon. This is certainly a trend that Azerbaijan shares with the other post-Soviet Muslim republics. Yet the return to Islam may not just be a return to a cultural heritage, but also a backlash against the globalization process, modernization, and Westernization, as has been the case in some Islamic states. When Western media and culture poured into the country after independence, it produced a conservative backlash in rural areas, as liberalization spread unevenly and mainly in the urban areas.[61]

Coupled with the Nagorno-Karabakh crisis, such "rural-urban divide" conditions appear ripe for radicalization. Thousands of Muslim Azeris were displaced and impoverished by the Christian-Armenian military. As the Palestinian-Israeli conflict demonstrated, poverty-stricken refugee camps are potentially dangerous breeding grounds for radical religious doctrine. Nowadays, both Sunni and Shia militant groups are operating in Azerbaijan.[62] Yet so far the Nagorno-Karabakh conflict has not definitely produced significant Islamic militants, which are detectable. This fact may or may not speak to the degree of Islamic moderation that Azerbaijan has experienced.

Even if militant or radical Islam has not taken deep roots in Azerbaijan, political Islam appears to be growing—a trend shared in neighboring Turkey. Various surveys conducted from 2001–2005 have demonstrated that political Islam is gaining approval.[63] One 2003–2005 comparative study conducted by a local firm

(PULS-S) found that the "Islamic model of state-building and public life is drawing more interest, and the number of supporters of Azerbaijan's strengthened relations with the Islamic nations is also rising."[64] Still, Azerbaijan's political leadership, dominated by the semi-authoritarian governance of Aliyev, has so far rejected fundamental and political Islam. In 2001, Aliyev created a state committee for relations with religious organizations. That committee monitors all religious activities, but keeps a close eye on the missionaries from Iran and Saudi Arabia.[65]

While Azerbaijan's Soviet history is a major factor in the revival of Islam, the politicization and radicalization of Islam is primarily due to external forces. Azerbaijan is geographically embedded in a region full of blossoming radical Islamic movements. Most radical Islamist groups operating in Azerbaijan are trained and/or supported from abroad. Iran, Saudi Arabia and the Persian Gulf region, Turkey, and the Russian Northern Caucasus (specifically Chechnya and Dagestan) are all sources with the geographic proximity to influence Azeri Islam. Saudi Arabia and Dagestan have been important sources of radical Sunni influence, but because of Azerbaijan's Shiite heritage, Iranian-supported Shiite movements are potentially more threatening to Azerbaijan.[66] As a result, the age-old dichotomy between Azerbaijan's Turkish and Iranian heritage is reemerging. Both Turkey and Iran have sponsored religious foundations in Azerbaijan, espousing moderate Sunni Islam and conservative Shia Islam respectively. Further implications of this geopolitical factor will be provided in the following discussion of Azerbaijan's greater geopolitical environment.

Contemporary Politics and Government in Azerbaijan

Government Structure

Based on its constitution, the new state of Azerbaijan is theoretically established as a secular and republican form of government, which derives its power from the people. The national government has three branches: the executive branch headed by the President of Azerbaijan, the judicial branch with the courts, and the legislative branch which consists of a single-chamber parliament led by a prime minister. Under the constitution, parliamentary representatives and the Republic's president are to be elected in free, open, and democratic elections by the people of Azerbaijan. (See Appendix G for Azerbaijan's constitution.)

Political Conditions

Despite the appearance of a check-and-balance system among the three branches of the government, Azerbaijan's executive branch, lead by President Ilham Aliyev, effectively holds an overwhelming share of the political power within the state structure. His tight grip on power resembles that of his father's, which some have described as "semi-authoritarian."[67] The manner in which he succeeded the presidency from his father, Heydar Aliyev, has raised some concerns about the real nature of political freedom and democracy in Azerbaijan. As his father's health failed, Ilham Aliyev ran for election as president in 2003. When the final election result was revealed, it showed Ilham Aliyev as the undisputed winner, having received 77 percent of all votes. His greatest opponent, the leader of Musavat Party (i.e., Isa Gambar) was reported to have received only 14 percent of the vote, while six other candidates split the remaining votes. OSCE observers criticized the election, citing widespread fraud, and the results provoked several clashes between security forces and demonstrators from opposition parties. Over 600 people were detained by security forces, a number of whom were opposition party leaders who had not directly participated in the violent demonstrations and election officials whohad refused to certify the results.[68]

The reports indicate that Ilham Aliyev also won a large majority of the votes in the October 2008 presidential election, in which he was seeking a second term. It was reported that he received 89 percent of the total votes in an election with 75 percent turnout of registered voters. International sources indicate that most of the opposition boycotted that election in protest of media control and unfair electoral conditions.[69] Still, these numbers may demonstrate that Ilham Aliyev does indeed have a significant amount of popular support. Either way, he appears to have firm control of the state of Azerbaijan. Moreover, the door for his lifelong presidency was opened in March of 2009, when a referendum was used to abolish presidential term limits.[70]

Important Political Players

Due to the apparent attempts to curtail free elections by Ilham Aliyev and his political party, the New Azerbaijan Party (YAP), it is important to observe the behavior of key opposition leaders and political parties for signs of growing internal instability in Azerbaijan. One significant opposition party is the AXC, which is the former president Elchibey's party; it continues to reflect a strong nationalistic stance. AXC has roughly 80,000 members, but it is a loose political grouping without a well-defined agenda. Isa Gambar and his New Equality Party (YMP) have continued to offer greater opposition. In fact, Gambar is a leading opposition candidate, and both Azeri officials and the OSCE representatives have stated that he was behind the violent riots in 2003. He and his party have also aligned themselves from time to time with Azadliq, an opposition block formed from a number of other opposition parties.[71]

Political Freedom, Civil Liberties, and Human Rights

Due to Ilham Aliyev's tight control of the Azeri state, Freedom House's index of international freedom (*Freedom in the World 2009*) lists Azerbaijan as "Not Free."[72] Freedom House rates Political Rights and Civil Liberties on a scale of 1–7, with 1 being the most free and 7 being the least free. Azerbaijan received a Political Rights score of 6 and a Civil Liberties score of 5. Freedom of speech is a constitutional right that is regularly infringed upon. The broadcast news media is largely pro-government. While there are opposition newspapers, they have poor circulation. Journalists are subject to threats and assaults, and according to the Committee to Protect Journalists, at least five journalists and editors were in prison in 2008 under various charges. Freedom of assembly is also abused by the Azeri government, particularly the right of the political opposition to assemble.[73]

Traditional religious minorities (Russian Orthodox Christianity and Judaism) are relatively well-treated by the government, but all other "nontraditional" religious minorities face difficult government regulations and restrictions. Some ethnic minorities, particularly Armenians, complain of discrimination in education, employment, and housing. Many of the Azeris displaced by the fighting in Nagorno-Karabakh also remain destitute, and they are still in miserable refugee camps.[74]

Such failures and abuses by the Azeri government are hidden by a lack of government transparency. This lack of transparency creates a permissive environment for corruption, which is endemic in Azerbaijan's government and bureaucratic structure. Azeri massive oil revenues have provided great incentive for such corruption. Azerbaijan was ranked 158 out of 180 countries surveyed in Transparency International's 2008 *Corruption Perceptions Index*.[75]

FOREIGN POLICY AND RELATIONS

United States and NATO

The United States has a strategic interest in Azerbaijan's energy. Though the United States does not really need Azeri oil for its domestic consumption, Washington has an interest in preventing Moscow's monopolization of energy resources. With such control, Russia might gain an OPEC-like ability to influence the oil prices, a potentially more dangerous prospect. Moreover, Washington has involved itself to keep the Islamic Republic of Iran (IRI) from economically benefiting from building an energy export relationship with Azerbaijan.

Still, American-Azeri ties have not always been steady. At first, the United States was very sympathetic toward the Armenian independence movement in Nagorno-Karabakh. Many Armenians immigrated to the States in the years of Ottoman brutality and after the conclusion of WWI. Today, Armenian-Americans constitute a powerful political lobby. For instance, there is a strong Armenian lobby in the state of Massachusetts that provided incentive for Senator John Kerry to propose the sanctioning of Azerbaijan under Section 907 of the Freedom Support Act, which the U.S. Congress passed in 1992. (See text of Section 907 in Appendix G.) Compared to the powerful Armenian lobby, Baku did not even have diplomatic representation (in Washington at that time) with which it might protest such a move.[76]

Both Presidents George H. W. Bush and Bill Clinton realized the negative consequences that Section 907 had for the future of American-Azeri relations, but neither president was able to convince the U.S. Congress to repeal that legislation.[77] Section 907 continued to hamper American-Azeri ties until January 2002, when George W. Bush finally managed to secure temporary suspension of the ban on U.S. aid to Azerbaijan. (See text of the Waiver of Section 907 in Appendix G.) The main reason for his success was the overnight shift in American domestic politics solely due to the attacks of September 11. Following the 9/11 terrorist attacks, American-Azeri relations suddenly became critical because Baku's cooperation was needed in Bush's War on Terror. Over-flight permission was essential for the United States and NATO to carry out the invasion of Afghanistan.[78] Baku seized the opportunity to take relations with Washington to a new level and approved U.S. overflight in return for the suspension of the aid ban.

There were two important factors that might have influenced Azerbaijan to seek a greater relationship with the United States. First, Moscow was initially cooperative with the U.S.-led operations in Afghanistan and friendly toward the idea of a war on terrorism. Russia's position made it possible for Azerbaijan and the United States to increase their cooperation without initially creating much tension between Baku and Moscow. Second, Azerbaijan may have perceived the proposed U.S. alliance as a means to counter the southern threat posed by Iran. Earlier in summer 2001, the disputes between Azerbaijan and Iran over the division of Caspian Sea energy resources had threatened to spill over into military conflict when Iran used naval ships to intimidate Azeri vessels and research vessels owned by British Petroleum (BP).

No matter what the reason, post-9/11 cooperation and the lifting of Section 907 had great positive ramifications in Azerbaijan. Even when anti-Americanism was internationally growing in reaction to the American invasion of Iraq, a survey conducted in 2006 revealed that most Azeris possessed a positive view of the United States. Azerbaijan even deployed troops to Iraq, the only other state with a Muslim majority population to join the United States in the occupation of Iraq besides Kazakhstan. Still, early decisions by Washington to provide relief to Yerevan during the conflict in Nagorno-Karabakh haunt the relatively new relationship with Baku. The temporary waiver of sanctions in Section 907 has been perceived by some Azeris as blackmail, simply because the waiver must be repeatedly renewed. This provides the United States with consistent political leverage over the Azeri government in return for cooperation. Azeris question why the United States would not simply repeal this ban, and why it continues to send foreign aid to Karabakh-Armenians.[79]

As Russia's attitude toward the United States has begun to sour, Baku leaders undoubtedly realized that being too cozy with the United States is a dangerous situation. The Russia-Georgia War highlights the recent tension that has arisen between Washington and Moscow. Azeri membership in NATO's PfP program is exactly the sort of cooperative security relationship of which Russia disapproves.[80] Though Azerbaijan is not a full-fledged NATO member, its PfP program includes far-reaching consequences for "military cooperation, defense modernization, democratic control of the armed forces, political consultations on security issues, peace support operations, security sector reform, civil emergency planning, [and] security related scientific, economic[,] and environmental cooperation."[81]

EU and OSCE

Just as NATO has been critical to bringing the United States and Europe together in security cooperation with Azerbaijan, the OSCE has been vital to Western Europe's security ties with Baku. The OSCE has been central to the development of security relations between Azerbaijan and Europe since Azeri independence, when the OSCE was the primary forum which attempted to negotiate a settlement between Baku and Yerevan.[82] The OSCE was a central European institution, since the EU structure did not officially emerge until 1993.

It was in 1999 that Europe-Azerbaijan relations really began to grow. That year a Partnership and Cooperation Agreement (PCA) was adopted between Europe and Azerbaijan. This was the first step toward political, economic, and institutional cooperation. The European Neighborhood Policy (ENP) followed years after the creation of the EU, and was a major step toward including Azerbaijan in the formulation of a foreign policy for the EU.[83] One of the primary goals of the EU in this respect is to minimize instability in neighboring states. "The European Security Strategy, adopted in December 2003, emphasizes the need for the EU to seek to build a belt of well-governed countries on its periphery."[84]

While the EU is incorporating Azerbaijan into its security belt, Baku is a particular case because of Europeans' interest in its energy sources. Energy projects in which both share an interest include the Deal of the Century, the BTC and BTE gas pipelines, and the BAK railway. Azeri-produced energy offers the opportunity to mitigate the EU's dependency on Russian fuel. Before the end of the Cold War, Russian energy was a significant source of imports. Now, the EU dependency on Russia is growing as Eastern European states becoming EU members. In 2006, 33 percent of the EU's oil and 40 percent of its gas came from Russia.[85] The BTC opened the door for diversification with Azeri oil imports, and plans for the Nabucco pipeline project promise greater potential. Nabucco plans propose a gas pipeline along the Caspian seabed from Turkmenistan to Baku that would attach to the BTE pipeline to feed Turkey and Europe.[86]

Russia, CIS, and CSTO

On December 8, 1991, Russia created the Commonwealth of Independent States (CIS), in an attempt to maintain ties with its former republics and facilitate cooperation in former Soviet space. Initially, Baku joined the organization, but when the nationalistic President Elchibey came to power, he terminated Azerbaijan's membership and distanced Azerbaijan from Russia.[87] Moscow soon focused on its own problems and offered little immediate reaction to Azeri action, but the Nagorno-Karabakh conflict offered Russia an opportunity to bring Azerbaijan back into the fold.[88] By refusing to intervene in the conflict and providing aid to Armenia, Moscow demonstrated that Baku must submit to Russian hegemony. Moscow unofficially supplied nearly $1 billion of arms and ammunition to Yerevan without any charges, which facilitated Armenians' war effort.[89] The disaster of this war for Baku is what ultimately produced the insurrection that drove Elchibey from office. But Elchibey's expulsion was not enough to satisfy Moscow. It wanted an Azeri president who would behave deferentially toward the Russian hegemony. Only after Heydar Aliyev requested CIS membership for Azerbaijan again did Russia intervene to bring a stop to the fighting.

For Russia, CIS membership of former Soviet Republics is an important security issue, because Moscow sees these states as its "Near Abroad" and an essential part of its geopolitical "sphere of influence." This way, Russian leaders view the Caucasus as a vital segment of their security sphere, which serves as a buffer between Russia and the greater Middle East. Although Moscow no longer maintains any major military bases in Azerbaijan (unlike Georgia and Armenia), it does still manage the Gabala radar station for its defense.[90] Cooperation through the CIS was supposed to offer protection of the national sovereignty for all its members, but Russia is clearly at the heart of this organization, which has been perceived as a new Russian attempt to maintain control over its former republics. As Russian ability and willingness to reassert control of its former republics increased under Putin's presidency, some CIS member states' leaders expressed opposition and said that there might be a need for a "dignified divorce" in order to maintain their own independence.[91] Another possible chink in the unity of the CIS appeared in 2006, when plans for a CIS anniversary meeting were canceled by Russia and Kazakhstan without the consultation of other members. Some speculated that this was the result of the Kremlin's "inability to garner support from other members for a plan to revamp the organization."[92] As Putin worked to reassert Moscow's dominance, Washington-led Western intrusion in the former republics became a concern for the Russian leadership. In particular, NATO's enlargement has increasingly been perceived as a source of threat.[93] Nowadays, Russia has its own security alternative to NATO, the CSTO. This organization was founded in 2002, but so far Azerbaijan has avoided joining.[94]

Moscow is not only interested in keeping Baku within its security structure, but it also has economic interests in Azerbaijan. As Western energy companies moved into the region after the USSR's collapse, Russia began to lose control of energy deposits that Soviet-era energy infrastructure had allowed it to dominate. This cost Moscow both energy revenues and political leverage. If additional Western energy pipeline projects, particularly a trans-Caspian pipeline (as called for under the Nabucco plan), are allowed to go forward, Russia could also lose its grip on Central Asian energy. Control of energy resources is vital to Moscow's interests, because Russian economic recovery has been based on energy income and Putin positioned Russia to become an Energy Superpower. As world energy prices rose in 2003, Lukoil reported revenue increases by 38 percent. This rapid growth boosted the Russian economy, which in turn translated into political popularity for Putin.[95] This popularity translated into the political capital that he needed to proceed with the centralization of power in pursuit of rebuilding Russian domestic status and international image.[96] Thus, beyond its economic benefits, energy is also seen as an essential factor in the international political power of Moscow.

Azerbaijan must take Russian energy interests into account when it makes foreign policy, because Moscow has demonstrated that it will act to protect its vital interests. Nevertheless, Baku has made some attempts to loosen Russian influence. Along with Georgia, Ukraine, and Moldova, Azerbaijan has created an international organization to provide an alternative to the CIS. Formed in 1997, that organization was named GUAM (from the first letter of each member country's name). It became GUUAM in 1999, when Uzbekistan joined. But the organization has demonstrated little impact, and in 2004, only two member states attended a GUUAM meeting held in Yalta. In 2005, Uzbekistan withdrew its membership and GUUAM returned to just GUAM. A year later, this organization did hold startling discussions regarding the creation of a mutual security force to replace Russian troops in Georgia, but this has turned out to be only talks so far.[97]

Thus, Azerbaijan has a demonstrated record of attempting to preserve distance with Russia, but when push has come to shove Baku has demonstrated deference to Moscow might. During the Russia-Georgia War, Azerbaijan remained relatively neutral. Some government officials even appeared to support Moscow's position. But reports that Russia supplied more weapons to Armenia demonstrate that Baku and Moscow remain at odds. Following in his father's footsteps, Ilham Aliyev will most likely continue to maintain a balanced foreign policy (with Western orientation) and a pragmatic position despite all conflicting national interests.[98]

Iran

When Azerbaijan gained its independence, it had an opportunity to reestablish its historically close relations with Iran.[99] But years of Soviet rule had undermined the historical ties that Shia Islam had created between Azeris and Iranians. Instead, the Azeri nationalism embraced by President Elchibey soon led to alarm for Iranians, who feared that Azeri nationalism would spawn attempts to join northwestern Iran with the new Azeri state. Because of the Nagorno-Karabakh conflict, however, Azerbaijan was in no position to engage in a second territorial conflict with the much larger and more powerful IRI. Tehran astutely emphasized this point by supporting Yerevan, demonstrating its ability to respond to Azeri threats against Iranian territorial integrity.[100]

It was not until Heydar Aliyev became president that Azerbaijan-Iranian relations would rebound. By abandoning nationalistic rhetoric on the status of Southern Azerbaijan (or the three Azeri-dominated provinces in northwestern Iran), Aliyev demonstrated pragmatism and a sober assessment of the possibilities for such reunification. Though some Azeris in northwestern Iran had demonstrated a desire for independence soon after WWII, and despite how Tehran regime had suppressed such Azeris desires, it is increasingly unlikely that South Azerbaijan might ever be joined to the Republic of Azerbaijan. First, the IRI possesses the military might and political will to use force to prevent such an event. Second, many Azeris in Iran have come to identify themselves as Iranians. Azeris are well integrated into the Iranian economy, society, and politics, especially after the 1979 Iranian Revolution. Some leading religious, business, and political leaders in Iran are Azeri, and the Ayatollah Ali Khamenei (the leader of the IRI) is himself of Azeri descent.[101] Because many Iranian-Azeris see themselves as having the upper hand in running the IRI, they are less motivated to leave Iran and join a weaker landlocked state with only one major export.[102]

Similar to Azeri demographic ties to northwestern Iran due to ethnicity, Iran also possesses demographic ties to Azerbaijan populations because of religious connection to conservative Shia in that republic.[103] Azerbaijan has reason to fear that Iran might use such ties for political leverage. IRI has demonstrated that it can manipulate sub-state movements to great effect by backing Hamas and Hezbollah.[104] Tehran has done this with little attention to some movements' Sunni or Shia orientations. In late 1990s, Heydar Aliyev attempted to reign in Iranian religious influence by prohibiting Iranian mullahs from teaching in Azerbaijan. In 2002, Azerbaijan went even further when it closed 22 *madrasas*. This prompted Tehran to seek out sympathetic Shia Azeri clergy, and to establish a relationship with them by providing education and financial support. These Iranian-backed clergy support conservative interpretations of Islam that threaten the secularist government in Azerbaijan. One survey found that nearly 37 percent of the population in the conservative southern region of Azerbaijan favors governance through Shari'a law now.[105]

In addition to their demographic clashes, Azerbaijan and Iran face a dispute over the division of Caspian Sea energy deposits. Azerbaijan has joined with Russia and Kazakhstan, supporting the legal division of the Caspian as a sea. Iran has opposed this, because it would gain a smaller share of energy deposits than if the Caspian were treated as a lake. Aliyev attempted to preempt such disagreements by incorporating Iran into his Deal of the Century in 1994. Nevertheless, this attempt to extend an olive branch was opposed by Washington. As American energy companies controlled almost a 40 percent share in the Azerbaijan International Operating Company (AIOC), Azerbaijan had little choice but to exclude IRI if it wanted U.S. participation. Tehran reacted sharply to Aliyev's decision to give in to American pressure. The Iranian foreign minister stated that the "nullification of the Azerbaijan-Iran treaty concerning Iran's participation in the consortium contradicts Azerbaijan's national interests and its previous statements. The consortium treaty may not come into force . . . unless the status of the Caspian Sea is decided."[106] When the legal status of the Caspian Sea was mentioned as a source of political leverage for Iran, the Azeri foreign minister replied that "it is not legal to draw parallels between the issue of the Caspian Sea's status and Azerbaijan's right to exploit its oil resources. Moreover, when Iran was party to debates in the international consortium, it never raised the issue"[107]

In the summer of 2001, the Azeri-Iranian disagreement threatened to become a military confrontation. On July 23, two Azeri research vessels working with BP, the Geofizik-3 and the Alif Hajiyev, were exploring approximately 93 miles southeast of Baku when Iranian military aircraft buzzed them several times. A short time later, an Iranian warship approached them and demanded that they relocate eight miles to the north. When the Azeri vessels protested that they were still in Azeri waters, the Iranian warship trained its guns on them.[108] This clash created a wave of concerns in the region, but soon both Tehran and Baku avoided increasing tensions by pulling back from their earlier positions.

Both Azerbaijan and Iran appear to favor greater economic cooperation via bilateral ties or multilateral ones through the Economic Cooperation Organization (ECO). However, their demographic and energy conflicts have complicated attempts to forge a close diplomatic relationship. In 2004, President Aliyev said that normal relations between these two states are possible if both countries refrained from interfering in one another's internal affairs. He stated that Azerbaijan was not interfering in Iranian domestic affairs and insinuated that Iran should behave in the same way: "We adhere to this principle and I am happy that Iranian-Azeri relations are being created on this basis."[109] One potential area for economic cooperation would be to build a railway linking Azerbaijan to the Persian Gulf.[110] Another is the continuing of natural gas swaps, in which Iran supplies Nakhichevan in return for Azeri gas supplies to northern Iran.[111]

Turkey

Turkey is not geographically connected to the mainland of the Azerbaijan Republic as Iran is. In fact, it only shares a 6.2-mile border with the isolated Nakhichevan territory, which is separated from Azerbaijan by Armenia.

Moreover, Turkey does not share Azerbaijan's Shia heritage. Despite these discon-
nections, however, there are growing ties between Turkey and Azerbaijan. Contrary to their historical experience when Ottomans tried to incorporate Azeri
territories into their Empire, Baku's political autonomy from Ankara is not a
question in the twenty-first century. In fact, the secular governments of both
republics means that sectarian conflict no longer holds the two states apart.
Nowadays, the shared Turkic ethnic and linguistic heritage has offered Turkey
and Azerbaijan a common ground on which to build friendly ties. Realizing the
advantages, Turkey has acted quickly to forge a relationship from these common
ties and was the first state to recognize the independence of Azerbaijan Republic.
Turkey's shared conflict with the Armenians also made it sympathetic toward the
Azeri side when war broke out. At least since the end of the Ottoman Empire
during WWI, Turks and Armenians have shared antagonism towards each other.

Under the idealistic and nationalist presidency of Elchibey, Baku was quite warm
to the idea of an ethno-cultural foundation for a relationship with Ankara. The
Azeri nationalistic rhetoric ended when Heydar Aliyev became president, and his
reconciliation with Moscow and Tehran distracted Azeri attention from the
Turkish-Azeri relationship, but a strong foundation had already been laid. Without
any reservations, Turkey supports Azerbaijan's territorial integrity and still has an icy
diplomatic relationship with Armenia. This led many Azeris to suggest that Turkey
is the only state that can really understand their difficult political situation.[112]

In addition to the shared linguistic heritage and ethnic conflict with the Armenians, Turkey and Azerbaijan also share a commitment to secularism. For Turkey,
this was imbued by Kemal Ataturk, who shaped the Turkish state after WWI. For
Azerbaijan, this was due to its Soviet heritage. Both governments remained secular and generally opposed to the application of Islamic law to the matters of
states. While Baku restricted Iranians from teaching religion in their republic,
moderate Turkish Sunni groups are allowed to teach Islam throughout Azerbaijan. Some experts even believe that these Sunni movements may now have a
greater influence in Azerbaijan than Shia Iranian organizations.[113]

Azerbaijan has also established a greater energy relationship with Turkey than
Iran. Turkey has become a significant energy consumer, offering a lucrative market for Azeri fossil fuel. In contrast, Iran is an oil exporter and is only interested
in limited energy swaps with Azerbaijan or serving as a middleman for the export
of Azeri energy to the international markets. The American-supported BTC
project offered the chance for Ankara and Baku to establish solid long-term economic ties that will most likely continue to grow in the foreseeable future.

Armenia

The defining issue and continuing roadblock in Azeri-Armenian relations is
the status of Nagorno-Karabakh. Though fighting stopped roughly a decade

ago, there has been no resolution to the conflict. Recent developments in the conflict included Nagorno-Karabakh's 2006 referendum, in which it declared its sovereignty as an independent state.[114] Such moves have only heightened tensions between Baku and Yerevan. In 2006 and 2007, brief fighting erupted along the border between Karabakh-Armenians and Azerbaijan.[115]

For Azerbaijan, conflict with Armenia has had several consequences. Because of Elchibey's alienation of Russia and Iran, both of those states developed closer ties with Armenia soon after Azerbaijan's independence. This laid a foundation for the sort of opposing triangular alliances that characterize the South Caucasus today: Russia, Iran, and Armenia versus the United States, Turkey, and Azerbaijan. Initially, however, the Armenians were a more organized political force in the United States. Because of their activism, the Armenian lobby successfully managed to get a ban on Washington foreign aid to Azerbaijan. For a solid and unobstructed Azeri-American relationship, this ban created a technical roadblock that is still a political problem between the two countries today.[116]

Georgia

Although there have historically been some territorial disputes between Georgia and Azerbaijan and religious tensions between the Christian Georgians and Muslim Azeris, these problems have largely been left behind in the current period. Firstly, such conflicts never became as bloody and entrenched as was the case between Azerbaijan and Armenia. Secondly, the reality of the region's geopolitics meant that the best route to build additional energy pipelines was through Georgia because of the troubled relationships with Armenia, Russia, and Iran. The BTC pipeline purposefully avoided Russia, Iran, and Armenia and cemented a lasting economic relationship between Georgia and Azerbaijan for now and the future.

Still, Azerbaijan's relationship with Georgia has been relatively limited. This is primarily because of Baku's aim to preserve a cordial relationship with Moscow. Georgia has proven unwilling to pursue a similar policy of deference. During the Russia-Georgia War in 2008, the Russian supply of natural gas to Georgia was cut off and Azerbaijan responded with emergency supplies for a short time before a reported problem with a compressor on the pipeline.[117] Despite its reservations and concerns about Moscow, Baku has learned its lessons, publically remained rather silent, and refused to criticize Russia directly, contrary to Georgian actions.

SUMMARY

The Nagorno-Karabakh conflict demonstrated that ethnic conflict continues to define the politics of the South Caucasus. Nowadays, religion does not appear to play as significant a role as it had historically when Sunni Ottoman, Shia Persian, and Christian Russian empires were aiming to establish their footholds in this region. However, religion still remains a demographic characteristic of importance in the Azeri-Iranian relationship. The general decline of Islam's significance in Azeri politics goes back to the Soviet era. This decline also opened the opportunity for Baku and Ankara to establish a relationship based on their shared ethnic and linguistic heritage. Yet it remains to be seen if Azerbaijan will be able to maintain its secular government in the face of Islamic resurgence, especially in the rural areas. Islam's resurgence also threatens to disrupt its orientation toward the West. In the long run, the revival of conservative Shia Islam could pull Azerbaijan back toward the IRI, especially when oil and gas run out and the West loses interest in this landlocked republic. Realizing that this is a real possibility, both Turkey and Iran have taken steps to increase their influence on the religious teaching in Azerbaijan. Thus, the historical Turko-Persian rivalry that characterized pre-Soviet Azerbaijan politics continues to persist, although Baku currently has much closer ties to Ankara than Tehran.

Probably the greatest geopolitical value of Azerbaijan is its energy resources. These have given Azerbaijan a prominent international position and political clout. However, it has also pulled Azerbaijan into dangerous international energy politics, including disputes over the international rivalry for export routes. Pipeline politics have significant implications for Azerbaijan's independence and the balance of power in the region. The northward orientation of Azerbaijan's old Soviet pipelines is indicative of the economic dependency bred by Russia. To break this traditional dependency, regional geopolitics allows Azerbaijan few options. Since Armenia and Iran are not politically viable options for pipelines, Azerbaijan turned to Georgia and the BTC plans that Turkey and the United States advocated.

The global geopolitical context in which Azerbaijan finds itself has also constrained its foreign policy. Washington's policy of isolating of Tehran has prompted Baku to avoid deep economic relations with Iran, despite their bilateral and multilateral (via ECO) ties. This is why Huntington's Clash of Civilizations perspective is not an accurate and suitable paradigm by which to examine international politics of this region, as we explain more in other sections of this work.

NOTES

1. CIA, "Azerbaijan," *The World Factbook* (Washington, D.C.: Central Intelligence Agency, 2009), https://www.cia.gov/library/publications/the-world-factbook/geos/aj.html (accessed May 18, 2009).

2. EIA, "Azerbaijan Energy Profile," (Washington, D.C: Energy Information Administration, May 15, 2009), http://tonto.eia.doe.gov/country/country_energy_data.cfm ?fips=AJ (accessed May 18, 2009).

3. Zbigniew Brzeziński, *The Grand Chessboard: American Primacy and Its Geostrategic Imperatives* (New York, NY: Basic Books, 1998), 41.

4. Johannes Rau, *The Nagorno-Karabakh Conflict Between Armenia and Azerbaijan: A Brief Historical Outline* (Berlin: Verlag Dr. Köster, 2008), 7.

5. Svante E. Cornell, "The Politicization of Islam in Azerbaijan," *CA-CI SR Paper* (October 2006): 15.

6. Ibid., 17.

7. Schaffer, 22.; Moshe Gammer, ed., *Ethno-Nationalism, Islam and the State in the Caucasus: Post Soviet Disorder* (New York, NY: Routledge, 2008), 205.

8. Rau, 21.

9. Christoph Zürcher, *The Post-Soviet Wars: Rebellion, Ethnic Conflict, and the Nationhood in the Caucasus* (New York, NY: New York University Press, 2007), 20.

10. Tadeusz Swietochowski, *Russia and Azerbaijan: A Borderland in Transition* (New York, NY: Columbia University Press, 1995), 68–69.

11. Rau, 26–27.

12. Swietochowski, 68–69, 103, and 105; Glenn E. Curtis, ed. *Azerbaijan: A Country Study* (Washington, DC: GPO for the Library of Congress, 1995), http://countrystudies.us/ azerbaijan/10.htm (accessed May 22, 2009).

13. Ole Høiris and Sefa Martin Yurukel, *Contrasts and Solutions in the Caucasus* (Aarhus: Aarhus University Press, 1998), 39–40.

14. Jamıl Hasanlı, *The Soviet-American Crisis Over Iranian Azerbaijan, 1941–1946* (Lanham, MD: Rowman & Littlefield Publishers, Inc., 2006), 225–228.

15. Ibid., ix–xii, 225–228, 252, and 255.

16. Farian Sabahi and Daniel Warner, eds., *The OSCE and the Multiple Challenges of Transition* (Burlington, VT: Ashgate Publishing Co., 2004), 26–27.

17. Rau, 26–27.

18. Zürcher, 164.

19. Georgeta Pourchot, *Eurasia Rising: Democracy and Independence in the Post-Soviet Space* (Westport, CT: Praeger Security International, 2008), 66.

20. Rau, 32–36.

21. Ibid., 37–38.

22. Ibid., 39.

23. Emil Souleimanov and Ondrej Ditrych, "Iran and Azerbaijan: A Contested Neighborhood," *Middle East Policy* XIV, no. 2 (Summer 2007): 104.

24. Murat Gül, "Russia and Azerbaijan: Relations after 1989," *Alternatives: Turkish Journal of International Relations* 7, no. 2 and 3 (Summer/Fall 2008): 56.

25. Rau, 39–40.

26. Gül, 57.

27. Cameron S. Brown, "Wanting Their Cake and Their Neighbor's Too: Azerbaijani Attitudes Towards Karabakh and Iranian Azerbaijan," *The Middle East Journal* 58, no. 4 (Autumn 2004): 572–573.

28. Rau, 40.

29. Pourchot, 66–67.

30. Rau, 45.

31. SIPRI. *SIPRI Yearbook 2008: Armaments, Disarmament and International Security* (Oxford: Oxford University Press, 2008), 187.

32. UN News Centre, "Armenia and Azerbaijan of Views on Nagorno-Karabakh During UN Debate," US News Centre, October 30, 2007. http://www.un.org/apps/news/story.asp ?NewsID=24169 (accessed September 2, 2009).

33. SIPRI, *SIPRI Yearbook 2008*, 187.

34. SIPRI, SIPRI Military Expenditure Database, http://milexdata.sipri.org/result.php4 (accessed August 16, 2009).

35. Dan Darling, "Azerbaijan Boosting Military Spending," *Forecast International*, May 9, 2007; CA-CI, "Azeri Military Budget to Equal Total Armenian State Budget," *Central Asia-Caucasus Institute* (March 22, 2006): 21.

36. Oleg Glashatov, "Azerbaijan Readies for a War for Karabakh. Would it Happen?" *Military Industrial Courier* (in Russian), UN Register of Conventional Arms.

37. Today.az, "Azerbaijan Shows MIG-29 Fighter Jets," Today.az (March 29, 2007), www.today.az/news/politics/38475.html (accessed September 2, 2009); ICG, "Nagorno-Karabakh: Risking War," Europe Report N187 (Brussels, Belgium: International Crisis Group, November 14, 2007), 13.

38. ICG, 13.

39. CRIA, "The Military Balance in Nagorno-Karabakh," Caucasus Update, *Caucasus Review of International Affairs* Issue 18 (January 19, 2009), http://cria-online.org/CU_-_file_-_article_-_sid_-_19.html (accessed September 2, 2009).

40. Sergey Minasian, "Azerbaijan Against RA and NKR: Military-Political Balance, Estimates of Military Capacities and Prospects of Development of Armed Forces," *Studies on Strategy and Security*, 2007.

41. World Bank, "Country Brief 2008: Azerbaijan" (World Bank Group, 2009), http://web.worldbank.org/WBSITE/EXTERNAL/COUNTRIES/ECAEXT/AZERBAIJANEXTN/0,,menuPK:301923~pagePK:141132~piPK:141107~theSitePK:301914,00.html (accessed January 5, 2009).

42. EIA, "Azerbaijan Energy Profile."

43. EIA, "Country Analysis Briefs: Azerbaijan" (Washington, D.C.: Energy Information Agency, November 2007), 7–8, http://www.eia.doe.gov/emeu/cabs/Azerbaijan/pdf.pdf (accessed June 10, 2009).

44. Nasib Nassibli, "Azerbaijan: Oil and Politics in the Country's Future," in *Oil and Geopolitics in the Caspian Sea Region,* Michael P. Croissant and Bulent Aras, eds. (Westport, CT: Praeger, 1999), 291.

45. EIA, "Country Analysis Briefs: Azerbaijan," 2.

46. Ibid., 2–3.

47. Ibid., 2–3.

48. Pourchot, 82.

49. EIA, "Country Analysis Briefs: Central Asia" (Washington, D.C.: Energy Information Administration, February 2008), 2–3.

50. Farian Sahahi, "Oil Diplomacy in the Caspian: The Rift between Iran and Azerbaijan in Summer 2001," in *The OSCE and the Multiple Challenges of Transition*, Farian Sabahi and Daniel Warner, eds. (Burlington, VT: Ashgate Publishing Co., 2004), 134.

51. Pourchot, 82.

52. IMF, *World Economic Outlook, April 2009* (Washington, D.C.: International Monetary Fund, 2009), 86, http://www.imf.org/external/pubs/ft/weo/2009/01/pdf/text.pdf (accessed September 2, 2009).

53. SIPRI, *SIPRI Yearbook 2008*, 186.

54. Macartan Humphreys, Jefferey Sachs, and Joseph E. Stiglitz, *Escaping the Resource Curse* (Columbia, SC: Columbia University Press, 2007), 5.

55. Ibid., 181.

56. SOFAZ, "Goals and Objectis," State Oil Fund of the Republic of Azerbaijan.

57. PRS Group, "Azerbaijan Country Forecast," in *Political Risk Yearbook* (Syracuse, NY: PRS Group, Inc., 2007), 19.

58. Zücher, 225.

59. Ibrahim El-Badawi and Samir Makdisi, "Explaining the Democracy Deficit in the Arab World," *The Quarterly Review of Economics and Finance* 46, no. 5 (February 2007), 813–831.

60. Cornell, "The Politicization of Islam in Azerbaijan," 21.

61. Ibid., 8.

62. The Middle East Journal, "Chronology: April 16, 2006–July 15, 2006," *The Middle East Journal 60*, no. 4 (Autumn 2006), http://www.accessmylibrary.com/coms2/summary_0286 -25444281_ITM; The Middle East Journal, "Chronology: October 16, 2007–January 15, 2008." *The Middle East Journal 62*, no. 2 (Spring 2008), http://www.accessmylibrary.com/ coms2/summary_0286-34442052_ITM.

63. Cornell, "The Politicization of Islam in Azerbaijan," 23.

64. Tair Faradov, "Religiosity in Post-Soviet Azerbaijan: A Sociological Analysis," *SIM Newsletter* 8 (September 2001), http://www.isim.nl/files/newsl_8.pdf (accessed April 10, 2009).

65. Sabahi and Warner, 135.

66. Cornell, "The Politicization of Islam in Azerbaijan," 9.

67. Martha Brill Olcott and Marina Ottaway, "Challenge of Semi-Authoritarianism," Carnegie Paper no. 7 (Washington, D.C.: Carnegie Endowment, October 1999), http://www .carnegieendowment.org/publications/index.cfm?fa=view&id=142 (accessed May 18, 2009).

68. Freedom House, *Freedom in the World 2009: Azerbaijan*, July 16, 2009, http://www .unhcr.org/refworld/docid/4a6452d2c.html (accessed August 19, 2009).

69. Ibid.

70. RIA Novosti, "Azerbaijan Votes to Remove Presidential Term Limits," RIA Novosti, March 19, 2009, http://en.rian.ru/world/20090319/120633154.html (accessed September 2, 2009).

71. PRS Group, "Azerbaijan Country Forecast," in *Political Risk Yearbook* (Syracuse, NY: PRS Group, Inc., 2007), 27–32.

72. Freedom House, "Country Report: Azerbaijan," *Freedom in the World Report* (Freedom House, 2009), http://www.freedomhouse.org/template.cfm?page=22&country=7560&year =2009 (accessed September 2, 2009).

73. Ibid.

74. Ibid.

75. Ibid.

76. Cornell, "The Politicization of Islam in Azerbaijan," 30.

77. Ibid., 9.

78. Sabahi and Warner, 132.

79. Cornell, "The Politicization of Islam in Azerbaijan," 8–9, 12, and 30.

80. Pourchot, 119.

81. Ministry of Foreign Affairs, "Information of Azerbaijan-NATO Cooperation," Georgian Ministry of Foreign Affairs.

82. RFE, "Nagorno-Karabakh: Timeline Of The Long Road To Peace," Radio Free Europe, February 10, 2006, http://www.rferl.org/content/article/1065626.html (accessed April 10, 2009).

83. Dov Lynch, "Shared Neighborhood or New Frontline? The Crossroads in Moldova," in *Russie.Nei.Visions 2006*, Thomas Gomart and Tatiana Kastueva-Jean, eds. (Paris: IFRI, 2006), 125.

84. Lynch, 125.

85. Energy.eu, "Energy Dependency," European Union, http://www.energy.eu/ (accessed January 21, 2009).

86. Alexander Cooley, "Principles in the Pipeline: Managing Transatlantic Values and Interests in Central Asia," *International Affairs* 84, no. 6 (2008): 1181; Andrew E. Kramer, "Putin's Grasp of Energy Drives Russian Agenda," *New York Times*, January 28, 2009, http://www.nytimes.com/2009/01/29/world/europe/29putin.html?_r=1&scp=2&sq=putin &st=cse (accessed January 28,2009).

87. Michael P. Croissant, *The Armenia-Azerbaijan Conflict: Causes and Implications* (Westport, CT: Greenwood Publishing Group, 1998), 83.

88. S. Neil MacFarlane, "The 'R' in BRICS: Is Russia an Emerging Power?" *International Affairs* 82, no. 1 (2006): 43, 46–47.

89. Rau, 53.

90. Rovshan Ismayilov, "Azerbaijan Ready to Discuss Russian-US Use of Radar Station," Eurasianet.org, June 8, 2007, http://www.eurasianet.org/departments/insight/articles/eav060807.shtml (accessed April 10, 2009).

91. Pourchot, 105.

92. Ibid., 106.

93. Ibid., 119.

94. PfP, " 'Rubezh 2008': The First Large-Scale CSTO Military Exercise," Partnership for Peace Information Management System, http://www.pims.org/news/2008/08/06/rubezh-2008-the-first-large-scale-csto-military-exercise (accessed April 10, 2009).

95. Milton F. Goldman, *Russia, the Eurasian Republics, and Central/Eastern Europe*, 11th ed. (Dubuge, IA: McGraw-Hill, 2008), 26, 35.

96. Ibid., 26.

97. Pourchot, 110.

98. Shahin Abbasov, "Azerbaijan: Russian Arms Scandal Feeds Baku's Support for Nabucco," Eurasianet.org, February 2, 2009, http://eurasianet.org/departments/insightb/articles/eav020409b_pr.shtml (accessed April 10, 2009).

99. For a more comprehensive analysis of Iranian-Azeri relations, see Houman Sadri and Nader Entessar, "Iranian-Azeri Dynamic Relations: Conflict & Cooperation in Southern Caucasus," *Rivista di Studi Politici Internazionali* [*Review of International Political Studies*] 76, no. 1, in English (Spring 2009): 59–79.

100. Cornell, "The Politicization of Islam in Azerbaijan," 43.

101. Adam Mendelson and Peter B. White, eds., "MEJ Author Pinar Ipek on Azerbaijan, Russia, and the World Energy Market," *MEI Bulletin* 60, no. I (March 2009): 8, http://www.mideasti.org/files/March%202009_lo.pdf (accessed April 10, 2009).

102. Based on author's informal interviews with diverse groups of Iranian-Azeris in three Azeri-dominated provinces of Eastern Azerbaijan, Western Azerbaijan, and Ardabil during the summers of 2002–2006.

103. In a conversation with the author, a former Iranian diplomat to Baku (who wanted to remain anonymous) stated that "beyond major cities, like Baku, the population of Azerbaijan are still devoted Shia Muslims." Interview conducted in summer 2007.

104. Robert Baer, *The Devil We Know: Dealing with the New Iranian Superpower* (Carlton North, Victoria, Australia: Scribe Publications, 2008).

105. Cornell, "The Politicization of Islam in Azerbaijan," 24 and 42–44.

106. Souleimanov and Ditrych, 104–105.

107. Ibid., 105.

108. Guy Dinmore and David Stern, "Azeri Leader Criticizes Iran Over Oil Claim in Caspian," *Financial Times*, August 30, 2001; Sabahi, 138.

109. RIA Novosti, "Iran, Armenia Agree to Strengthen Bilateral Cooperation in the Sphere of Regional Security," RIA Novosti, December 26, 2001, http://web.lexis-nexis.com (accessed June 14, 2006).

110. Sevindzh Abdullayeva and Viktor Shulman, "Iran Wants Wider Relations with Azerbaijan: Foreign Minister," ITAR-TASS News Agency, November 28, 2005, http://web.lexis-nexis.com (accessed June 14, 2006).

111. Rovshan Ismayilov, "Azerbaijan and Iran: Dangerous Liaisons?" EurasiaNet.org, January 19, 2006, http://www.eurasianet.org/departments/insight/articles/eav011906a.shtml (accessed April 10, 2009).

112. Brown, 573–574; Arminfo News Agency, "Azerbaijan FM: Problem with Opening of Boundary Connected Not Only with Armenian-Azerbaijani Conflict, but also with Relations Between Turkey and Armenia," Arminfo News Agency, May 31, 2004, http://web.lexis-nexis.com (accessed July 21, 2006).

113. Sabahi and Warner, 23.

114. The Middle East Journal, "Chronology: Oct 16, 2006–January 15, 2007," *The Middle East Journal 61*, no. 2 (Spring 2007).

115. The Middle East Journal, "Chronology: July 16, 2007–October 15, 2007," *The Middle East Journal 62*, no. 1 (Winter 2008); The Middle East Journal, "Chronology: Jan. 16, 2008–April 15, 2008," *The Middle East Journal 62*, no. 3 (Summer 2008).

116. Cornell, "The Politicization of Islam in Azerbaijan," 30.

117. The Middle East Journal, "Chronology: January 16, 2006–April 15, 2006," *The Middle East Journal 60*, no. 3 (Summer 2006).

CHAPTER 3

Armenia

Map 3.1 Armenia and Original Political Borders

Designed by Albert Citron. Used with Permission.

Photo 3.1 Armenian President

Serzh Sargsian (left), President of the Republic of Armenia Shaking hands with United Nations Secretary-General Ban Ki-moon United Nations Headquarters, New York, USA, September 26, 2008. (# 198171 UN Photo by Eskinder Debebe.)

In the South Caucasus, Armenia is positioned with the greatest geographic challenges. Armenia has long been landlocked, without even access to the Caspian Sea and the energy resources in that basin. Not only is Armenia physically isolated in the rugged Caucasus, but it has also been politically isolated. To the east and the west, Armenia shares disputed borders with Azerbaijan and Turkey. With both of these Turkic neighbors, Armenia has a long history of ethnic, religious, and territorial disputes. The only other states with which Armenia shares a border are Iran (to the south) and Georgia (to the north). This has led some to argue that Armenia's geographic position has been the single greatest factor influencing its troubled history.[1] Though Armenia once occupied a much larger territory than it does today, Armenia is also now the smallest state in the region, occupying only about 11,484 square miles (Map 3.1).

PRE-SOVIET HISTORY

The Armenian people emerged from indigenous Hurro-Urartean tribes and migrating Indo-European peoples who mixed in the mountainous geographic area that spans Asia Minor and the Caucasus. The difficulty of the terrain in the region kept the Armenians isolated, even from one another, preventing the

Photo 3.2 Armenian Minister of Foreign Affairs

Vartan Oskanian, Minister for Foreign Affairs of the Republic of Armenia High-level Dialogue on Interreligious and Intercultural Understanding and Cooperation for Peace, United Nations Headquarters, New York, USA, October 4, 2007. (# 157028 UN Photo by Marco Castro.)

establishment of any one central political power for the early Armenians.[2] It was under the Yervandunis that the first Armenian dynasty was established, who were appointed as regional governors by the increasingly powerful Medes in the sixth century BC. Later, the Persians, who replaced the Medes in 550 and ruled until 331 BC, kept this dynasty in power. The Yervandunis' dynasty continued to rule Armenia with a fair degree of autonomy even after Alexander the Great brought an end to the Persian Empire.[3] Together, the political autonomy of the Armenians and their geographic isolation encouraged their development into a cohesive and distinct people group.[4]

When the Roman Empire began to expand into Asia Minor, Armenia found itself caught between Roman advancing legions and the Parthian kingdom that had established itself in Persia. Armenia became the frontier between these two great powers, essentially a buffer state. At that time, Armenia was ruled by the Artashesian dynasty, which attempted to maintain power by playing the Romans and Parthians against each other.[5] Eventually, however, the Armenians came to ally themselves with Rome, which was followed by conversion to Christianity in 314–315.[6] This established a Western orientation among Armenians and laid a religious foundation that would separate Armenians from the Muslim Arabs, Turks, and Persians who later became dominant forces in the region. Once the Byzantine Empire fell, Armenia was completely cut off from the Christian West, leading Armenia into what contemporary Armenians call the "dark centuries."[7] Repeated invasions by the Muslims, the Mongols, and the conqueror Tamerlane savaged the Armenian population.[8] These pressures scattered the Armenians, creating the first Armenian diasporas from those who could flee to Europe.[9]

When a new Armenian ruling class began to reemerge, they had close ties to a Christian Georgian kingdom, which rose to power between the twelfth and thirteenth centuries. The Georgian city of Tbilisi, now the capital of Georgia, became a major center for Armenians during this time.[10] But Armenians remained caught between powerful Muslim empires: the Ottomans and the Safavids. In the sixteenth century, the Turkic-Persian tensions that defined Azerbaijan also influenced Armenia. Just as Armenia had been the frontier between the Romans and the Parthians, Armenia became the buffer between the Ottoman Turks and Safavid Persians. This time, however, the Armenians would not ally themselves with either power; instead, they appealed to Christian Europe and Russia for support.[11] Nevertheless, they remained isolated from Europe, because the might of the Muslim empires did not begin to crack until the late 1800s.

As Tsarist Russian forces began their conquest of the Caucasus, Armenia's hopes for a strong Christian ally became more possible. The Treaty of Turkmenchay, which pushed the Persian Empire back, gave Russia control of eastern Armenian lands. Then the Russo-Turkish War of 1877–1888 brought further Armenian lands under the Russian Empire with the conquest of the cities of Kars and Ardahan. Both these cities are now a part of Turkey, but at the time they had large Armenian populations. A great many Armenians lived even further to the West, deeper within the boundaries of the Ottoman Empire in what is now modern-day Turkey.[12] Though Russia conquered Armenian lands without the intent of allowing the Armenians political independence, the Tsarist Empire was largely perceived as the protector of the Armenian people, since it had liberated them from their Muslim neighbors. Some have argued that this historical reliance on foreign powers has been ingrained in the Armenian psyche, and plays a role in Armenia's reliance on Russia even today.[13]

This tie between the Armenians and Russians excited ethnic and religious tensions between Armenians and their Turkic Muslim neighbors in what are now modern Turkey and Azerbaijan. Furthermore, Russian rule led to massive demographic shifts in the Caucasus. Between 1828 and 1830, approximately 130,000 Armenians immigrated into the South Caucasus with Russian encouragement. At least 18,000 of these Armenians settled in the Nagorno-Karabakh region, creating the problematic demographic overlap with Azeris that would be the source of ethno-religious violence for over a century to come.[14]

Attempts to "Russify" the Armenian population under the Tsar did create some tension with Armenians, but the Muslim Turks always remained a greater threat to Armenians.[15] Those Armenians who lived within the Ottoman Empire generally faced oppression and, sometimes, sporadic violence. They longed for independence from Muslim rule. As Russia rolled Ottoman borders back, Armenian revolts increased during the late nineteenth century. From the perspective of the Ottoman Turks, then, the Armenians increasingly became a troublesome group of people that threatened the integrity of the already unstable Ottoman-Russian border. Waning relative to the rising European powers, the Ottomans were constantly on the defense and the situation of the Christian Armenians provided a constant political excuse for Russia and other European states to intervene in Ottoman affairs or seize territory. Due to this situation, Ottoman Turks increasingly began to identify Armenians as enemies (and a Fifth Column). Thus, both unofficial and official oppression of Armenians increased as fighting escalated in WWI. As Russian forces pressed further into Ottoman lands, Ottoman forces relocated Armenians from their traditional homes, a move that was accompanied with ethnic violence and massacres that are now referred to as the Armenian Genocide of 1915. Although the United States has yet to officially recognize those events as genocide (mainly due to the political wedge this would drive into the valuable American-Turkish ties), an estimated 1.5 million Armenians were killed in 1915. If those numbers are accurate, then one-third to even one-half of the total Armenian population worldwide was killed at that time.[16]

This violence decimated Armenian populations in the Caucasus and Asia Minor, leaving only those Armenians behind Russian borders untouched. But when the Bolshevik Revolution forced Moscow's early withdrawal from WWI, even those Armenians were left vulnerable to Ottoman troops. Not only did Armenians lose their Russian protectors at this time, but when the TDFR fell apart, Armenians also found themselves at war with Azeris and Georgians. Georgia and Armenia engaged in brief military confrontations over the regions of Lori and Akhalkalak, but Yerevan had its worst conflicts with Baku. In the territories of Nakhichevan, Zangenur, and Karabakh there were intense ethnic conflicts in which both sides were aggressors.[17] For instance, Armenian forces won decisive victories in Zangenur and destroyed some 115 Azeri settlements, killed around 7,000 Azeris, and displaced roughly 50,000 others.[18] Fighting between Azerbaijan and Armenia was not as decisive in Nakhichevan and Karabakh, and ethnic fighting in those territories did not have a chance to resolve itself before the victorious Bolshevik forces reasserted Russian control in the South Caucasus.

SOVIET HISTORY

Despite Russia's debilitating Revolution, the Ottoman Empire was not able to take full advantage of the chaos in the South Caucasus because of the defeats it was suffering at the hands of the other Allied nations. The defeat of the Ottomans, however, offered the Armenians a chance to reclaim lands that they had historically lived in. But Turkish forces were quickly reorganized under the leadership of Mustafa Kemal Ataturk, and the new Turkish national army rapidly restored the core of the Ottoman Empire in the Anatolian peninsula, establishing the modern Republic of Turkey. Facing the advance of Turkish forces, the Armenians once again had to choose between Turkish or Russian rule. Armenia submitted to Bolshevik troops and was incorporated into the new Soviet Union.

The weight of the Soviet Empire froze the territorial disputes that had been raging between Armenia and its neighbors. But this did not lead to resolution of these old conflicts. Instead, new administrative borders drawn by the Soviets complicated the geographic integrity of Armenia. Despite the fact that Nagorno-Karabakh was, by that time, predominantly populated by Armenians, it remained within the borders drawn for Azerbaijan. Armenians at large, and particularly those in Nagorno-Karabakh were never satisfied with this division, but Soviet administrators by and large refused to consider the unification of Nagorno-Karabakh with Armenia.

The desire of Armenians can be understood in light of their sense of territorial loss and mistreatment at the hands of Turks. Some estimate that the territory once occupied by Armenians was once six times larger than the territory of Soviet Armenia, the smallest of all Soviet Republics.[19] Though the Soviets eventually made Nagorno-Karabakh an autonomous political entity within Azerbaijan, the Armenian population was still in an uneasy position when the Soviet Union began to collapse. Soviet recognition of Armenians as a distinct ethnicity and Moscow's efforts to recognize their political autonomy allowed Armenian nationalism to strengthen without ever allowing it to be satisfied by real political unification. The Soviets even relocated Azeris from Armenia, so that Armenia was soon the most ethnically homogenous republic in the USSR.[20]

Public debate over Nagorno-Karabakh began to gain momentum in the years after Khrushchev, as Armenian protestors became bolder. On April 24, 1965, major demonstrations were held in the Armenian capital city of Yerevan to mark the fiftieth anniversary of the Armenian deportations under the Ottomans. At the same time, the protestors called for the "reestablishment" of Nagorno-Karabakh under Armenian control.[21] Despite the new energy of Armenian demands, the Communist Party largely ignored the growing movement. But when Gorbachev began his reforms of the Soviet Union, promoting *glasnost* (i.e., openness or transparency) and *perestroika* (i.e., restructuring), Armenians found now room to express their desire for unification. In 1988, Armenians in Nagorno-Karabakh applied to be incorporated with Armenia and voted to politically separate from Azerbaijan. Gorbachev continued the Communist Party's refusal to grant such autonomy but realized the growing trouble in the region and attempted to squash it though a carrot and stick approach—providing greater economic aid to

Nagorno-Karabakh while firing high-ranking officials and stationing larger numbers of troops in the area.[22]

In Azerbaijan, Armenian attempts to separate Nagorno-Karabakh caused alarm and led to ethnic violence against Armenians. During the last years of the USSR several anti-Armenian *pogroms* were carried out in limited locals in Azerbaijan.[23] On opposing sides in both countries, Armenians and Azeris abused each other, but violence in Azerbaijan was the most pronounced. This, in turn, increased Armenian worries and furthered the historical enmity between the Christian Armenians and Turkic Muslims. As the Soviet Union began to fall apart, Armenians and Azeris fled from their homes to their respective republics in the hundreds of thousands. Once Soviet military support of Azerbaijan's territorial integrity came to an end after the Moscow *putsch* in August of 1991, Armenians in Nagorno-Karabakh felt confident enough to declare independence and prepared for the inevitable military confrontation with Azerbaijan.[24]

INDEPENDENCE AND DEVELOPING SECURITY OF THE STATE

On August 23, 1990, the former Soviet Republic of Armenia declared itself an independent state. Two months later, Levon Ter-Petrossian (see Appendix B for biography) was elected as the first Armenian president. Ter-Petrossian was, like most Armenian politicians who gained power at the time, in tune with Armenian nationalism. Yet his legacy as president came to demonstrate a touch of Soviet-style authoritarianism through his strong presidency that also included a touch of pragmatism, which makes him appear quite moderate when compared to the strident nationalism that has characterized many of Armenia's other politicians.[25] Because of Ter-Petrossian's nationalism, however, his election proved far more unifying for Armenia than the election of Mutalibov in Azerbaijan. The new political unity provided Yerevan with focus and stability that would provide it an early advantage in its conflict with Baku. Immediately after independence, the primary issue on the Armenian agenda was the independence of Nagorno-Karabakh. President Ter-Petrossian initially attempted to distance Yerevan from officially appearing to support Nagorno-Karabakh due to international pressure. However, the issue was simply too salient, and Armenia was soon undeniably engaged in the war for Nagorno-Karabakh.

War for Nagorno-Karabakh

When Armenia and Azerbaijan gained their independence, both quickly received international recognition, which included recognition of their Soviet-demarcated borders. Yerevan had officially agreed to its Soviet borders in January of 1992, so under international law, Armenia was open to criticism if it attempted to violate Azeri borders. Under Ter-Petrossian's cautious leadership,

Armenia initially attempted to avoid blatantly challenging Azerbaijan for this reason. Instead of trying immediate unification with Nagorno-Karabakh, Armenia recognized Nagorno-Karabakh's 1991 declaration of independence. In this way, Yerevan could frame the conflict as a civil war in Azerbaijan, and not a war between Armenia and Azerbaijan.[26]

Armenians, however, were not going to stand by and watch their brothers fight the war with Azerbaijan alone. Ter-Petrossian himself had risen to his political position as a member of the Karabakh-Armenian movement.[27] In the disputed region, Armenians had the numerical advantage, because they accounted for nearly three-fourths of the local population.[28] Karabakh-Armenian forces were joined by fighters from Armenia and by former Soviet military units formed in the area.[29] Yet, at the outset, the war appeared far from determined because of the large military that Baku had inherited from the USSR.[30]

The first objective of Armenian forces was to break out from Nagorno-Karabakh and to establish a transportation corridor with Armenia, through which aid and military supplies could travel. This objective required the capture of the Azeri towns of Shusha and Lachin. After having driven west toward Armenia to secure this supply line, Armenian forces began to expand to the north, south, and west. Between July and October of 1993, the cities of Aghdara (July 7), Aghdam (July 23), Jabrayil (August 23), Fizuli (August 23), Gubadley (August 31), and Zangilan (October 23) were captured by advancing Armenians.[31] Azerbaijan's domestic political chaos weakened the coordination of its military response in a conflict in which its enemy was more unified and resolved.

By the end of 1993, the fact that Armenia was completely committed to the war effort in Nagorno-Karabakh was quite undeniable. As Armenian advances moved further and further beyond the borders of Nagorno-Karabakh and deeper into Azeri territory, international condemnation of Yerevan began to grow.[32] Yet, before Armenian forces were halted by Russian intervention, the Armenian offensive continued until 20 percent of Azerbaijan's Soviet territory was occupied.[33] When the Bishkek Protocol finally brought an end to hostilities in May of 1994, Armenian forces had succeeded in physically uniting Nagorno-Karabakh to Armenia and establishing a wide defensive buffer around the disputed region. (See text of the cease-fire agreement in Appendix G.)

Despite Azerbaijan's refusal to recognize Nagorno-Karabakh as independent or as a part of Armenia, the region has maintained de facto independence for nearly two decades now and would be extremely costly for Azerbaijan to retake. Yet, at the international stage, Nagorno-Karabakh has yet to receive significant recognition of its independence. When it attempted to issue its first constitution in 2006, this move was vigorously opposed by the EU, the OSCE, and European Council (EC).[34] A final, lasting resolution to the conflict remains elusive because of the strong historical animosities that continue to persist between Armenians and Azeris. It remains a political "hot topic" in Armenia, and any politician who engages in negotiations faces the possibility of being labeled a traitor. In fact, President Ter-Petrossian's willingness to seek out a compromise with Baku was one of the factors that eventually led to his resignation. His compromising willingness, coupled with his growing authoritarianism and the difficult economic situation in Armenia, undermined his legitimacy with the public. The last straw was his attempt to manipulate the presidential election in 1996. Public outcry was so great that it forced his resignation, allowing Robert Kocharian (see Appendix B for biography), Armenia's ultra-nationalist prime minister, to rise to the presidency.[35]

Status of Armenia's Military

Like Azerbaijan, Armenia has an interest in growing its military capabilities in order to pursue its interests in Nagorno-Karabakh. Yet its slower economic recovery left it with less revenue to invest. Still, from 1998 to 2005, Armenia spent a larger percentage of its GDP on its military than Azerbaijan. Armenia's military expenditures have increased by 125 percent in real terms from 1998 to 2007. In 2006, Armenia spent 2.8 percent of its GDP on its military, as compared to Azerbaijan's 3.6 percent. For Armenia, this translated into total expenditures of US$157 million.[36] Figures for 2008 appear to demonstrate $217 million of expenditures in constant U.S. dollars (2005), as compared to Azerbaijan's US$697 million.[37] Yet, Serzh Sargsian (Armenia's Defense Minister, see Appendix B for biography) has expressed confidence that increases since 2006 allow Yerevan to effectively counter Azeri forces in the event of new hostilities.[38]

Just as Armenia's military expenditures do not match those of Azerbaijan, neither do its declared weapons acquisitions. The only major arms transfer to occur in recent years was Armenia's purchase of 10 SU-25s from Slovakia in 2005.[39] However, the amount of undeclared acquisitions is difficult to measure, and Yerevan's close ties with Moscow allow it the opportunity to potentially hide real acquisitions. For instance, in January of 2009, Azerbaijan accused Russia of supplying Armenia with $800 million worth of weapons, including tanks, armored personnel carriers, grenade launchers, rockets, and ammunition. Although both Moscow and Yerevan denied the transfer, the deployment of weapons and armaments to the Russian 102nd Army base in Armenia has clearly allowed Armenia to strengthen its position. That base is reported to have 74 tanks, 224 armored vehicles, 60 towed artillery systems, 14 aircraft, and an S-300 missile system. Yet, the number of Russian personnel stationed at that base would prohibit Russia from being able to mobilize these assets on a large scale, which has led to speculation that Moscow is willing to "lend" this equipment to Yerevan in the case of a war.[40]

This sort of cooperation with Russia potentially allows Armenia to skirt the Conventional Armed Forces in Europe Treaty that it has accused Azerbaijan of breaking. In addition, Baku alleged that Yerevan exceeded its limits by hiding its forces in Nagorno-Karabakh.[41] Other reasons that Armenia may feel it does not have to match increases in Azerbaijan's military spending include the advantage of its defensive position and the fact that it remains under the Russian security umbrella provided by the Collective Security Treaty. Armenian forces along the border between Nagorno-Karabakh and Azerbaijan hold all the strategic heights and have their northern flank protected by the Mrov Mountains and their southern flank protected by the Aras River and Iranian territory. That leaves only a little more than a 74-mile front line, which Armenian forces have been fortifying since 1994.[42] A number of Western and Russian military experts argue that Azerbaijan still lags behind Armenia in real military capability, and given these defensive advantages, Armenia still appears to possess a formidable defensive capability.[43]

Armenia's Economic Isolation

Although the war for Nagorno-Karabakh was a military success, there were severe economic consequences that Armenia suffered as a result. Under the Soviet Union, 85 percent of Armenia's rail traffic passed through Azerbaijan.[44] From the onset of the hostilities, Armenia lost access to trade routes through Azerbaijan. This was soon followed by the loss of trade routes through Turkey, as that state closed its borders to Armenia in support of Azerbaijan. The isolation brought by the war with Azerbaijan compounded the economic crash that impacted all of the former Soviet Republics. Between 1991 and 1993, the size of the Armenian economy fell by 60 percent.[45]

In order to maintain international trade, Armenia could rely only on transportation routes through Georgia and Iran, but the Armenian-Iranian border was still largely closed, with only a single road to connect the two. Thus, Georgia became the vital transit state for Armenia's trade, providing it with a connection to Russia that was necessary for Armenia to continue to function. Despite the fact that the railways and roads between Georgia and Armenia are in poor condition, these routes now account for 70 percent of Armenia's total international trade.[46]

Once trade was cut with Azerbaijan, one of the most severe losses suffered by Armenia was in the area of energy. The Soviet-era natural gas pipeline system designed to supply much of Armenia's heating needs originated in Azerbaijan. With the cutoff of Azeri pipelines, Armenia had to rely on its own hydropower generation and on fuel trucked in through Georgia for energy. While there was an alternative gas pipeline that ran through Georgia, that line was repeatedly disabled by Azeri-perpetrated sabotage. Moreover, the gas flow to Armenia was also interrupted by the domestic turmoil within Georgia, which experienced its own separatist conflicts and civil war. The halt to hostilities in Nagorno-Karabakh did nothing to improve Armenia's energy crisis. Energy continued to be a problem through 1998, when a major earthquake forced the closure of Armenia's only nuclear plant—the source of one-third of Armenian electricity at the time.[47]

The energy crisis in Armenia perpetuated economic troubles as its industry lacked the fuel to continue manufacturing. In order to solve its energy problems, Armenia pursued privatization in the late 1990s and into 2000. This opened the door for growing Russian energy companies to enter the Armenian market. In 2002, Armenia turned over the Hrazdan thermal power plant, the Sevan-Hrazdan hydropower cascade, and financial control of the Madzamor nuclear plant to several Russian companies in return for the forgiveness of $96 million in debt to Russia.[48] This sort of arrangement occurred again in 2006, when Russia gained further holdings in Armenian assets in exchange for not increasing the gas prices charged to Armenian customers.[49] As a result, Moscow now has significant control of Armenia's critical energy resources—a situation that could allow Russia major political leverage. Because of the geopolitics of the region, however, Armenia has been left with very few choices in this matter. In 2008, 100 percent of the 48 tb/d of oil and 72 bcf of gas that Armenia consumed had to be imported.[50] Now, the reality is that Armenia's privatizing reforms and the presence of Russian companies have stabilized its energy sector and allowed this country to begin an economic recovery.

Between 1994 and 2000, the average GDP growth in Armenia was 5 percent. Since 2001, that has now accelerated to around 11 percent.[51] One reason that Armenia was economically able to survive in such a bleak economic time was the great number of remittance payments received from the large international Armenian diaspora. These funds sustained Armenians and have been used in the rebuilding of the Armenian economy.[52] As Armenia continues to seek economic growth, however, Armenian reliance on Russia and international aid may become hindrances. International aid and remittances can breed dependency.[53] Such funds are sources of easy cash for Yerevan government, which appears to be reluctant to surrender this source of economic control. It seems that Armenian leaders prefer that money flow into their hands through foreign aid rather than foreign direct investment (FDI).[54]

Status of Armenia's Economy

Despite earlier attempts to isolate Armenia by Turkey, the country has relatively experienced remarkable economic growth over the past several years. In October 2009, Armenia and Turkey signed a protocol through the Swiss mediation process to establish diplomatic ties and open their common border, closed by Ankara since 1993. However, this agreement has not been formally and mutually approved by both sides, as the date of writing this work (Tables 3.1–3.4, Graphs 3.1–3.4).

On the positive side in 2007, the annual percentage change of Armenian economy in its Real GDP was 13.8. However, when the global recession hit,

Table 3.1 Armenian Export Volume

	1998	1999	2000	2001	2002	2003	2004	2005	2006	2007	2008
US	11.567	16.008	37.861	52.268	46.888	57.187	97.098	109.514	65.816	75.895	38.360
EU	77.499	107.706	109.766	92.207	200.441	263.520	255.167	453.114	472.162	515.106	456.979
Japan	0.061	0.062	0.212	0.078	0.801	0.106	0.217	1.119	0.313	4.703	0.504
China (m)	0.124	0.067	0.573	0.066	4.050	4.597	21.750	9.245	0.464	7.872	7.770
Russia	39.986	33.856	44.560	60.501	64.634	94.418	77.898	119.004	121.156	201.543	220.724
CIS (8)	28.404	10.239	11.291	14.754	13.752	14.701	15.919	21.136	34.552	62.712	69.737
Iran	31.392	34.161	30.089	31.870	31.469	22.479	30.560	28.513	29.643	38.499	49.034
Turkey	2.988	1.129	1.528	1.130	1.436	1.155	2.021	2.473	2.371	3.033	1.959
Azerbaijan	0.000	0.000	0.000	0.000	0.000	0.000	0.000	0.000	0.000	0.000	0.000
Armenia	9.573	11.100	15.989	12.413	16.607	18.674	29.062	46.833	54.649	87.869	97.440
Georgia Subtotal	201.594	214.328	251.869	265.287	380.078	476.837	529.692	790.951	781.126	997.232	942.507
World Subtotal	220.516	231.669	300.488	341.632	504.473	685.599	722.911	973.921	985.108	1152.220	1067.160

(m) = mainland; CIS (8) = Belarus, Kazakhstan, Kyrgyzstan, Moldova, Tajikistan, Turkmenistan, Ukraine, Uzbekistan.
Source: IMF's Direction of Trade Statistics.

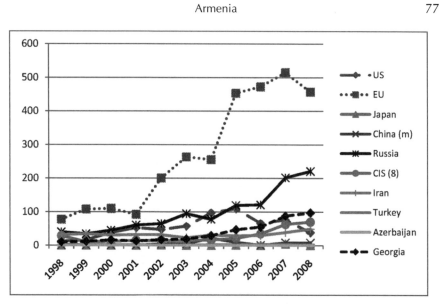

Graph 3.1 Armenian Export Volume

Armenia's fragile economy also declined like Azerbaijan's, and the percentage change dropped to 6.8. Through 2009, Armenia's GDP is projected to decline, perhaps even into negatives, before moving toward a slow recovery. Its economy remains vulnerable, but the IMF projects that Armenia should be able to continue reducing its current account balance.[55]

Ordinarily a weak economy might be correlated with internal instability. However, Armenians demonstrated significant national solidarity during the

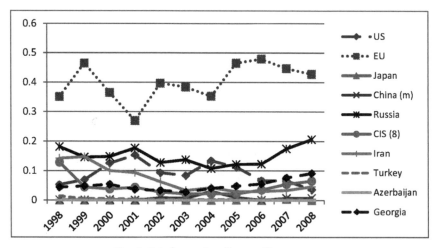

Graph 3.2 Armenian Export Percentage

Table 3.2 Armenian Export Percentage

	1998	1999	2000	2001	2002	2003	2004	2005	2006	2007	2008
US	5.25%	6.91%	12.60%	15.30%	9.29%	8.34%	13.43%	11.24%	6.68%	6.59%	3.59%
EU	35.14%	46.49%	36.53%	26.99%	39.73%	38.44%	35.30%	46.52%	47.93%	44.71%	42.82%
Japan	0.03%	0.03%	0.07%	0.02%	0.16%	0.02%	0.03%	0.11%	0.03%	0.41%	0.05%
China (m)	0.06%	0.03%	0.19%	0.02%	0.80%	0.67%	3.01%	0.95%	0.05%	0.68%	0.73%
Russia	18.13%	14.61%	14.83%	17.71%	12.81%	13.77%	10.78%	12.22%	12.30%	17.49%	20.68%
CIS (8)	12.88%	4.42%	3.76%	4.32%	2.73%	2.14%	2.20%	2.17%	3.51%	5.44%	6.53%
Iran	14.24%	14.75%	10.01%	9.33%	6.24%	3.28%	4.23%	2.93%	3.01%	3.34%	4.59%
Turkey	1.36%	0.49%	0.51%	0.33%	0.28%	0.17%	0.28%	0.25%	0.24%	0.26%	0.18%
Azerbaijan	0.00%	0.00%	0.00%	0.00%	0.00%	0.00%	0.00%	0.00%	0.00%	0.00%	0.00%
Georgia	4.34%	4.79%	5.32%	3.63%	3.29%	2.72%	4.02%	4.81%	5.55%	7.63%	9.13%
Armenia Subtotal	91.42%	92.51%	83.82%	77.65%	75.34%	69.55%	73.27%	81.21%	79.29%	86.55%	88.32%

(m) = mainland; CIS (8) = Belarus, Kazakhstan, Kyrgyzstan, Moldova, Tajikistan, Turkmenistan, Ukraine, Uzbekistan.
Source: IMF's Direction of Trade Statistics.

Table 3.3 Armenian Import Volume

	1998	1999	2000	2001	2002	2003	2004	2005	2006	2007	2008
US	96.301	85.669	102.675	84.201	54.155	90.968	89.123	111.492	106.297	145.753	168.679
EU	280.301	268.543	317.644	269.631	275.956	350.38	343.354	506.461	620.633	979.467	1075.37
Japan	6.189	2.35	3.822	2.89	0.464	16.418	12.667	23.719	39.947	104.864	49.7225
China (m)	9.96	4.888	5.413	7.811	10.128	31.449	38.496	65.585	111.074	194.763	193.488
Russia	191.403	181.348	137.158	173.648	192.898	174.908	159.687	242.632	304.171	494.461	605.342
CIS (8)	11.858	10.352	16.586	26.188	77.021	169.234	213.291	259.925	356.603	537.904	633.1471
Iran	63.913	78.45	82.328	78.121	62.615	51.281	62.285	89.167	0.002	0.002	41.12
Turkey	56.78	40.152	40.462	33.756	38.232	40.887	44.805	66.928	95.423	130.631	53.5513
Azerbaijan	0.002	0	0	0	0	0.013	0	0.002	0	0	0
Georgia	26.83	26.856	19.801	18.503	31.47	10.581	13.127	19.212	35.462	46.334	53.0558
Armenia Subtotal	743.537	698.608	725.889	694.749	742.939	936.119	976.835	1385.123	1669.612	2634.179	2873.476
World Subtotal	902.389	842.738	884.733	876.814	986.762	1279.49	1350.7	1801.74	2191.61	3267.73	3509.66

(m) = mainland; CIS (8) = Belarus, Kazakhstan, Kyrgyzstan, Moldova, Tajikistan, Turkmenistan, Ukraine, Uzbekistan.
Source: IMF's Direction of Trade Statistics.

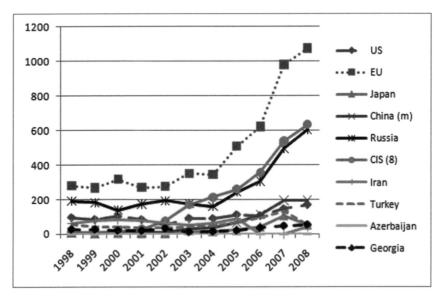

Graph 3.3 Armenian Import Volume

difficult economic times ushered by the collapse of the USSR and the war with Azerbaijan. This seemingly indicates that economic fluctuations in Armenia will not upset the political status quo. Nevertheless, the smaller size of the Armenian economy does threaten its external security, because it has comparatively less to spend on its military than Azerbaijan.[56] In order to compensate for this disadvantage, Armenia has incentive to maintain a close relationship with Russia, particularly through international organizations like the CIS and the CSTO.

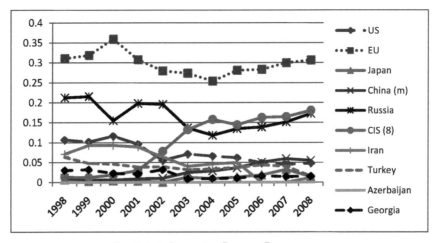

Graph 3.4 Armenian Import Percentage

Table 3.4 Armenian Import Percentage

	1998	1999	2000	2001	2002	2003	2004	2005	2006	2007	2008
US	10.67%	10.17%	11.61%	9.60%	5.49%	7.11%	6.60%	6.19%	4.85%	4.46%	4.81%
EU	31.06%	31.87%	35.90%	30.75%	27.97%	27.38%	25.42%	28.11%	28.32%	29.97%	30.64%
Japan	0.69%	0.28%	0.43%	0.33%	0.05%	1.28%	0.94%	1.32%	1.82%	3.21%	1.42%
China (m)	1.10%	0.58%	0.61%	0.89%	1.03%	2.46%	2.85%	3.64%	5.07%	5.96%	5.51%
Russia	21.21%	21.52%	15.50%	19.80%	19.55%	13.67%	11.82%	13.47%	13.88%	15.13%	17.25%
CIS (8)	1.31%	1.23%	1.87%	2.99%	7.81%	13.23%	15.79%	14.43%	16.27%	16.46%	18.04%
Iran	7.08%	9.31%	9.31%	8.91%	6.35%	4.01%	4.61%	4.95%	0.00%	0.00%	1.17%
Turkey	6.29%	4.76%	4.57%	3.85%	3.87%	3.20%	3.32%	3.71%	4.35%	4.00%	1.53%
Azerbaijan	0.00%	0.00%	0.00%	0.00%	0.00%	0.00%	0.00%	0.00%	0.00%	0.00%	0.00%
Georgia	2.97%	3.19%	2.24%	2.11%	3.19%	0.83%	0.97%	1.07%	1.62%	1.42%	1.51%
Armenia Subtotal	**82.40%**	**82.90%**	**82.05%**	**79.24%**	**75.29%**	**73.16%**	**72.32%**	**76.88%**	**76.18%**	**80.61%**	**81.87%**

(m) = mainland; CIS (8) = Belarus, Kazakhstan, Kyrgyzstan, Moldova, Tajikistan, Turkmenistan, Ukraine, Uzbekistan.
Source: IMF's Direction of Trade Statistics.

Finally, as that of a small state, the Armenian economy is closely tied to that of few trade partners. To detect the trade patterns of this republic with global and regional powers, the IMF trade data was again collected, tabulated, and graphed. Following the same method used for Azerbaijan, the first table and graph show the volume of Armenian exports, followed by the statistics that illustrate the percentages of trade with major and minor powers. Then, the same format was used to analyzed the trends in Armenian imports volume as well as import percentages. From the data, tables, graphs, and statistics, one can make the following observations.
For exports:

1. The export volume shows steady growth with all major partners.
2. There is no significant trade with Azerbaijan and Turkey.
3. The export percentages, however, indicate diverse trade patterns.
4. The EU takes the first place as the destination of Armenian exports.
5. The percentage of exports to the EU, however, has major ups and downs.
6. As expected, Russia (ranking second) and the CIS are significant trade partners.
7. Georgia is a consistent and gradually growing export destination.
8. Iran and the United States are major export destinations, but both show a downturn trend.

For imports:

1. Again, the volumes indicate steady import growth with trade partners.
2. Again, there is no trade with Baku, and declining trade with Ankara.
3. Again, Russia and the CIS are major trade partners.
4. The imports from Iran and the United States are significant, but have been decreasing.
5. Trade with Georgia has almost remained the same level for the entire period.

Role of the Armenian Diaspora

War and economic pressures after Armenian independence have driven nearly 25 percent of Armenia's population to emigrate since 1991.[57] This has drained Armenia of significant groups of young people and highly skilled workers and contributed to the historical dispersion of Armenians. The turbulent history of this republic has led many Armenians to seek refuge abroad, scattering them internationally. While this whittled away the strength of the Armenian state in the South Caucasus, diaspora Armenians have provided an important political and financial support for the modern Armenian state.

Today the total population of Armenia is 3.5 to 4 million people, while almost two times that number (7 to 8 million) live abroad.[58] In the United States, there is an Armenian population of approximately 1 million, 1.5 million in Russia, and around another million spread throughout Europe, the Middle East, and

Latin America.[59] The Armenians abroad have become organized representatives for Armenia in their countries of residence. Moreover, they even began to exert influence on the foreign policy of their countries of residence, particularly in states that possess democratic processes like the United States.[60] Diasporas are usually very committed to the preservation or restoration of their nation, and conflict-generated diasporas like the Armenians tend to maintain very strong ties to their historic homeland and people.[61]

Indeed, the 1915 Ottoman violence against Armenians is central to Armenian consciousness. Today, one of the primary objectives of the Armenian diaspora is to solicit international recognition of Ottoman Turkish violence during WWI as genocide. The Armenian diaspora has also committed itself to supporting the independence of Karabakh-Armenians, the survival of the Armenian state, and the growth of democracy in Armenia.[62] The diaspora has furthered these goals by providing significant financial support to Armenia and Nagorno-Karabakh through remittances, and by encouraging foreign aid to Armenia. Diaspora remittances have been used to construct highway connections between Armenia and Nagorno-Karabakh and for reconstruction after the war.[63]

Although the Armenian diaspora has provided vital support for the Armenian state, at times the diaspora community is at odds with itself. The Soviet Iron Curtain separated Russian-Armenians from the diaspora in the West for around 70 years, which produced different perspectives between Western and Eastern Armenians.[64] For example, Western Armenians tend to take a dim view of Yerevan dependency on Moscow and place a great deal of emphasis on the growth of democracy in Armenia.[65] Just how close Armenia should remain to Russia is a contentious issue.

Contemporary Government and Politics in Armenia

Government Structure

According to its constitution, the Republic of Armenia is established as a secular republican form of government that derives its power from the people. The national government has three branches: the executive branch headed by the President of Armenia, the judicial branch with its law courts, and the legislative branch which consists of a single-chamber parliament led by a prime minister. Under the constitution, parliamentary representatives and the president are to be elected in free democratic elections. (See Appendix G for Armenia's constitution.)

Political Conditions

The freedom and fairness of Armenian elections have been questioned since independence, and the political powers of its presidents have become very significant.[66] While the Armenian electoral system appears to be more open and free than that of Azerbaijan, there are serious questions about the health of democracy in Armenia. In the presidential elections of 2008, when President Sargsian was elected, opposition parties appeared to be hindered in their ability to organize. When election results awarded Sargsian 53 percent of the vote, several international monitors questioned the results, citing voting irregularities. Backers of former President Ter-Petrossian, who claimed to have won the election, took to the streets in protest. When security forces reacted, 10 people were killed and at least another 200 were injured.[67]

Important Political Players

President Sargsian's political party, the ruling party of Armenia, is known as the Republican Party (HHK). Sargsian is a close ally of former President Kocharian, and both are important players to watch in the shape of Armenian domestic politics and for the future of Nagorno-Karabakh. Since the 2008 presidential election, Ter-Petrossian has become a major opposition leader. During that election, he was endorsed by many of the small opposition political parties in Armenia. He was also endorsed by the former ruling party, the Armenian Pan-National Movement (HHSh), and the People's Party (HZK). The HZK is notable because it is the party of Stepan Demirchian, who was the main opposition candidate in the 2003 presidential election where he faced Kocharian. Other major opposition leaders include Raffi Hovannisian, Artashes Geghamian, Vazgen Manukian, and Aram Karapetian.[68]

Political Freedom, Civil Liberties, and Human Rights

Due to "the inability of the opposition to successfully compete" in the 2008 elections, Freedom House downgraded Armenia's Political Rights rating to a 6. It received a better Civil Liberties score of 5, considering that the scale is 1 through 7 with 1 as the best score. The overall ranking that Armenia received from Freedom House, then, is "Partly Free." Freedom of speech is a right that is unofficially infringed upon by Armenian officials. The broadcast media is largely controlled by political pressure from above, and one particularly independent television station, A1+, was closed through a licensing decision. Violence against journalists also continues to be a problem.[69]

As far as religious freedoms are concerned, Armenia rates relatively high, as most religious groups have not reported serious infringements on their rights. However, the Armenian Apostolic Church is granted some rights not afforded to others. Around 90 percent of the Armenian population identifies themselves as members of that church. Jehovah's Witnesses have been jailed for refusing to serve in the Armenian military. The small number of ethnic minorities in Armenia appear to be treated relatively well, although there are some complaints about discrimination by police.[70]

Government transparency is also an issue in Armenia. It was ranked 109 out of the 180 countries surveyed in Transparency International's 2008 *Corruption Perceptions Index*. Reports indicate that bribery is common among government officials; and corruption appears to be a problem in Armenian law enforcement agencies. Elected officials and bureaucrats are rarely removed under charges of corruption. This state of affairs undermines the openness of the Armenian political system and may be tied to cynical attitudes of Armenians toward their government.[71]

FOREIGN POLICY AND RELATIONS

United States and NATO

At the time of independence, Yerevan was positioned very positively in relation to Washington, a fact in no small part due to the role of the Armenian diaspora.[72] The United States was sympathetic to Armenians in Nagorno-Karabakh and their pursuit of independence. For example, Senator John Kerry, backed by the large Armenian lobby in the state of Massachusetts, proposed the addition of Section 907 to the Freedom Support Act in 1992 in order to sanction Azerbaijan for its violence against Armenians. At the time, Baku did not even have diplomatic representation in Washington.[73]

Because of this political situation, Armenia also received large amounts of foreign aid from the United States. But American-Armenian relations began to weaken as it became more apparent to the world that the war in Nagorno-Karabakh had two different stories, and not just the one told by Yerevan. At the same time, the United States began to realize the strategic value of Azerbaijan due to its energy wealth. The importance of Azerbaijan reached even greater heights when the "War on Terror" began.

Yerevan's ties with Tehran and its complicated connection with Ankara have also worn on the American-Armenian relationship. For Washington, the strategic relationship between the United States and Turkey is even more important than ties between the United States and Azerbaijan because of the Turkish role in spreading moderate Islam, its democratic example, and its role for the projection of U.S. military might. Even President Barack Obama, who before the election was willing to recognize the Ottoman violence in 1915 as genocide, has refused to use that term because of the damage it would cause to Turkish-American relations. Instead, he has stated that this is an issue that Ankara and Yerevan should work together to resolve.[74]

Still, the United States has continued to maintain ties with Armenia, continuing to provide some aid, supporting democratic development, and urging Armenia to cooperate with NATO through the PfP program. Armenia became a participant in the PfP program in 1994 and even deployed troops in Kosovo.

Then, in 2005, Armenia received its first approved Individual Partnership Action Plan (IPAP). This cooperation with the Western security structure allows Armenia to maintain some separation from Russia.[75] However, Armenia has made it clear that it is not seeking NATO membership, something that would clearly upset Russia.

EU and OSCE

For Armenia, Europe offers even greater economic opportunity than the United States does. The EU offers a large market and multilateral European organizations hold both economic and political promise. Armenia has consistently grown closer to the EU. In 1999, the EU-Armenia Partnership and Cooperation Agreement (PCA) went into effect. In 2004, Armenia gained a place in the EU's ENP program. Armenia's ENP action plan was then approved in 2006, and soon after Armenia began implementing the objectives of that plan.[76]

Similar to the actions of Armenian diaspora in the United States, the Armenian diaspora in Europe generated sympathy for the Armenian cause during its early years of independence. In Europe, the Armenian diaspora has used its political power to oppose Turkey's membership into the EU.[77] In the long run, however, Armenia is strategically less important for the EU than Azerbaijan is. This is mainly due to Europe's growing energy demands, which Azerbaijan can supply, especially via the new pipeline lines.

The EU's plan with Armenia through the ENP structure is primarily motivated by another strategic concern. That is to create a stable belt of neighboring states around Europe, as mentioned earlier. The OSCE plays an important role in this strategy, and its involvement in the Nagorno-Karabakh conflict has been an important part of European-Armenian relations. The OSCE has served as a forum for negotiations and facilitating the peace process.[78] Yet, the OSCE has had little success in resolving this conflict; and it has developed tension with Armenians because of its criticism of Nagorno-Karabakh's attempts to gain international recognition.

Russia, CIS, and CSTO

The relationship between Moscow and Yerevan has a long, complicated history. Although in some ways Moscow has been the traditional protector of Armenians, Russia has prevented Armenia from gaining complete political autonomy throughout its history. Even today, Russia continues to be a constraint on Armenian sovereignty, through its control of Armenian energy and its role as a regional hegemon via international organizations like the CIS and CSTO.

At the time of independence, the war for Nagorno-Karabakh made security the top priority for Yerevan. In order to protect itself, Armenia agreed to allow

Russia to maintain military bases on its territory and to have Russians patrol its borders.[79] Unlike Georgia and Azerbaijan, Armenia has never left the CIS, and it has welcomed Russia's establishment of the CSTO and regularly participated in war games of this security organization.[80] In this manner, Armenia has deferred to Russia as the regional security manager.

Following immediately behind (and associated with) security concerns in Armenian foreign policy priorities has been the issue of energy. Armenia has almost entirely been dependent on Russia for hydrocarbon energy supplies. Russia has willingly supplied this energy and significantly invested in the Armenian energy sector. This has established what appears to be a long-term economic partnership, but one that has a built-in dependency ties.

Despite this potential negative impact, Armenian-Russian relations appear to be firmly established. The Russia-Georgia War warned Armenia of Moscow's willingness to act in order to maintain its dominance in the region, but this does not appear to have shaken Armenian-Russian ties. So, considering the historical ties of Yerevan and Moscow and the importance of Russian security aid and energy resources for Armenia, it appears unlikely that the new Armenian President Sargsian (a nationalist following in Kocharian's footsteps) will rock the boat on bilateral ties between these two states.[81]

Iran

At first glance, the traditional Christian-Muslim rivalry in the Caucasus may suggest that the Muslim Persians should perceive the Christian Armenians as an enemy. Such simplistic assertions would certainly support the Clash of Civilizations argument. However, a closer observation of the historical relationship between Armenia and Iran shows a very different story.

The connections between the two nations go back to the time of the Safavid Dynasty, which invited Armenian artists and technicians to come to Iran during the early process of the modernization of Persia. In fact, so many Armenians moved to Iran that they developed significant communities along with their churches, businesses, and community centers in Isfahan (Capital of the Safavids) and later in Tehran. They also established major Armenian communities in the cities of Urumieh (capital of the Iranian Western Azerbaijan province), Tabriz (capital of the Iranian Eastern Azerbaijan province), Jolfa in Iranian Azerbaijan, and another city of Jolfa in the province of Isfahan.

Even with the establishment of the Islamic Republic, the Armenian communities have maintained their special status and remained loyal to Iran. In fact, many Armenians voluntarily joined the Iranian military during the Iran-Iraq War. The IRI regime considers those Armenians who lost their lives as *shahid* (or martyr, a term exclusively used for dead Muslim soldiers). In the honor of martyred Armenians, the IRI has named some streets and made large murals of their brave acts.

The establishment of friendly ties between these two nations demonstrates that contemporary international politics are not merely driven by ethnic or religious differences. Instead, the Armenian-Iranian ties show a pragmatic consideration of shared history and geopolitical realities. For Armenia, there are great economic benefits to pursuing closer ties with Iran, while Tehran considers a mix of economic and security reasons to reach out to Yerevan. Regarding security, for example, Iranian support for Armenia has given it more political leverage over Azerbaijan. This way, the IRI can counter any attempts by the nationalists in Baku to sow trouble among Iranian-Azeris.

Regarding business and economics, in 2000, there were important discussions of a three-way economic union between Armenia, Turkmenistan, and Iran. On this topic, Armenia has expressed great interest.[82] Friendly diplomatic and economic relations have also trickled down into attempts to further security cooperation. On December 26, 2001, presidents Mohammad Khatami (Iran) and Robert Kocharian (Armenia) declared that Tehran and Yerevan had agreed to build up bilateral cooperation in the sphere of regional security and stability.[83]

Yet Armenia knows that Iran is a volatile friend to have. Perhaps to downplay their relationship for the Azeris, President Robert Kocharian stated in 2002 that, "There is no serious military aspect in our relations."[84] At that time, he talked about the good, neighborly relations between both states; and how they were working to increase trade and economic cooperation. A specific example of this cooperation is the Iranian-Armenian gas pipeline, which was completed in 2007 after laying 62 miles of pipe across Iran and 25 miles through Armenia.[85] This route is projected to supply Armenia with almost 53 million cf of gas annually.[86] This pipeline allows Armenia to diversify its energy imports and to decrease its dependence on Russian energy in the long run.

Turkey

Yerevan's relationship with Ankara remains very icy, and its nature is nearly as troubled as Yerevan's ties to Baku. Turkish-Armenian tension is primarily the function of territorial disputes, the issue of Armenian genocide, and their disagreements over Nagorno-Karabakh status. Turkey has strongly defended Azerbaijan's territorial integrity, a stance that fits with Turkey's similar opposition to Armenian claims to its territory. Because of their shared territorial conflicts, Baku leaders have expressed numerous times that Ankara can really relate to deep dimensions of Azeri conflict with Armenia.[87] The closeness of the Turkish-Azeri ties has led Armenians to see that alliance as the continuation of historical conflicts with Turks and an attempt to "keep Armenia helpless and vulnerable."[88] Thus, the Turkish-Azeri ties have a psychological impact on many Armenians.

The Armenian diaspora has often increased tension with Turkey through its attempts to lobby foreign governments to recognize the Armenian Genocide of

1915. In the United States, the diaspora's attempts to push genocide recognition through the U.S. Congress has even created tension between the United States and Turkey.[89] The Turkish government officially refuses to acknowledge the massacre of Armenians during WWI as genocide, which serves to undermine any hope for new ties between these states.[90]

Yet not all Armenians feel that recognition of the Armenian genocide is necessary for rapprochement. Turkish-Armenians constitute the largest Christian population in Turkey, at approximately 70,000 in number. These Armenians generally support a more rapid resolution to Turkish-Armenian disputes, since this impacts their daily lives in Turkey. In contrast, the Armenian diaspora at large has much less reason to put the past behind them. Mesrob II, the eighty-fourth patriarch of the Armenian Orthodox community in Turkey, has expressed that hopes for any Armenian-Turkish relationship are constantly hindered by returning to the issue of genocide.[91]

Opening economic ties with Turkey would certainly be one of the most significant steps toward breaking Armenia's trade dependencies on Moscow. Attempts to achieve rapprochement, however, have accomplished very little. When Armenians offered to open relations with Turkey without any preconditions in 2002, Turkey was slow to reciprocate, responding that Armenia needed to resolve its conflict with Azerbaijan and renounce claims to certain sections of Turkish territory.[92] In 2003, Armenia made a renewed effort in which such concessions were considered.[93] Afterwards, Turkey declared that it would consider reopening its border with Armenia.[94] But in 2004, the Turkish government announced that it was suspending relations because Armenia was not living up to its expectations.[95]

In 2005, the IMF added its voice to the issue, stating that it would be critical for Yerevan to achieve the normalization of ties with Ankara.[96] Turkey also has reasons to seek an economic relationship with Armenia. For instance, the resolution of the Turkish-Armenian border dispute is something that the EU has strongly requested.[97] In 2006, however, negotiations stalled again, and the Armenian Foreign Minister Vardan Oskanyan said that Turkey did not appear willing to open diplomatic relations.[98]

Still, improving ties with Armenia appears to be on the agenda of the ruling Justice and Development Party (AKP) in Turkey. On September 6, 2008, Turkish President Abdullah Gul visited Armenia for a football (soccer) match between their national teams.[99] Some reports seemingly suggested that both opposing sides were preparing to reopen roads across their borders.[100] Additionally, there is still the possibility that the Kars-Gumru railway could be reopened.[101]

Azerbaijan

The dispute over Nagorno-Karabakh remains the main obstacle holding Azerbaijan and Armenia apart. During their initial struggle to solicit international support for their respective causes, Yerevan gained the edge with the help of the Armenian diaspora. In fact, the diaspora has become well organized and a major force to be reckoned with in Armenian-Azeri relations. In the past, many Azeri politicians argued that the Armenian lobby in the United States was the greatest obstacle to negotiations and to the establishment of friendly ties between the United States and Azerbaijan.[102] Certainly, Section 907 of the Freedom Support Act served to erect a barrier to U.S.-Azeri ties that has only recently been broken down. In addition to successfully limiting Azerbaijan's ability to receive foreign aid, the Armenian lobby managed to place Armenia in the enviable position as the highest (per capita) recipient of U.S. foreign aid in the former Soviet Union.[103]

Yerevan's initial success at isolating Baku from Europe and the United States meant that Azerbaijan's relationship with Turkey received even more emphasis. In turn, the growth of Azeri-Turkish ties reinforced the feeling of Armenians that the Azeris were their historic Turkic Muslim enemies, despite the fact that historically Azeris have been differentiated from the Sunni Turks by their Shia and Persian heritage. The animosity still felt between Armenians and their Turkic neighbors remains a hindrance to any final resolution to Armenian territorial disputes.

Nowadays, European states and the United States have taken a more neutral stance on the Nagorno-Karabakh conflict than they originally did during its early stages. The West has withheld its recognition of Nagorno-Karabakh until both parties can reach a mutually satisfactory agreement. Not only do the United States and EU desire to see peace more firmly established in the region, but there are also hopes that resolution of the frozen conflict might allow Armenia to establish economic and political relationships with Turkey and Azerbaijan. They expect that such improved relationships might even draw Yerevan away from their "too close for comfort" connections with Moscow and Tehran.

Recently, there have been signs of slow, measured movement toward an eventual settlement. For instance, both Azeri president Ilham Aliyev and Armenian president Serzh Sargsian met together during a CIS summit in June 2008.[104] Since then, other meetings and reports of progress have continued to appear from time to time through 2009. Still, there remains little visible or substantive progress on the disputed issues at hand.[105]

Georgia

Historically, Georgia and Armenia have shared some similarities as Christian nations in an area of the world that is largely Muslim. Traditionally, both nations have long been defined by their religion as Christian, and both embraced advancing Russian forces in order to escape the rule of Muslim empires. By the time of their independence, however, their separate ethnic identities had become more

important than their shared historical experiences and common religious heritage. Nationalism produced territorial tensions along their border. Even more
important than such border tensions, the current Republics of Armenia and
Georgia have taken a very different diplomatic position toward Russia since
gaining independence.

Nevertheless, Georgia is vital for Armenian economic ties to Russia. Therefore,
Yerevan has placed a great deal of emphasis on establishing friendly ties with
Tbilisi. Without Georgia, Armenia could not easily extend its trade ties to
Russia, Europe, or the Black Sea region. The lion's share of Armenia's international
trade now transits Georgian territory. Thus, while Armenia has demonstrated
willingness to aggressively and relentlessly pursue ethnic unity (in the war for
Nagorno-Karabakh), it has downplayed nationalist tension over areas of Georgian
territory that have large Armenian populations. Rather than seeking the unification
of Georgia's Javakheti region to the Armenian motherland, Yerevan has pragmatically attempted to silence such discussions in order to protect its vital economic
relations with Georgia.[106] Armenia has also worked with Georgia to settle the status
of their shared border.[107]

These days, Armenia also holds important economic and strategic opportunity
for Georgians as well. The Armenian-Iranian gas pipeline that was completed in
2007 could be extended to Georgia, offering the Georgians the means to further
reduce their energy dependency on Russia. Tehran has made it clear that it is very
open to this idea. Such pipeline extension is a possibility that has major benefits
for the IRI, because access to Georgia may eventually also provide Iran with
pipeline connection to the European markets.[108] Moreover, both Armenia and
Georgia would benefit from such transportation line and the growth of trade
along their routes.[109]

Furthermore, Armenian close ties with Russia do not always have to be a strain
on the Yerevan-Tbilisi relationship. In 2004, Saakashvili said that "Armenia can
be of help to us, insofar as she maintains close ties of friendship with Russia."[110]
Though hope for Russia-Georgia rapprochement has dimmed in light of the
2008 war, their improved relationship is always a possibility for the future. Armenia has attempted to avoid taking sides in that conflict, and it has an interest in
the normalization of Georgia-Russia ties because Russian transportation blockades of Georgia are disruptive for the Armenian economy.[111]

SUMMARY

Throughout its history, Armenia has had to struggle to maintain its identity
amidst the rise and fall of other major powers. This eventually led Armenia to turn to
external powers (e.g., Romans, Persians, and Russians) for support—a pattern of
behavior that still appears to persist. From Yerevan's perspective, upon Armenian
independence, the greatest threat to the unity of the Armenian people was Azerbaijan.

The complexity of the Soviet-era borders between these two Republics was convoluted, inviting ethnic conflict. In response, Yerevan acted swiftly and decisively to separate Nagorno-Karabakh from Azeri control.

Comparatively, Armenian actions demonstrated significant resolve and unity, while Azerbaijan was in political disarray in the early stages of the post-independence era, despite its energy wealth and large military. During that conflict, Armenia endured terrible economic times, as trade plummeted and energy grew scarce. The economic isolation imposed on Armenia due to their negative relations with Turkey and Azerbaijan, however, made it essential for Yerevan to maintain whatever trade outlet options it had left. Therefore, even the very nationalist Armenian presidents (e.g., Kocharian and Sargsian) have downplayed ethnic conflict with Georgia. Cementing ties with Tbilisi allowed Armenia to secure access to Russian markets and energy resources.

Another intriguing example of where Armenian nationalism has not resulted in conflict is in Armenian-Russian ties. Nationalism in both Georgia and Azerbaijan has played a large role in moving these states away from the Russian orbit and "sphere of influence." Why not in Armenia? Yerevan's decision to maintain its ties with Moscow may be also seen as a natural and "rational choice," since Russia has historically supported Armenians against their Muslim Turkic neighbors. However, there are also strong geopolitical reasons for this orientation that may be understood when Armenia's position is contrasted with that of its South Caucasus neighbors.

Both Armenia and Azerbaijan have chosen potential allies with which they do not share a border (i.e., Russia and Turkey, respectively). This means that their primary allies are major states with which neither state had the complication of border disputes. Armenia is physically separated from Russia by Georgia, and Azerbaijan is geographically separated from Turkey by Georgia and Armenia. Having such buffer areas reduces the threat that the stronger allies may pose to these NIS, simply because of the geographic and political difficulties that Moscow would have to annex Armenia or Ankara could have to absorb Azerbaijan.

Furthermore, Armenia shares ties with the large Russian-Armenian population while Azerbaijan shares a similar ethnic heritage with the Turks. There is also a similar geopolitical logic to this pattern of alliances that can be found in relation to energy. The Azeri economy is dependent on the sale of its energy to Turkish and Western markets, while in a reverse manner, Armenia's economy is so far dependent upon energy imported from Russia. In the end, these geopolitical constraints meant that both alliances became focused on transportation routes and energy pipelines running through Georgia. The next chapter concentrates on a closer analysis of the Georgian affairs and their security and geopolitical position within the region.

NOTES

1. Anahide Ter Minassian, "Enjeux, Les Armeniens Au 20eme Siecle. Vingtieme Siecle," *Revue d'Histoire* 67 (July–September 2000), 135.

2. Razmik Panossian, *The Armenians: From Kings and Priests to Merchants and Commissars* (New York, NY: Columbia University Press, 2006), 33–35.

3. Ibid., 35.

4. Nina Garsoïan, "The Emergence of Armenia," in *Armenian People from Ancient to Modern Times*, vol. I, Richard G. Hovannisian, ed. (New York, NY: Palgrave Macmillan, 2004), 42.

5. Panossian, 39.

6. Anne E. Redgate, *The Armenians* (Oxford: Blackwell, 1998), 115–116.

7. Panossian, 61.

8. Christopher Walker, *Armenia: The Survival of a Nation*, 2nd ed. (New York, NY: St. Martin's Press, 1990), 31.

9. Panossian, 65.

10. Ibid., 67 and 87.

11. George Bournoutian, "Eastern Armenia from the Seventeenth Century to the Russian Annexation," in Richard Hovannisian, ed., *The Armenian People from Ancient to Modern Times*, vol. II (New York, NY: St. Martin's Press, 1997), 34–36.

12. Bournoutian, 98–105.

13. Panossian, 111.

14. Rau, 21.

15. Ronald Suny, "Eastern Armenians Under Tsarist Rule," in Hovannisian, *The Armenian People from Ancient to Modern Times*, 129–137.

16. Panossian, 161, 231.

17. David Marshall Lang, "Independent Georgia (1918–1921)," excerpt from *A Modern History of Soviet Georgia*, David Marshall Lang (London: Weidenfeld and Nicolson, 1962), http://www.conflicts.rem33.com/images/Georgia/Lang_9a.htm (accessed May 21, 2009).

18. Rau, 26–27.

19. Khachig Tölölyan, "The Armenian Diaspora as a Transnational Actor and as a Potential Contributor to Conflict Resolution," *Diaspora: Journal of Transnational Studies* (2006): 1; Panossian, 277.

20. Rau, 32; Panossian, 277.

21. Nahaylo, Bohdan and Victor Svoboda, *Soviet Disunion: A History of the Nationality Problem in the USSR* (New York, NY: Macmillan, 1990), 147.

22. Rau, 32–33.

23. Thomas de Waal, *Black Garden: Armenia and Azerbaijan through War and Peace* (New York, NY: New York University Press, 2003), 40.

24. Zürcher, 64; Rau, 32–36.

25. Stephan A. Astourian, "From Ter-Petrosian to Kocharian: Leadership Change in Armenia," *Berkeley Program in Soviet and Post-Soviet Studies Working Paper Series* (Winter 2000–2001), 43, http://bps.berkeley.edu/publications/2000_04-asto.pdf (accessed May 18, 2009); Thomas Goltz, *Azerbaijan Diary: A Rogue Reporter's Adventures in an Oil-Rich, War-Torn, Post-Soviet Republic* (New York, NY: M. E. Sharpe, 1998), 315.

26. de Waal, 161.

27. Laurence Ritter, "Getting Ready for a Political Come-back? Levon Ter Petrosian Breaks His Silence," Caucaz Europenews, December 13, 2004, http://www.caucaz.com/home_eng/breve_contenu.php?id=88 (accessed May 24, 2009).

28. de Waal, 12.

29. Rau, 37–38.

30. Croissant, 46.

31. Ibid., 39.

32. de Waal, 213.

33. Murat Gül, "Russia and Azerbaijan: Relations after 1989," *Alternatives: Turkish Journal of International Relations* 7, 2 & 3 (Summer & Fall 2008): 56.

34. Rau, 45.

35. Astourian, 2, 47, and 56.

36. SIPRI, *SIPRI Yearbook 2008: Armaments, Disarmament and International Security* (Oxford: Oxford University Press, 2008), 187.

37. SIPRI, SIPRI Military Expenditure Database, http://milexdata.sipri.org/result.php4 (accessed August 16, 2009).

38. Arminfo, "Armenian Defense Chief Unfazed by Bigger Military Spending in Azerbaijan," Arminfo, November 6, 2006 (translation from Russian, World News Connection, National Technical Information Service, NTIS, US Department of Commerce); Dan Darling, "Azerbaijan Boosting Military Spending," *Forecast International* (May 9, 2007). http://www.forecast international.com/press/release.cfm?article=110 (accessed January 31, 2010).

39. ICG, "Nagorno-Karabakh: Risking War," Europe Report N187, International Crisis Group, November 14, 2007, 13.

40. Alexander Jackson, "The Military Balance in Nagorno-Karabakh," *Caucasus Review of International Affairs* 18 (January 19, 2009), http://cria-online.org/CU_-_file_-_article_-_sid_-_19.html (accessed September 2, 2009).

41. Jasur Mamedov, "Azerbaijan Flexes Military Muscles," *Institute for War and Peace Reporting*, July 19, 2007.

42. ICG, 13–14.

43. Wayne Merry, "Diplomacy and War in Karabakh: An Unofficial American Perspective," *Central Asia–Caucasus Institute* (October 25, 2006).

44. de Waal, 87.

45. Aaumya Mitra et al., *The Caucasian Tiger: Sustaining Economic Growth in Armenia* (Washington, D.C.: The World Bank, 2007), 6.

46. Mitra et al., 5 and 109.

47. Gevorg Sargsayan, Ani Balabanyan, and Denzel Hankinson, *From Crisis to Stability in the Armenian Power Sector: Lessons Learned from Armenia's Energy Reform Experience* (Washington, D.C.: The World Bank, 2006): 2.

48. Ibid., 6.

49. Vladimir Papava, "On the Essence of Economic Reforms in Georgia, or How European Is the European Choice of Post-Revolution Georgia?" *TEPAV* 3, http://www.tepav.org.tr/karadeniz/kei.html (accessed May 23, 2009).

50. EIA, "Armenia Energy Profile," Washington, D.C.: Energy Information Administration, http://tonto.eia.doe.gov/country/country_energy_data.cfm?fips=AM (accessed March 24, 2009).

51. Mitra et al., 3.

52. Ibid., 4.

53. Jan Soykok, "Armenian Tragedy, But Who Is Responsible?" *Journal of Turkish Weekly* (January 6, 2005), http://www.turkishweekly.net/news/1320/armenian-tragedy-but-who-is -responsible.html (accessed January 31, 2010).

54. Lara Tcholakian, "Armenian Diaspora Looks for Presidential Vote to Promote Stable Growth," Eurasianet.org, February 18, 2003, http://www.eurasianet.org/departments/ business/articles/eav021803_pr.shtml (accessed May 23, 2009).

55. IMF, *World Economic Outlook, April 2009* (Washington, D.C.: International Monetary Fund, 2009), 86, http://www.imf.org/external/pubs/ft/weo/2009/01/pdf/text.pdf (accessed September 2, 2009).

56. SIPRI, *SIPRI Yearbook 2008*, 186.

57. Ken Stier, "Study Highlights Inefficiencies and Evils of Armenian Emigration," Eurasianet.org, April 16, 2002, http://www.eurasianet.org/departments/business/articles/ eav041602_pr.shtml (accessed April 21, 2009).

58. Bahar Baser and Ashok Swain, "Diaspora Design Versus Homeland Realities: Case Study of the Armenian Diaspora," *Caucasian Review of International Affairs* 3, no. 1 (Winter 2009), 52.

59. Mitra et al., 550–551.

60. Yossi Shain, "Ethnic Diasporas and US Foreign Policy," *Political Science Quarterly* 109, no. 1 (January 2005): 2.

61. Baser and Swain, 48; Terrence Lyons, "Diasporas and Homeland Conflict" (Workshop on "Contentious Politics," Washington, DC, March 15, 2004).

62. Tatoul Manaseryan, "Diaspora: the Comparative Advantage for Armenia," Armenian International Policy Research Group (January 2004): 2.

63. de Waal, 256.

64. Baser and Swain, 56.

65. Bercovitch, Jacob, "A Neglected Relationship: Diasporas and Conflict Resolution," in *Diasporas in Conflict: Peace-Makers or Peace-Wreckers?* Hazel Smith and Paul Stares, eds. (Tokyo: United Nations University Press, 2007).

66. Stephan A. Astourian, "From Ter-Petrosian to Kocharian: Leadership Change in Armenia," *Berkeley Program in Soviet and Post-Soviet Studies Working Paper Series* (Winter 2000–2001), http://bps.berkeley.edu/publications/2000_04-asto.pdf (accessed May 18, 2009).

67. Freedom House, "Country Report: Armenia," *Freedom in the World Report* (Freedom House, 2009), http://www.freedomhouse.org/template.cfm?page=22&year=2009&country =7557 (accessed September 2, 2009).

68. Rueben Meloyan, Opposition Leaders Reluctant to Back Ex-President, *Radio Free Europe*, November 19, 2007, http://www.armenialiberty.org/content/Article/1591618.html (accessed September 2, 2009).

69. Freedom House, "Country Report: Armenia."

70. Ibid.

71. Ibid.

72. Shain, 12.

73. Svante E. Cornell, "The Politization of Islam in Azerbaijan," *CA-CI SR Paper* (October 2006): 30.

74. Today's Zaman, "Its up to Turkey, Armenia to Resolve History Row, Says Obama," *Today's Zaman*, April 6, 2009, http://www.todayszaman.com/tz-web/detaylar.do?load =detay&link=171673 (accessed May 24, 2009).

75. NATO, "NATO's Relations with Armenia," North Atlantic Treaty Organization, February 24, 2009, http://www.nato.int/issues/nato-armenia/index.html (accessed May 23, 2009).

76. Armenian Foreign Ministry, "European Neighborhood Policy: ARMENIA," Armenian Foreign Ministry, April 3, 2008, http://www.armeniaforeignministry.am/doc/id/memo _eu.pdf (accessed May 23, 2009).

77. Baser and Swain, 57.

78. Liz Fuller, "Nagorno-Karabkh: OSCE to Unveil New Peace Plan," Eurasianet.org, April 9, 2005, http://www.eurasianet.org/departments/insight/articles/pp040905.shtml (accessed May 23, 2009).

79. Emil Danielyan, "Georgian Transit Ban Hinders Russian Military Presence in Armenia," Eurasianet.org, October 10, 2008, http://www.eurasianet.org/departments/insight/articles/ eav101008a.shtml (accessed May 24, 2009); Sergei Balgov, Armenia and Russia Reassert Bonds Amid Georgia's Crisis," Eurasianet.org, November 17, 2003, http://www.eurasianet.org/ departments/insight/articles/eav111703.shtml (accessed May 24, 2009).

80. Asbarez.com, "CSTO Rubez War Games Begin in Armenia," Asbarez.com, July 22, 2008, http://www.asbarez.com/2008/07/22/csto-rubezh-war-games-begin-in-armenia/ (accessed May 24, 2009).

81. RIA Novosti, "Russia, Armenia to Set Up Joint Air Defense Network," RIA Novosti, February 13, 2009, http://en.rian.ru/russia/20090213/120124464.html (accessed May 24, 2009).

82. AFX News Limited, "Turkmenistan, Iran Discuss Caspian Sea Status; Armenia Seeks 3-Way Union," *AFX News Limited*, November 28, 2000.

83. RIA Novosti, "Iran, Armenia Agree to Strengthen Bilateral Cooperation in the Sphere of Regional Security," RIA Novosti, December 26, 2001.

84. ITAR-TASS, "There Is Not Military Aspect in Armenia-Iran Ties: Leader," ITAR-TASS News Agency, March 14, 2002.

85. ITAR-TASS, "There Is Not Military Aspect in Armenia-Iran Ties: Leader"; Georgeta Pourchot, *Eurasia Rising: Democracy and Independence in the Post-Soviet Space* (Westport, CT: Praeger Security International, 2008), 81.

86. RIA Novosti, "First Stage of Work on Iran-Armenia Gas Pipeline Project to Begin Soon," RIA Novosti, December 26, 2000.

87. Arminfo News Agency, "Azerbaijan FM: Problem with Opening of Boundary Connected Not Only with Armenian-Azerbaijani Conflict, but also with Relations between Turkey and Armenia," Arminfo News Agency, May 31, 2004.

88. Shain, 6.

89. Carl Hulse, "US and Turkey Thwart Armenian Genocide Bill," *The New York Times*, October 26, 2007, http://www.nytimes.com/2007/10/26/world/americas/26iht-26cong .8062989.html?_r=1 (accessed January 31, 2010).

90. BBC, "Plan to Improve Turkey's Relations with Armenia Said Shelved," British Broadcasting Corporation, January 16, 2001; Savannah Waring Walker, "World Briefing," *New York Times*, September 27, 2000, http://www.nytimes.com/2000/09/27/world/world-briefing .html?pagewanted=1 (accessed January 31, 2010).

91. Today's Zaman, "An Interview with Mesrob II, the 84th Patriarch of Turkey's Armenian Orthodox Community," *Today's Zaman*, September 17, 2007.

92. Saadet Oruc, "Armenia Wants Diplomatic Relations with Turkey . . . But What About Ankara?" *Turkish Daily News*, June 30, 2002.

93. Ugur Ergan, "New Approach Reported in Relations between Turkey, Armenia," *Financial Times*, June 6, 2003.

94. Financial Times, "Turkey to Restore Relations with Armenia, Armenian TV Says," *Financial Times*, June 6, 2003.

95. Arminfo News Agency, "Development of Armenia-Turkey Relations Suspended," *Arminfo News Agency*, May 31, 2004.

96. Financial Times, "IMF: Armenia Needs Good Relations with Turkey to Further Boost Its Economy," *Financial Times*, July 21, 2005.

97. Arminfo News Agency, "EU Interested in Normalization of Armenia-Turkey Relations," *Arminfo News Agency*, April 5, 2006.

98. Arminfo News Agency, "RA FM: Turkey Is Not Ready to Establish Diplomatic Relations with Armenia," *Arminfo News Agency*, June 9, 2006.

99. Kamer Kasim, "The Impact of the Armenian Diaspora in Turkey's Relations with Armenia," *The Journal of Turkish Weekly* (March 9, 2009): 2, http://www.turkishweekly.net/print.asp?type=1&id=66480 (accessed April 20, 2009).

100. Gayane Abrahamyan, "Armenian Village Plans for Turkish Border Openings," Eurasianet.org, April 16, 2009, http://www.eurasianet.org/departments/insightb/articles/eav041609.shtml (accessed May 23, 2009).

101. Baser and Swain, 61.

102. Shain, 7.

103. Human Rights Watch, *Azerbaijan: Seven Years of Conflict in Nagorno-Karabakh* (New York, NY: Human Rights Watch, 1994), 78.

104. Alima Bissenova, "Azerbaijan, Armenian Presidents Meet on CIS Forum Sidelines," *CA-CI Analyst* (June 6, 2008), http://www.cacianalyst.org/?q=node/4884 (accessed May 24, 2009).

105. Eurasianet.net, "Armenia, Azerbaijan Presidents Meet," Eurasianet.net, May 8, 2009, http://eurasianet.net/departments/news/articles/eav050809b.shtml (accessed May 24, 2009).

106. Regnum News Agency, "Georgia Is Becoming Hostage to Azeri-Turkish Alliance: Interview with Pavel Chobanyan," *Regnum News Agency*, July 10, 2006: 1, http://www.gab-bn.com/juillet_06/Ge1-%20Georgia%20is%20becoming%20hostage%20to%20Azeri%20Turkish%20alliance.pdf (accessed May 21, 2009).

107. Caucaz Europenews, "Georgia, Armenia Discuss Border Delimination," Caucaz Europenews, February 21, 2007, http://caucaz.com/home_eng/depeches.php?idp=1536&PHPSESSID=5fa14f0afa45094e55c33cce6e13f542 (accessed May 24, 2009).

108. Robert Parsons, "Caucasus: Georgia, Armenia Consider Options after Russia Pipeline Explosions," Radio Free Europe, February 1, 2006, http://www.rferl.org/content/article/1065318.html (accessed May 23, 2009).

109. UNDP, "Study of Economic Relations between Georgia and Armenia: The Development of Regional Trade Related Growth in Samtskhe-Javakheti," United Nations Development Programme, May 13, 2008, 5, http://undp.org.ge/new/files/24_248_868263_cbc-eng.pdf (accessed May 21, 2009).

110. Rosbalt, "Mikhail Saakashvili: Armenia Can Help Georgia Repair Relations with Russia," Eurasia21.com, March 12, 2004, http://www.eurasia21.com/cgi-data/news/files/149.shtml (accessed May 21, 2009).

111. Haroutiun Khachatrian, "Armenia Concentrates on Balancing Act between Russia and Georgia," Eurasianet.org, November 8, 2006, http://www.eurasianet.org/departments/insight/articles/eav110806a.shtml (accessed May 20, 2009).

CHAPTER 4

Georgia

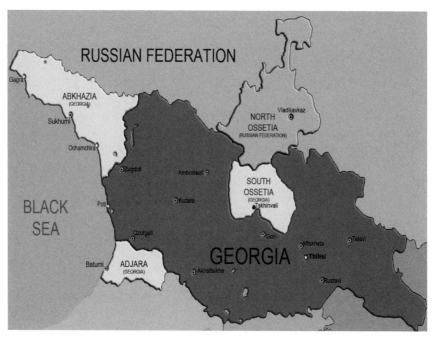

Map 4.1 Georgia and Separatist Regions

Designed by Albert Citron.

Photo 4.1 Georgian President

Mikhail Saakashvili (left), President of Georgia Shaking hands with United Nations Secretary-General
Kofi Annan United Nations Headquarters, New York, USA, September 21, 2004. (# 39737 UN Photo
by Mark Garten.)

Georgia's central position atop the South Caucasus region has the potential to
make it a major hub for regional trade. Adjacent to both Armenia and Azerbaijan,
Georgia offers both states an outlet for trade and transportation routes (Map 4.1).
As has been noted, while Azeri-Armenian relations remain frigid, both states must
rely on Georgia. Azerbaijan needs Georgian territory to reach Turkey, and Armenia
needs Georgian territory to reach Russia. Georgian territory also stands between the
South Caucasus and Europe. It is the only state in the region to have access to the
Black Sea, which makes it a hub for energy pipelines and oil tankers. While
Azerbaijan's energy resources have made it the most geopolitically strategic state
in the South Caucasus, the necessity of Georgian territory for regional pipelines
makes it geopolitically pivotal. Through Georgia, Azerbaijan exports to Turkey and
the West, and also through Georgia, Armenia may import from Russia.
As the West seeks to pull more energy toward itself, it has realized that Georgia
offers the opportunity to pull energy out of the Caspian Sea basin without a
Russian middleman. For Russia, then, Georgia is the spigot through which the
West's access may be pinched off. The 2008 war between Russia and Georgia, then,
has immense ramifications for the regional security and geopolitical future of the
region as well as international trade.

Photo 4.2 Georgian Ministry of Foreign Affairs

From the Web site of the Georgian Foreign Ministry, http://www.mfa.gov.ge/index.php?lang_id=ENG&sec
_id=30&info_id=10046 Grigol Vashadze (left), Foreign Minister of Georgia Meeting with Secretary of State
Hillary Clinton, Washington, D.C., USA, April 14, 2009.

PRE-SOVIET HISTORY

The territory of the modern Georgian state is the historical crossroads through the
Caucasus Mountains, connecting the North Caucasus to the South Caucasus. That
territory has endured repeated invasions, seen the movements of various peoples,
and inherited a legacy of conflicts between Christianity and Islam as well as the East
and the West. After being incorporated into the Byzantine Empire, the Georgian people became Christians. Like the Armenians, their Christian heritage has endured,
though they have had to tolerate periods of Islamic rule too. The Muslims conquered
Georgian territory in the seventh century, and from that time on, Georgian territory
"was almost always divided into two primarily princely states (Kartli/Tbilisi in the east
and Ergesi/Kutaisi in the west) that were as often at each other's throats over issues of
royal succession as they were revolting against their feudal overlords (e.g., Arabs,
Persians, Mongols, Seljuk, and Ottomans)."[1]

Because of these divisions, a cohesive Georgian identity took more time to form
than the development of Armenian or Azeri identities. "The first time the word
'Sakartvelo,' or 'place of the Georgians,' appears in the chronicles is 1008, during a
brief and almost coincidental unification of western and eastern Georgia under Bagrat
III and his mixed Armeno-Georgian-Abkhazian family line. That state's capital was at

Kutaisi; Tbilisi remained a Muslim garrison town, as it had been for almost 400 years."[2] Due to this mix of ethnic heritages, Christianity has been one of the most defining characteristics of Georgians. As the Russian Empire gained strength in the north, Georgians, just like the Armenians, sought Moscow's protection against its Muslim rulers. In the late eighteenth century, both Georgian principalities turned to Russia's Catherine the Great at different times for support against the Persians, Turks, and even each other. Finally, in 1783, the Orthodox-Christian Georgians decisively chose Russian rule over the Muslims. Because of Georgia's geographic position atop the South Caucasus, this decision opened the region to further Russian expansion.[3]

By 1801, Georgia had been completely absorbed into the Tsarist Russian Empire, and Moscow was positioned to be the single most influential power over Georgia until the end of the Cold War. Georgia briefly enjoyed a period of independence between 1918 and 1921, when the Tsarist Russian Empire was torn apart in the Bolshevik Revolution. Independence, however, came with a number of problems, even then. During that early attempt to create a Georgian state, the Ossetian people staged a revolt in support of the Bolshevik Russians.[4] This event was an early warning for the role that Georgia's ethnic heterogeneity would play in producing insecurity after Georgian independence in the 1990s. When the Bolshevik army returned Russian control to Georgia in 1921, that unresolved ethnic conflict was postponed.[5]

SOVIET HISTORY

After integration into the USSR structure, Georgia was joined with three different ethno/religious/political entities created by the Soviets. Abkhazia was the largest of these regions. Abkhazians are not Georgian by descent, and Abkhazia has been a historically distinct region that was only captured by Russia in 1864. As Russian forces advanced, more than half of the Muslim Abkhazian population fled from their homeland into Ottoman Turkey. This opened up territory in the region for Georgians and Russians for expansion and settlement. Under Soviet restructuring, motivated by Lenin's commitment to national self-determination, Abkhazia was federated with Georgia. South of Abkhazia, another Muslim region, Adjaria, was incorporated with Georgia as an autonomous region. Adjaria, too, had old Ottoman-Muslim ties, and it remains heavily Muslim, though it was ceded to Russia in 1877. Despite their Muslim faith, Adjarians are actually Georgian by ethnicity. The final region to be granted autonomy within the greater Georgian political entity was South Ossetia. Of Persian descent themselves, the Ossetian people intermarried with Georgians, Chechens, Russians, and Circassians. The Ossetians not only intermarried but settled on both sides of the Caucasus Mountains. This is why there is a North Ossetia on the Russian side of the Caucasus Mountains today. Ossetians in Georgia were granted an autonomous district within Georgia, while North Ossetia was made an autonomous republic.[6]

Ten years after Georgia was brought into the Soviet Union, Abkhazia was made an autonomous republic in Georgia, with similar status to that of Adjaria. Political integration with Georgia, in addition to loss of territory to Georgian settlers, created concern among the Abkhazian people left in the area. In 1978, Abkhazians requested independence from Georgia in order to join Russia. Moscow, however, as in the case of the Armenians in Nagorno-Karabakh, would allow no greater autonomy. As a result, by 1991, ethnic Abkhazians accounted for only 17 percent of the population then inhabiting Abkhazian territory.[7]

Therefore, in the case of Georgia, the USSR once again encouraged nationalist identities without recognizing those identities with the complete independence that they desired. This is a major reason Georgia would face separatist conflicts upon its independence. Even before the Soviet Union's collapse, nationalist tensions had grown volatile.[8] By 1989, tensions were on the rise, and Moscow responded with military force. Soviet paratroopers were used to put down demonstrations in Georgia's capital city of Tbilisi.[9] A political dissident who had been imprisoned by Moscow, Zviad Gamsakhurdia (see Appendix C for biography) became the leader of the Georgian nationalist movement. In the parliamentary elections of 1990, his Roundtable/Free Georgia coalition won 155 of 250 seats.[10] As Georgian nationalists consolidated their political control, the South Ossetians once again attempted to assert their independence. They declared themselves separate from Georgia and sought unification with their kinsmen in North Ossetia and the greater Russian Federation.[11]

INDEPENDENCE AND DEVELOPING SECURITY OF THE STATE

On April 9,1991, the parliament of Georgia officially declared independence. A month later, Gamsakhurdia was elected to the presidency with 86 percent of the total vote. His election slogan, "Georgia for Georgians," only excited the fears of Abkhazians and Ossetians.[12] Early in 1991, the Abkhazians, like the Ossetians, also expressed their preference to remain a part of the Russian Federation rather than lose their autonomy to Georgian nationalists.[13] Adjarians, too, refused to surrender their political autonomy. Though the Adjarians, Georgian by descent, did not try to remain federated with Russia, the Adjarian president, Aslan Abashidze, refused to pay any taxes to Georgia or to allow Adjarians to be recruited for the Georgian national army.[14]

Separatist Conflict: Abkhazia, Adjaria, and South Ossetia

Once in office, Gamsakhurdia aimed to consolidate the Republic of Georgia. While he allowed Adjaria to maintain some autonomy, he directed his focus toward thwarting South Ossetian independence. He officially ended South Ossetia's political autonomy and employed force to halt the Ossetian independence movement. The first round of fighting between Ossetians and Georgians was in full swing by October of 1991. Georgia appeared to have the advantage in such fighting, but Gamsakhurdia's strident nationalism also alienated Russia. Since he viewed the CIS as an attempt by Russia to continue to exert control over Georgia, he refused to join the CIS. He also openly expressed his disgust with Gorbachev and Gorbachev's foreign minister, Eduard Shevardnadze (see Appendix C for biography), who was a native Georgian. Because of Gamsakhurdia's enmity with Gorbachev, a reformer that the West viewed with admiration, many Western leaders were inclined to take a dim view of Gamsakhurdia. As Georgia began to descend into political chaos, Gamsakhurdia was surrounded by many political enemies and no external supporters. It was in this period when a Georgian opposition movement, led by several warlords, forced him out of office.[15]

However, when Gamsakhurdia fled Tbilisi in January of 1992, he refused to surrender his vision for Georgia. After fleeing first to Azerbaijan, then to Armenia, and finally to Chechnya, he organized a rebellion against the new Georgian president, Eduard Shevardnadze. After the coup that had overthrown Gamsakhurdia, Shevardnadze returned to Georgia and sought political leadership. He was elected president on October 11, 1992. His election, however, was hardly a unifying event. It was boycotted by the Abkhazians and Ossetians, as well as Gamsakhurdia's nationalist supporters. Under the circumstances of Shevardnadze's return and election, rumors circulated that Moscow had manipulated events to effect the change in Georgian leadership.

Even if Shevardnadze may have had Russian favor, he still was in charge of a country that was falling apart. While he was attempting to consolidate power against Gamsakhurdia's nationalists, Abkhazia made its own move to gain independence. Shevardnadze was forced to turn his forces to counter this threat to Georgian territorial integrity. By August of 1992, pitched fighting had clearly broken out between Georgians and Abkhazians. Despite the internal divisions among the Georgians, Georgian forces gained the early advantage and pushed the Abkhazian fighters back to the cities of Gudauta and Tkvarcheli. Yet as the conflict wore on, the Abkhazians received support from other Caucasus peoples, including freedom fighters from Chechnya. Lack of discipline among the Georgian forces meant that after their initial victories, they began to fall apart. The Abkhazians, on the other hand, were reorganizing. While Moscow denied any involvement, there were also signs that the Russian military had unofficially begun to back the Abkhazians. Reports of fighter-bomber attacks on Georgian positions were made several times, even though the Abkhazians had no air force. When Georgia shot down a Russian MIG-29 with a fully uniformed Russian pilot, Moscow still continued to deny any involvement.[16]

With external aid, Abkhazian forces rallied, and they launched an offensive that surrounded the major city of Sukhumi. Though Shevardnadze himself led Georgian forces in the city, it fell to Abkhazian forces, and he barely escaped.

The Abkhazian offensive recaptured all Abkhaz territory, driving Georgian civilians out. Between the years of 1992 and 1993, 10,000 to 15,000 soldiers and civilians were killed and around 250,000 people were displaced. The crushing defeat at Sukhumi gave Gamsakhurdia another chance to bid for power, and this placed Shevardnadze in a dangerous position. It was only because of his ties to Moscow and accepting CIS membership for Georgia that Shevardnadze was able to maintain his position. In return for bringing Georgia back in line with Moscow, he received Russian tanks to give him an edge over Gamsakhurdia's forces. The Ossetians, Abkhazians, and Adjarians were free to run their own affairs while Shevardnadze continued to shore up his power base. The internal conflict came to an end finally when Gamsakhurdia mysteriously turned up dead—with a reported gunshot wound to the head in an act of suicide or assassination. In the meantime, Russian troops (or so-called "peacekeepers") were deployed in the disputed Abkhazian and South Ossetian borders to prevent further conflicts.[17]

Russian intervention essentially made the separation of Abkhazia and South Ossetia a permanent situation which led to de facto independence. Mediation efforts by organizations like the OSCE also failed to bring real resolution, so tensions continued to persist. In 1998, Georgian militias demonstrated the failure by stirring up violence again in Abkhazia, provoking an Abkhazian retaliation in which around 200 Georgian guerillas were killed and another 50,000 Georgians displaced.[18] Skirmishing also flared up in 2001. In the end, the continuation of these separatist conflicts and Shevardnadze's relative inability to resolve them undermined popular support for his presidency.[19]

He also appeared unable or unwilling to control the corruption and crime that had spread through Georgia in the years of political chaos. It should be remembered that he rose to power on the heels of a coup instigated by local warlords. Generally, Shevardnadze maintained what had become the status quo, refusing to reopen conflicts with the separatists, seeking to remain in line with Russia, and encouraging modest economic gains without running afoul of Georgia's powerful warlords and criminals. These factors led to dissatisfaction with Shevardnadze's rule among the poverty-ridden Georgian people.[20]

This dissatisfaction laid the foundation for the ousting of Shevardnadze and the subsequent election of the nationalist Mikheil Saakashvili in the Rose Revolution of 2003. Saakashvili's election signaled a reopening of these conflicts. In 2004, President Saakashvili demonstrated assertiveness that set him apart from Shevardnadze when he engaged in a "serious skirmish" with South Ossetian separatists as he cracked down on smuggling and the drug trade in Georgia. Using his momentum from both domestic and international approval, Saakashvili also succeeded in bringing Adjaria firmly into Georgia. President Abashidze initially opposed Saakashvili in an attempt to maintain power, but he was no match for Saakashvili along with international pressure, particularly when some such pressures were applied by Turkey. Ankara still possesses a special political influence among Adjarians because of their Ottoman history. Thus, Turkish support of Saakashvili facilitated the peaceful removal of Abashidze on May 6, 2004.[21] Further consolidation on Georgian territory was accomplished in 2006, when control of the Kodori Gorge in upper Abkhazia was restored after the ruling warlord in that region was defeated by Georgian forces. Saakashvili even demonstrated a willingness to reverse Georgian isolation of Abkhazia and South Ossetia and to encourage economic engagement in order to make the possibility of future federation with Georgian state a more palatable reality.[22]

One of the major roadblocks to any reunification, however, continued to be the position Moscow had taken between Georgia and the separatist regions. Saakashvili's regime began to pressure Russian forces to withdraw from Abkhazia and South Ossetia in 2005 and 2006. However, Abkhazia and South Ossetia made it clear that they still desired a Russian military presence, and Moscow appeared disinterested in complying with Tbilisi requests. In the 2006–2007 time period, despite the presence of Russian troops, there were several acts of violence along the Abkhazian-Georgian border, including several alleged rocket attacks by the Abkhazians. Thus, tension levels remained high on both sides under Saakashvili's leadership. Moreover, Georgian concerns mounted as it became more and more likely that Tbilisi may never reintegrate its separatist regions.

When the leaders of the separatist republics compared their situation to the Kosovars in Serbia, Putin joined them in warning that independence for Kosovo would be perceived as a legal precedent for the independence of Abkhazia and South Ossetia. This reinforced the perception that Moscow favored the permanent separation of these republics from Georgia. By 2008, Abkhazia and South Ossetia had been independent for nearly a decade and a half. Abkhazia reiterated its demands for UN, EU, and OSCE recognition of its independence, and the Kremlin took steps to establish new ties with Abkhazia. Moscow backed the withdrawal of old CIS sanctions that had been placed on Abkhazia during the early years of the conflict, while the Russian *Duma* encouraged Putin to recognize both Abkhazia and South Ossetia as independent states. New Russian troops were deployed to Abkhazia during 2008, including troops with orders to repair the railway connecting Russia to Abkhazia.[23]

This bolstering of Russian support for the separatists closely preceded Georgian action in South Ossetia in August of 2008. Russian troops, already in the separatist regions, provided cause for retaliation when fired upon by the Georgian military; and they constituted the initial forces to support the subsequent Russian invasion of Georgia. In that invasion, the recently repaired railway to Abkhazia facilitated the ability of the Russians to open a second front, invading not only from the north but also from the northwest.[24]

Status of Georgia's Military

Although Georgia has managed to avoid disputes with its South Caucasus neighbors, its separatist conflicts have been long and bloody. In addition to a desire to create a military that can effectively respond to separatism, Tbilisi has aimed to rapidly modernize its military in order to facilitate its efforts to gain NATO membership. After hitting a low point at 0.6 percent of GDP in 2000, Georgian military expenditures have increased more than 10 times in real terms.[25] In 2006, Georgia spent an astounding 5.2 percent of its GDP on military expenditures. That is a larger percentage of GDP than either Azerbaijan or Armenia spent on their militaries between 1998 and 2006 (around US$362 million).[26] Over the last several years, that amount has continued to increase. In 2007, Georgian defense expenditures in constant U.S. dollars (2005) rose to $720 million, and then declined slightly in 2008, to $651 million.[27]

After President Saakashvili took office in January of 2004, he turned toward the West for foreign aid and began to seek NATO membership in order to counter the Russian hold on Abkhazia and South Ossetia. As Georgia began its intensification process with NATO, this brought in additional military aid, particularly from the United States.[28] Immediately following 9/11, Washington provided more than $34 million in military aid (equal to 70 percent of Georgia's 2002 military budget), with $20 million of that money marked for use in the expulsion of Chechen fighters in the Pankisi Gorge.[29] In 2006 and 2007, the United States granted another $10 million in military assistance.[30]

The push to join NATO has been Georgia's primary justification for its rapidly increasing military expenditures, but a stronger military simultaneously strengthened Georgia's position versus Abkhazia and South Ossetia. These two issues are closely related. However, Saakashvili seemingly realized that bringing either separatist region back under Georgian control would be difficult, if not impossible. The decrease in expenditures from 2007 to 2008 was actually cited as a step to demonstrate Georgia's commitment to a peaceful reunification similar to what occurred in Adjaria. Nevertheless, the 2008 Russia-Georgia War has upset this course of action and darkened the future of the Georgian military.[31]

According to a CNN report during the war, Georgia had a total troop strength of 26,900, of which 17,000 were in the army, while Russian total troop strength was reported to be 641,000 with 320,000 in the army. The Georgian military is primarily armed with Soviet-era weapons, which at the time of the engagement, included roughly 80 T-72 tanks, 150 armored vehicles, a similar number of artillery pieces, 7 SU-25 ground attack fighters, 7 attack helicopters, and 150 surface-to-air missiles.[32] After the war, reports indicated that Georgia had 170 dead and 400 injured in addition to the loss of 70 tanks and armored vehicles, 10 artillery systems, 4 BUK-1M air defense systems, 2 fighters, 3 boats, 4,000 automatic weapons, and large amounts of ammunition.[33]

According to a U.S. military assessment that was leaked to *The New York Times*, the Georgian forces are "highly centralized, prone to impulsive rather than deliberative decision making, undermined by unclear lines of command and led by senior officials who were selected for personal relationships rather than professional qualifications."[34] Little has yet been done about this, though President Saakashvili replaced the defense minister after the conflict. Rebuilding Georgia's military will certainly take significant time and money. Equipment losses totaled around US$400 million, and the fighting has severely damaged the morale of Georgian soldiers. At the same time, the Georgian Defense Ministry's budget for 2009 has fallen from even the 2008 level, to around US$540 million, which is not enough to maintain the existing military forces, replace lost equipment, and train replacements for those killed in action.[35]

Separatism and Dependency in the Georgian Economy

As the USSR collapsed and separatist conflicts took their toll, the Georgian economy suffered a devastating collapse in the early 1990s. At that time the Georgian economy was primarily sustained by Black Sea tourism, various agricultural products, and mining.[36] All of these sectors suffered after the Soviet collapse, but tourism in particular was decimated because of the fighting in Georgia. Abkhazia's separation also meant the loss of significant coastal areas that had supported tourism. From 1992 to 1993, Georgia's GDP shrank by a shocking 80 percent.[37] It was not until Shevardnadze had consolidated power as president and had restored a sense of political stability that the Georgian economy could begin to slowly recover. But this recovery was inhibited by government corruption and the black market, both of which had gained deep roots in the lawlessness that had endured during the chaotic early years of independence.

From 1994 until his ousting in 1998, Shevardnadze did take serious steps to reform and revitalize the economy, following the liberal policies of the "Washington Consensus" that the West and international institutions like the IMF had prescribed. By 1997, the results of his reforms were beginning to really become visible, producing a 10–11 percent growth rate. Under his presidency, one of the major steps in international trade was the construction of the Baku-Sups oil pipeline with Azerbaijan. That pipeline played a significant role in spurring economic growth. But Georgian economic growth under Shevardnadze stagnated between 1998 and 2003, undermining his successes. International currencies crises in neighboring Russia in 1998 and Turkey in 2000 contributed to this economic slowdown. By 2003, 13 years after Georgian independence, its economy could still only boast 73 percent of its economic growth from 1990.[38]

The apparent failure of Shevardnadze to maintain economic growth was one of the factors leading to his ousting, along with public dissatisfaction due to corruption. When the Rose Revolution came in 2003, however, it caused surprisingly little economic dislocation. Economic growth in that year approached 8.6 percent, and the newest oil pipeline project (i.e., the BTC pipeline) that Shevardnadze had begun continued without interruption.[39] Thus, despite public dissatisfaction with Shevardnadze's leadership, it appears that he did lay a strong foundation for economic growth, but it was President Saakashvili who would politically benefit from the 2003 upswing in the economy.

Saakashvili's regime continued its compliance with the advice of the West and international organizations, moving rapidly to implement further economic reforms, and more actively pursuing future economic integration with the EU. Under Saakashvili, a new wave of privatization attempts began, but one of the interesting consequences of the opening Georgian economy was the amount of Russian investment that came in. Russian companies began buying up significant amounts of Georgian assets in the summer of 2003.[40] Gazprom also opened negotiations with Georgia for ownership of the gas pipeline to Armenia. Russian investment, particularly in the energy sector, promised to bring cash. Yet, as in the case of Armenia, Russian investment also threatened to give Russian companies, which are under the influence of the Moscow government, significant political leverage over Tbilisi. The political consequences of Gazprom's ownership of the pipeline to Armenia were so significant that Washington's intervention convinced Tbilisi to leave those talks.[41] The ability of the Kremlin to manipulate energy markets for political gain was exhibited later in 2006, when Gazprom announced increases in energy prices to Georgia on the verge of winter. As an alternative to high gas prices in the colder months, Gazprom offered to lower prices in return for a greater stake in Georgia's energy assets. These are exactly the sort of tactics used in Armenia, but in Georgia they excited accusations of Russian economic blackmail.[42]

Like Yerevan, Tbilisi cannot supply its own domestic energy consumption. Nearly all of Georgia's 14 tb/d oil consumption in 2007 and its 52 bcf of gas consumption in 2006 were imported. Approximately 60 percent of total gas imports are supplied by Russia, while Georgia is able to obtain the other 40 percent from Azerbaijan.[43] Friendly ties with Baku, then, clearly offer Tbilisi a chance to be less dependent on Russian energy than Armenia is. Still, even though Georgia has resisted Russian monopolization of its energy sector at the prompting of Washington, 60 percent of gas imports are a significant source of political leverage for Moscow. Other sectors of Georgian economy are also highly vulnerable to external influence from the Kremlin. Tourism along the Black Sea coast has historically been dominated by Russian tourists, a flow of revenue that Moscow can manage because it can control the flow of travel to Georgia. Russia has also imposed trade sanctions on Georgian wine, damaging the agricultural sector, and banned Georgian guest workers in Russia. This last step has strangled the flow of remittances from Georgians who could not find work at home.[44]

In order for Georgia to decrease its economic dependency on Russia, it needs to increase trade through primarily pipelines, roads, and railways to the east and west. Indeed, it has already begun to encourage this sort of infrastructure, as Georgia's geopolitical position is ideal for an East-West energy corridor. Azerbaijan, Turkey, the EU, and the United States all support this orientation as it benefits them economically and politically. The BTC and BTE pipelines passing through Georgia have opened the Caspian basin's energy to the West, preventing complete Russian monopolization of such resources. Furthermore, if plans for a trans-Caspian pipeline ever come to fruition, then Central Asian energy could also be accessed by the West without the Russian middleman. If Georgia can maximize trade to its east and west while retaining its role as a hub for north-south trade between Russia and Armenia, it can realize great economic opportunity for diversification. In particular, if Georgia can successfully connect to the Iran-Armenia gas pipeline, it might be able to further reduce its dependency on Russian gas. However, the 2008 Russia-Georgia War may supply Moscow with further motivation to stand in the way of such attempts.

Status of Georgia's Economy

Under Saakashvili's leadership, the Georgian economy has continued to improve from its former shambles. In 2007, the annual percentage change in its Real GDP was close to Armenia's at 12.4. The global economic recession, however, hit the Georgian economy even harder. Its percentage change dropped to 2.0. Throughout 2009, Georgia's GDP was projected to decline. The IMF, however, projects that Georgia's GDP is likely not to slow as much as Armenia's will before moving toward a slow recovery. Still, Georgia's Current Account Balance is not projected to improve.[45]

The economic decline, coupled with fallout from the war, threatens to produce internal instability and security challenges in Georgia. Since the war, there have been several large anti-Saakashvili protests. One of the more recent major protests, held on April 2, 2009, was attended by thousands of Georgians demanding Saakashvili's resignation.[46] The decline in the Georgian economy does threaten its external security, because it has fewer funds to spend on its recently damaged military machine. In order to compensate for such disadvantages, however, Tbilisi does not have a great power on which it can always rely. Despite their expressions of sympathy and past foreign aid, Europe and the United States clearly have limits in their own commitment to Georgia (Tables 4.1–4.4, Graphs 4.1–4.4).

This brings the necessity of an analysis of Georgian trade patterns with the global and regional powers. As explained in previous chapters, the IMF trade data was collected, tabulated, and graphed to observe special economic trends in the past decade. The result can be summarized in the following sections.

In terms of exports, the volume of Georgian exports grew relatively rapidly. A distinct upward trend occurred in 2002, with steadily increasing growth and a very dramatic upswing from 2006 to 2008. This means that the economy was

Table 4.1 Georgian Export Volume

	1998	1999	2000	2001	2002	2003	2004	2005	2006	2007	2008
US	13.909	16.273	7.138	9.053	13.978	15.358	21.230	26.749	58.863	171.995	221.636
EU	69.123	109.729	76.390	61.890	65.529	81.638	111.367	165.216	188.490	415.449	611.372
Japan	0.598	1.338	0.381	1.039	0.691	0.223	0.626	1.441	0.518	0.499	3.170
China (m)	1.461	1.361	0.908	1.045	1.176	1.172	3.307	5.599	10.351	13.220	10.429
Russia	57.558	45.292	68.607	74.399	60.960	83.941	104.533	153.925	75.657	53.550	52.896
CIS (8)	30.437	45.179	27.308	47.835	58.112	97.318	143.371	130.652	153.288	184.619	216.224
Iran	0.000	0.000	6.801	4.311	3.317	3.426	4.501	4.681	2.699	4.020	5.079
Turkey	82.727	84.808	74.497	68.568	53.738	82.549	118.607	121.809	124.919	199.535	476.768
Azerbaijan	22.909	8.623	20.080	9.976	29.248	16.625	25.327	83.448	92.167	92.220	105.284
Armenia	24.391	24.414	13.633	12.508	20.994	30.762	54.455	39.928	73.621	72.866	60.962
Georgia Subtotal	303.113	337.017	295.743	290.624	307.743	413.012	587.324	733.448	780.573	1207.973	1763.820
World Subtotal	330.798	361.041	325.994	317.347	349.405	465.266	644.824	850.993	980.897	1498.080	2497.870

(m) = mainland; CIS (8) = Belarus, Kazakhstan, Kyrgyzstan, Moldova, Tajikistan, Turkmenistan, Ukraine, Uzbekistan.
Source: IMF's Direction of Trade Statistics.

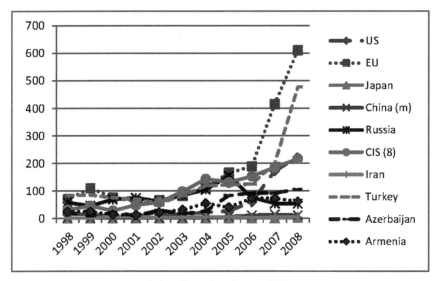

Graph 4.1 Georgian Export Volume

already improving slightly before Shervardnadze was ousted. In volume, the EU and Turkey are Georgia's top two partners (similar to imports). The CIS is next (similar to imports) but has been almost tied with the United States over the past two years. This is a remarkable rise in importance for Washington as an export partner. Russia, historically important, has been declining as an export partner, which would fit with the economic embargoes that Moscow has been

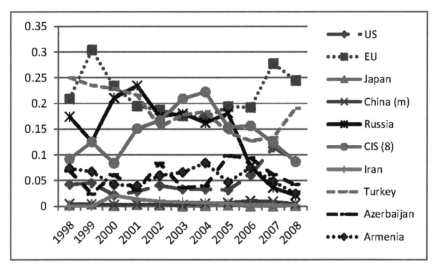

Graph 4.2 Georgian Export Percentage

Table 4.2 Georgian Export Percentage

	1998	1999	2000	2001	2002	2003	2004	2005	2006	2007	2008
US	4.20%	4.51%	2.19%	2.85%	4.00%	3.30%	3.29%	3.14%	6.00%	11.48%	8.87%
EU	20.90%	30.39%	23.43%	19.50%	18.75%	17.55%	17.27%	19.41%	19.22%	27.73%	24.48%
Japan	0.18%	0.37%	0.12%	0.33%	0.20%	0.05%	0.10%	0.17%	0.05%	0.03%	0.13%
China (m)	0.44%	0.38%	0.28%	0.33%	0.34%	0.25%	0.51%	0.66%	1.06%	0.88%	0.42%
Russia	17.40%	12.54%	21.05%	23.44%	17.45%	18.04%	16.21%	18.09%	7.71%	3.57%	2.12%
CIS (8)	9.20%	12.51%	8.38%	15.07%	16.63%	20.92%	22.23%	15.35%	15.63%	12.32%	8.66%
Iran	0.00%	0.00%	2.09%	1.36%	0.95%	0.74%	0.70%	0.55%	0.28%	0.27%	0.20%
Turkey	25.01%	23.49%	22.85%	21.61%	15.38%	17.74%	18.39%	14.31%	12.74%	13.32%	19.09%
Azerbaijan	6.93%	2.39%	6.16%	3.14%	8.37%	3.57%	3.93%	9.81%	9.40%	6.16%	4.21%
Armenia	7.37%	6.76%	4.18%	3.94%	6.01%	6.61%	8.44%	4.69%	7.51%	4.86%	2.44%
Georgia Subtotal	91.63%	93.35%	90.72%	91.58%	88.08%	88.77%	91.08%	86.19%	79.58%	80.63%	70.61%

(m) = mainland; CIS (8) = Belarus, Kazakhstan, Kyrgyzstan, Moldova, Tajikistan, Turkmenistan, Ukraine, Uzbekistan.
Source: IMF's Direction of Trade Statistics.

Table 4.3 Georgian Import Volume

	1998	1999	2000	2001	2002	2003	2004	2005	2006	2007	2008
US	150.150	73.040	69.595	63.993	68.043	90.770	110.914	148.313	129.761	267.037	645.150
EU	374.289	229.319	188.435	240.854	231.320	430.777	617.571	671.498	947.898	1260.940	1489.720
Japan	3.604	7.579	7.320	3.177	3.952	2.488	5.933	8.337	39.542	97.626	251.098
China (m)	6.739	2.455	2.910	3.832	8.717	23.168	28.904	46.713	103.332	203.871	314.703
Russia	112.851	63.514	98.792	93.469	121.620	161.095	257.771	384.350	558.766	655.031	758.449
CIS (8)	57.322	92.225	66.536	77.326	80.097	103.240	215.144	336.649	480.547	671.588	768.293
Iran	0.000	0.000	5.880	6.315	8.097	6.996	15.158	26.000	40.301	48.958	64.353
Turkey	180.510	125.621	111.466	107.144	89.677	112.136	202.089	283.006	522.560	746.083	1096.210
Azerbaijan	84.607	78.896	56.690	73.185	79.894	93.791	156.398	233.420	318.525	355.790	406.194
Armenia	10.531	12.210	15.812	10.286	8.565	11.199	26.229	39.294	40.246	82.057	99.805
Georgia Subtotal	980.602	684.859	623.436	679.581	699.982	1035.660	1636.111	2177.580	3181.478	4388.981	5893.975
World Subtotal	1230.780	859.414	727.745	755.917	794.097	1143.520	1848.040	2490.760	3677.610	5291.910	7218.630

(m) = mainland; CIS (8) = Belarus, Kazakhstan, Kyrgyzstan, Moldova, Tajikistan, Turkmenistan, Ukraine, Uzbekistan.
Source: IMF's Direction of Trade Statistics.

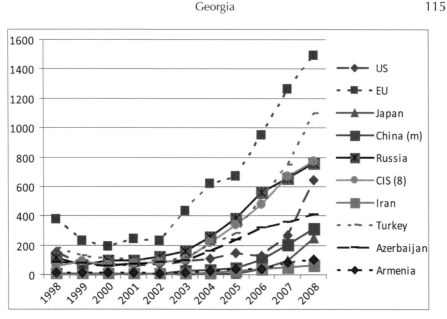

Graph 4.3 Georgian Import Volume

imposing on Tbilisi. Trade with China and Iran is generally not at a significant level during this period. Exports with Azerbaijan and Armenia are relatively stable, with Baku at a higher level.

Using the percentages of exports illustrates the relative importance of Georgia's export partners (in relationship to one another) for their share of Georgia's total world export. Here, one of the most interesting trends is that Russia's share is dropping dramatically since 2005. Moreover, the share of the CIS has also been

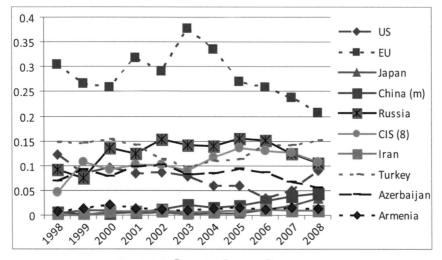

Graph 4.4 Georgian Import Percentage

Table 4.4 Georgian Import Percentage

	1998	1999	2000	2001	2002	2003	2004	2005	2006	2007	2008
US	12.20%	8.50%	9.56%	8.47%	8.57%	7.94%	6.00%	5.95%	3.53%	5.05%	8.94%
EU	30.41%	26.68%	25.89%	31.86%	29.13%	37.67%	33.42%	26.96%	25.77%	23.83%	20.64%
Japan	0.29%	0.88%	1.01%	0.42%	0.50%	0.22%	0.32%	0.33%	1.08%	1.84%	3.48%
China (m)	0.55%	0.29%	0.40%	0.51%	1.10%	2.03%	1.56%	1.88%	2.81%	3.85%	4.36%
Russia	9.17%	7.39%	13.58%	12.36%	15.32%	14.09%	13.95%	15.43%	15.19%	12.38%	10.51%
CIS (8)	4.66%	10.73%	9.14%	10.23%	10.09%	9.03%	11.64%	13.52%	13.07%	12.69%	10.64%
Iran	0.00%	0.00%	0.81%	0.84%	1.02%	0.61%	0.82%	1.04%	1.10%	0.93%	0.89%
Turkey	14.67%	14.62%	15.32%	14.17%	11.29%	9.81%	10.94%	11.36%	14.21%	14.10%	15.19%
Azerbaijan	6.87%	9.18%	7.79%	9.68%	10.06%	8.20%	8.46%	9.37%	8.66%	6.72%	5.63%
Armenia	0.86%	1.42%	2.17%	1.36%	1.08%	0.98%	1.42%	1.58%	1.09%	1.55%	1.38%
Georgia Subtotal	**79.67%**	**79.69%**	**85.67%**	**89.90%**	**88.15%**	**90.57%**	**88.53%**	**87.43%**	**86.51%**	**82.94%**	**81.65%**

(m) = mainland; CIS (8) = Belarus, Kazakhstan, Kyrgyzstan, Moldova, Tajikistan, Turkmenistan, Ukraine, Uzbekistan.
Source: IMF's Direction of Trade Statistics.

dropping since 2006. Intriguing is that the relative roles of almost all listed trade partners have been declining. In fact, only exports to Turkey relatively rose from 2007 to 2008. By the end of the decade, in the balance between Washington and Moscow, the Georgians' exports to the United States are relatively higher than to (geographically next-door) Russia.

In regard to imports, the volume of Georgian imports has been drastically on the rise. As was the case for exports, the EU and Turkey are Georgia's leading partners. Russia and the CIS are next, nearly tied in the volume of their imports. The volume of Russian imports has not fallen off as their exports have. Thus, Moscow is still supplying Tbilisi, even if it is refusing to buy from this republic. Only with Iran and Armenia have the trends in volume growth been relatively lethargic. In 2002, imports began to rise across the board. Thus, export growth was matched by import increase. By 2008, Washington had almost reached the import levels from Moscow and the CIS.

Finally, the relative importances of Georgia's import partners are demonstrated by the import percentages graph. This graph shows that Georgia's share of imports has been increasing from China, Japan, and Turkey. While the share of imports from the United States was in decline until 2006, it began to rise after that time. Moreover, the imports from the EU have been relatively declining, while no one else has made up the difference.

Georgia's Rose Revolution

Beyond the separatist movements of the 1990s, the single most significant sociopolitical shift in Georgian domestic politics was the democratic "Rose Revolution" that occurred in 2003. Shevardnadze's popularity had been on the decline over the course of his 11-year presidency, dragged down through the perceived failures in resolving the separatist challenge, restoring economic growth, and eliminating corruption and crime, and for his deference to Moscow. An old Soviet-style politician, Shevardnadze consolidated his rule over the years until most of the power of the Georgian state was held by a small group of elites close to him.[47] Such issues undermined Shevardnadze's political legitimacy among the Georgian public. The legitimacy of his presidency began to fracture further when, in an attempt to curb public criticism, Shevardnadze began to intimidate the relatively free Georgian media along with other dissenters. In the face of his growing authoritarianism, political opposition parties began to gain strength.[48]

The strength of opposition parties grew to such an extent that, when parliamentary elections came around in 2003, it appeared that Shevardnadze's political party stood to lose a number of seats. Electoral fraud was not uncommon in elections up until this point, but in 2003, Shevardnadze's party made a blatant attempt to rig the election in their favor in order to retain power.[49] The national reaction was outrage. Yet as tens of thousands of Georgians organized to demonstrate, the rallies occurred peacefully, urged on by the Georgian media. Moreover, the opposition forces were reportedly supported, financed, and advised by some of the Western states.[50] For instance, George Soros and the Open Society Georgia Foundation played a significant role.[51] When Shevardnadze called out the army to control or suppress the demonstrations, the protestors disarmed the tension by presenting the soldiers with roses, meeting the threat of force with a gesture of shared patriotism. During these demonstrations many soldiers laid down their arms.[52] Instead of becoming dispersed, the movement continued to swell until November 22. On that day, when Shevardnadze attempted to bring his illegitimate parliament into session, demonstrators stormed the parliamentary building and forced Shevardnadze to flee. He resigned the next day.[53]

Saakashvili was the opposition leader who led the demonstrators into Parliament on November 22. Riding the popular movement, he was elected president in January of 2004.[54] The results of that democratic election were praised in the West (particularly the United States) as a victory for the spread of democracy and self-determination. This provided the foundation for a new era in Tbilisi's relationship with Washington, Western European capitals, and Western international institutions like NATO.

This revolution marked the beginning of similar democratic movements across the former Soviet Republics. Ukraine had its "Orange Revolution" in 2004; and Kyrgyzstan experienced the "Tulip Revolution" in 2005. Though Moscow may not have immediately perceived the democratic revolution in Georgia as a negative occurrence, the subsequent revolutions have deepened Russian concerns due to their political ramifications. In at least Georgia and Ukraine, these movements resulted in the election of nationalist, pro-Western leaders who have attempted to buck Russian dominance. The spread of these democratic revolutions may also be linked to the Kremlin leaders' fear of the continuing encroachment of Western institutions (i.e., NATO and the EU) into Russian "Near Abroad" and their historical "sphere of influence."

Contemporary Government and Politics in Georgia

Government Structure

According to its constitution, the Republic of Georgia is established as a secular, republican form of government that derives its power from its citizens. Similar to the other republics, the national government has three branches: the Executive Branch headed by the President, the Judicial Branch along with the courts, and the Legislative Branch which consists of a single-chamber parliament led by a Prime Minister. Based on the constitution, parliamentary representatives and the president are to be regularly elected in free, open, and democratic elections. (See Appendix G for Georgia's constitution.)

Political Conditions

The freedom and fairness of elections in Georgia have long been in question. The Rose Revolution appeared to offer the possibility of new, free elections, as the Georgian people exercised their collective voice to force President Shevardnadze from office. Nevertheless, the presidency of Saakashvili is now viewed in many corners as the same sort of hyper-presidentialism, or even authoritarianism, that the other South Caucasus states appear to face.[55]

In late 2007, political opposition to Saakashvili began to harden. There were several large protests against Saakashvili's leadership before the end of that year as opposition groups called for early elections. The government responded with a violent police crackdown and declared a state of emergency. Under that state of emergency, street protests were restricted and opposition media was restricted. Saakashvili responded to demands for early elections by declaring January 5, 2008 for the presidential election and resigning from the presidency in order to run again. The rapidity of his moves made it difficult for the opposition to organize for the elections. He won the election with 53 percent of the vote but amid reports of voting irregularities and accusations of vote-rigging from the opposition. Levan Gachechiladze, the presidential candidate of the National Council opposition bloc, placed second with 27 percent and claimed that fraud pushed Saakashvili over the 50 percent threshold, thus preventing a runoff.[56]

These days, in the wake of the disastrous war with Georgia, Saakashvili's political position has become increasingly precarious. Opposition groups are growing in number as former allies of Saakashvili have begun to abandon him.[57] With the election of President Barack Obama, it remains to be seen if Washington will continue to be as ardent a friend to Saakashvili as his domestic support erodes.

Important Political Players

Saakashvili's political party is the United National Movement (ENM). Former defense minister Irakli Okruashvili and his Movement for United Georgia were one of the major opposition leaders of the 2007 protests. He was arrested for corruption, released when he recanted accusations that Saakashvili had political enemies murdered, and was granted political asylum in France.[58] After the 2008 war, Saakashvili's political position was further degraded, when the former speaker of the Georgian Parliament, Nino Burjanadze, announced that she was leaving Saakashvili's party. Later, she founded the Democratic Movement–United Georgia. Another opposition leader, Irakli Alasania, former envoy to the United Nations, has formed Alliance for Georgia. The most radical of these opposition leaders is Levan Gachechiladze, head of United Opposition.[59]

Political Freedom, Civil Liberties, and Human Rights

Due to the irregularities that have been reported in presidential and parliamentary elections, reports of intimidation, and apparent abuses of state resources by the National Movement, Freedom House has marked Georgia as a "Partly Free" state. The state of Georgia's Political Rights and Civil Liberties were both given a rating of 4. Their rating is based on scale which ranges from 1 to 7, with 1 as the best score. The restriction of opposition media and the aggressive police response to some opposition protests have been the main reason to question the state of freedom and rights in Georgia. Moreover, there are instances of gerrymandering in electoral districts and other electoral irregularities.[60]

Freedom of religion is not an issue for the predominant Georgian Orthodox Church and traditional minorities like Jews and Muslims. However, harassment and discrimination by the Orthodox churches and law enforcement officials have been reported against newer groups, like Baptists, Pentecostals, and Jehovah's Witnesses. The rights of ethnic minorities in non-separatist areas of Georgia appear to be respected, and there are few complaints of discrimination.[61]

As with the other South Caucasus states, transparency has been an issue. As Georgia has attempted to grow closer to both the EU and NATO under Saakashvili's leadership, reforms have begun in order to combat graft and corruption in the government. Nevertheless, judicial reforms have been slow; and the judicial branch is mired in charges of corruption as well. The police forces have had a major cleansing process to remove corrupt officials. Today, Georgia has the highest transparency rating of the South Caucasus states. However, it still ranks only 67 out of the 180 in the world according to Transparency International's 2008 *Corruption Perceptions Index*.[62]

FOREIGN POLICY AND RELATIONS

United States and NATO

Diplomatic ties between the United States and Georgia opened soon after independence in 1992. Since then, Washington has become, according to the Georgian Ministry of Foreign Affairs, "one of the main international guarantors of Georgia's sovereignty and territorial integrity."[63] This is because the United States has consistently and regularly backed Tbilisi in its desire to resolve the separatist disputes without any loss of territory. Furthermore, Washington has strengthened Georgia's position by providing military training, economic aid, and diplomatic support in the international community.

Energy, security, and democracy constitute three major U.S. priorities in its relationship with Georgia. As should be clear by now, Georgia is vital to the establishment of East-West energy routes to the Caspian Sea basin. The BTC and BTE pipelines have accomplished this goal, and they must be maintained in order to prevent a greater Russian monopoly on regional energy. The energy politics of the region, however, took a backseat following the tragic events of 9/11. Afterward, Georgia became more important in U.S. security calculations. Together, Georgia and Azerbaijan have granted over flight permission to the United States that has created an air corridor that NATO aircraft may use to reach Afghanistan. As a result, now "practically all flights between NATO territory and Afghanistan cross Georgian and Azeri airspace."[64]

Since the 9/11, Georgia and the United States have also joined in cooperation on two major programs designed to improve Georgian defense forces. These programs are the Georgia Train and Equip Program (GTEP) and the Sustainment and Stability Operations Program (SSOP). Begun in 2002, GTEP has invested 64 million dollars into Georgia's military, primarily to increase its ability to carry out counterterrorism operations. Also in 2002, the United States deployed 200 special force troops to train Georgian soldiers.[65] This sort of military cooperation has boosted Georgia's strength versus Ossetia and Abkhazia and provided it with an opportunity to even strengthen its position in the face of Russia. Georgia demonstrated its eagerness for this new security relationship in the post-9/11 world by participating in the American-led coalition in Iraq, deploying the third largest contingent of foreign troops, after the United States and the United Kingdom.[66]

The Rose Revolution resulted in the further deepening of American-Georgian ties. After Saakashvili's election in 2003, security cooperation was followed with new levels of economic aid. For instance, in 2005, the United States initiated what is called the Millennium Program. This program has encouraged international investment in Georgia and committed $295 million to the development of Georgian infrastructure and its private sector.[67] U.S. political support for Georgia's integration into western institutions also increased at that time; and the United States began to push more fervently for Georgian membership within NATO.[68]

When Saakashvili was elected, Georgia was already a participant in NATO's PfP program (it had been since 1994).[69] Though all three states in the region have engaged in some level of membership through the PfP program, Georgia has certainly been the most active in its attempts to grow closer to NATO.[70] In October of 2004, NATO approved Georgia's first IPAP. Georgia's progress since then eventually led to its invitation into Intensification Dialogue in 2006.[71] This demonstrated rapid compliance with the process to NATO membership, and in April of 2007, the United States endorsed the NATO Freedom Consolidation Act, which proposed the admission of Albania, Croatia, Georgia, and Macedonia as new NATO members.[72]

Once Georgia reached the point where NATO membership was a real possibility, however, the issue of separatism emerged as the major roadblock. These unresolved conflicts present potential points of crisis in the future, but more importantly these disputed areas involve Russian troops. Thus, if Georgia were granted

NATO membership, it would be able to request NATO military intervention in the event of a war with Russia. However, war with Russia is not a prospect that NATO members want to risk. As a result, Georgia's membership process came to a halt in 2007, as NATO turned its attention to possible resolutions of the separatist conflicts.[73]

The persistence of these conflicts over the years, however, left little hope that Georgia would receive membership anytime soon. The NATO summit held in Bucharest emphasized this reality, not long after Kosovo's independence was recognized in early 2008. Well aware of Russian opposition to NATO's continued eastward expansion, Germany and other European states opposed any further integration of Georgia and Ukraine. Therefore, the debate over the granting of Membership Action Plans (MAPs) for Georgia and Ukraine has been suspended. In place of these MAPs, NATO leaders offered only the comment that Georgia would undoubtedly receive NATO membership sometime in the future.[74] This gave Russia time to increase the roadblocks to Georgian membership in NATO, and the motivation to act before that nebulous future time for Georgian membership materialized.

EU and OSCE

Similar to the United States, the EU and its member states share a tri-fold interest in Georgia based on energy, security, and democracy. Unlike the United States, however, the EU imports Caspian energy to meet its actual domestic consumption, giving it an even greater interest in the region's energy politics. Even before the USSR had fallen, Western Europe had developed a heavy reliance on Russian energy exports. Because of this, the BTC and BTE pipelines through Georgia are of strategic value for European energy security, supplying non-Russian imports necessary for energy import diversification. In fact, diversification of energy imports is a strategic objective for the EU, and in pursuit of this objective, the EU has proposed plans to extend the BTC and BTE pipelines with a trans-Caspian line that would open access to Central Asian oil and gas.[75]

The EU and Georgia, like the other Caucasus states, established an effective PCA in 1999. That year, Georgia was also admitted to the EC and the World Trade Organization (WTO). In 2001, the EU Cooperation Coordination Council was created to provide further guidance for Georgia-EU relations. Georgia's EU integration process, like its NATO integration, accelerated after Saakashvili's election. In 2004, Tbilisi gained a place in the EU's ENP program. Also in that year, the EU initiated a Rule of Law Mission in Georgia (EUJUST THEMIS), which brought about a new phase of cooperation within the European Security and Defense Policy (ESDP) structure.[76]

After Georgia became an ENP member, the EU became more involved in the conflicts with Abkhazia and South Ossetia. On February 21, 2006, the EU expressed support for the territorial integrity of Georgia and backed Georgian attempts to make progress on a peaceful settlement with South Ossetia. In 2007, the EU initiated a fact-finding mission which was directed to determine the possibility of implementing the EU-Georgia ENP Action Plan within both Abkhazia and South Ossetia. This was an attempt to increase border control, cement mutual ties, and increase the incentives for a peaceful settlement.[77]

Outside of NATO's role in security, the OSCE has been one of the other most important security organizations to which Georgia belongs. The OSCE has also been central to European-Georgian relations since independence. In 1992, the OSCE created a specific Mission to Georgia, which has remained focused on a resolution to the separatist conflicts with Abkhazia and South Ossetia. Since 1993, the OSCE has also had a role in monitoring the Georgia-Abkhaz border through the UN-led peace process. The OSCE Mission to Georgia also monitors Joint Peace Keeping Forces (JPKF) deployed in the Georgia-Ossetian conflict zone.[78]

Despite its long record of active involvement, however, the OSCE appears to have little ability to influence Moscow's role in preserving those frozen conflicts. One political analyst has flatly stated that the OSCE "can either function as a 'community' in consensus with Russia and remain irrelevant, or give up on the consensus with Russia and risk ceasing to function at all."[79] The unwillingness or inability of the EU and the OSCE to act at great odds to Russia has been repeatedly demonstrated. This was evident by European objections to Georgia's NATO membership; and the OSCE's inability to prevent the crisis in South Ossetia from descending into a war between Russia and Georgia.

Russia, CIS, and CSTO

Under its first president, the nationalistic Gamsakhurdia, Georgia quickly moved away from Moscow after leaving the USSR. Georgian nationalism tinged with anti-Russian feelings has provided a tension in Russian-Georgian relations that probably only met its lowest ebb under President Shevardnadze. Georgia's repeated efforts to buck membership in the CIS and its attempts to gain ever greater integration into Western institutions have produced negative reactions in the Kremlin. There are several important strategic reasons why this behavior irritates the Russians, beside any feelings that they may possess for their special role in the former Republics.

Georgia is a part of a security buffer that the former Soviet Republics form around the Russian Federation. Georgia's attempts to gain NATO membership threaten to poke a major hole in this buffer zone, bringing NATO right up to the Russian border in the Caucasus. Even Georgia's westward economic orientation has security implications for Moscow. Membership in the EU would reduce Russia's economic influence to some degree, but the most important security aspect of Georgia's economic orientation is its western energy pipelines. These pipelines threaten Russia's ability to monopolize Caspian energy resources. Russia's ability to control energy resources coming out of the Caspian region guarantees it economic security and provides political leverage.

Therefore, for Russia to lose its historical influence over Georgia is a major security concern. If Georgia can be made compliant with Russian wishes, then Moscow might gain the ability to control NATO's air access to Central Asia as well as Western energy access to the Caspian basis and beyond. Since independence, however, Georgians have remained relatively uncooperative from the Russian perspective. The Rose Revolution established a democratic process in which pro-Russian candidates have a very difficult time gaining office because of the ties between Georgian patriotic feeling and anti-Russian sentiments. Since Georgia provided, in some ways, the spark for the other democratic "color revolutions" that followed in Ukraine and Kyrgyzstan, it is not a stretch to see how some Russian leaders might fear that Georgia would lead other former republics away from the Russian Federation orbit. For instance, Georgia has urged the creation of organizations, like GUAM, that exclude Russia.

To counter the Georgian threat to its perceived security, Russia does potentially have the ability to leverage the 60 percent of Georgian gas consumption that it supplies. However, Russia's ability to control the future of Georgia's separatist conflicts provides an even greater source of political and security leverage. With Russian troops in Abkhazia and South Ossetia, Moscow has a major say in whether or not these republics will ever gain independence, be absorbed into the Russian Federation, or rejoin Georgia. When Saakashvili took office and began to implement a very assertive approach to Moscow and the separatist regions, he threatened to upset the status quo that Russia had established in the region. It was obviously well before 2008 that the status of the separatist republics was closely linked to Georgia's NATO membership process, giving Georgia incentive to seek resolution and Russia incentive to increase the permanence of Abkhazian and South Ossetian independence.

Lead-up to Russia-Georgian Hostilities

Russia has used its economic leverage and the separatist conflict in tandem to leverage Georgia. Simultaneously, Moscow imposed a discriminatory visa regime on Georgia and began distributing Russian passports in the separatist regions. Effectively, the distribution of passports enabled Russia to claim greater numbers of citizens in these areas, bolstering its right to act in defense of these people. For instance, 80 percent of South Ossetians are now also Russian citizens.[80] In addition, the Kremlin also began to co-opt the security forces of Abkhazia and South Ossetia. In 2004, several Russians were appointed to serve as the heads of separatist security forces. General Sultan Sosnaliev and Major General Vasily Lunev were appointed, respectively, as the Abkhazian and the South Ossetian defense ministers.[81] In 2006, Russian energy was cut off to Georgia by suspicious explosions that damaged gas pipelines and electrical power lines. Several months later, Moscow banned the sale of Georgian wine—80 percent of which was sold in Russia. Relations grew even worse in September of 2006, when Tbilisi arrested several Russians on allegations of spying. Moscow responded by announcing economic retaliatory measures.[82]

In 2007, Kremlin's tactics changed to include more military aspects. On March 11, 2007, an unmarked Russian military helicopter (which was identified as a Mi-24 HIND-E) fired an air-to-surface missile at a building in Chkhalta, Georgia. Then later, on August 6 of that year, there was another incursion into Georgian airspace and a missile fired by at least one Russian airplane near the village of Tsitelubani. The aircraft was identified as a Russian Su-24M fighter jet, which also fired a surface-to-air missile before it was tracked returning to the Russian airspace. That missile failed to detonate, but elicited angry reactions in Georgia. Moscow dismissed both occurrences as Georgian plots to smear Russia; and some officials claimed that both aircraft must have been operating under Georgian command. Playing off of the Russian story, South Ossetia used the incident as an opportunity to request additional Russian military support for air defense against Georgia. However, the idea that Tbilisi would have instigated these events appears to have weak foundations. An international team sent by the OSCE and the JPKF to investigate verified that, in the August 6 incident, the fighter jet originated from and returned to Russian airspace. In addition, they reported that the Georgian air force does not own any Su-24M fighters or even have the capabilities to launch the specific Kh-58 missile type that was recovered.[83]

In 2008, the Kremlin began to increase its support of Abkhazia when it backed the withdrawal of CIS sanctions, deployed additional troops, and began to repair its railway with Abkhazia.[84] The Russian military support, coupled with Russian efforts to tie the separatist republics to Moscow through citizenship and security cooperation, amounts to what has been described as a process of "creeping annexation."[85] The possibility that Abkhazia and South Ossetia would not only remain de facto independent, but they might also become de facto members of the Russian Federation, appeared to be a not-distant reality. On April 16, 2008, Putin opened direct trade, transportation, and political ties with both breakaway regions of Georgia. That announcement was followed by the deployment of Russian paratroops and artillery within Abkhazia.[86]

The Russia-Georgia War

On July 15, 2008, Moscow added to the concentration of troops it had in the region when it began military exercises in the North Caucasus. When those exercises concluded on August 2, most of the troops that had been involved remained positioned in North Ossetia instead of returning to their home bases in Pskov and Novorossiysk.[87] Therefore, when Georgian troops launched their attack on the South Ossetian capital Tskhinvali on the evening of August 7, Russian troops were already prepositioned for an invasion. Some reports even indicate that advance units of Russian forces had already crossed into South Ossetia before the Georgian attack had even begun.[88]

The Georgians launched their invasion of South Ossetia on claims that they were responding to rocket attacks that had been originating from South Ossetia. The Kremlin, on the other hand, maintained that its "peacekeepers" had been fired upon by advancing Georgian troops and used this justification for its invasion of Georgia. This constituted Russia's first invasion of another state since the Soviet invasion of Afghanistan in 1979. Over the course of the next 10 days, the Russian military completely drove the Georgians out of South Ossetia, opened a second front from Abkhazia and along the Georgian Black Sea coast, and drove deep into Georgian territory.[89] Fighting was relatively brief, very decisive, and one-sided in favor of the Russians, while the attention of the world was focused on the Beijing Olympic Games. With its small military completely crushed, Tbilisi had little option but to agree to a cease-fire. And with that defeat, plans for membership in NATO and for reunification of the separatist regions appear to have been dealt a deathblow. (See text of the cease-fire agreement in Appendix G.)

Iran

Georgia-Iran relations have been friendly, with limited diplomatic and economic ties. The fact that these two states do not share a border may contribute to the lack of conflict in their relationship, as repeatedly in the South Caucasus common borders have often played a role in ethnic conflict. Both states also share some mutual interests. For IRI, trade routes and pipelines with Georgia would allow a bridge to European markets, while for Georgia such opportunities would bring economic benefits that could reduce the influence of Moscow.

Reportedly, Tbilisi is ready to grant Tehran access of Black Sea ports, which would be the first step in opening a new route to Europe.[90] These sorts of discussions have been ongoing, and Georgia has expressed keen interest in becoming Iran's link to Europe in the Great Silk Road transportation project.[91] When Georgia's gas pipeline with Russia was damaged by explosions in 2006, it temporarily relied on Iran for natural gas imports.[92] Moreover, the Armenia-Iran pipeline could be extended a little further north into Georgia, which would allow Georgia permanent access to Iranian gas resources.

Iran's status as an international pariah has been cause for some caution on Georgia's part, but even in the middle of the crisis over the Iranian nuclear program Tbilisi has remained pro-Iran. On May 30, 2003, Georgian Deputy Foreign

Minister Kakha Sikharulidze issued a statement on the tensions between the United States and Iran. He said that "[a]ll the controversies between two states should be resolved through dialogue" and "the hope is that the controversial issue of Iran's possible links with international terrorism will be settled peacefully."[93]

During the Russia-Georgia War, Tehran took no official stance on the conflict, only to expressing its desire that the conflict would come to a swift conclusion. These sentiments appear to be a function of the mixed interests Iran had in the conflict. On the one hand, just like Russia, Iran has been threatened by the increasing proximity of NATO. A halt to NATO's regional expansion is a positive development from the Iranian perspective. On the other hand, Iran has its own national interests that it would like to advance in the Southern Caucasus. From Tehran's perspective, the war had shifted the balance of powers in the region toward Russia.[94]

Turkey

Tbilisi and Ankara have had historically strained relationships which are the result of centuries of Muslim-Christian tensions, ethnic conflicts, and territorial disputes since the Ottoman Empire era. However, that past has been set aside by both states. Since gaining independence, Georgia has developed political, economic, and security cooperation with Turkey. Ankara immediately recognized Tbilisi's independence and even took an active role in mediating the first hostilities between Georgia and South Ossetia. Economically, both states have worked hand-in-hand to establish the BTE and BTC pipelines. Regarding security, between 1991 and 2001, the United States and Turkey provided $94 million and $13 million, respectively, for strengthening of the Georgian military. Since 2000, the Turkish and Georgian militaries have engaged in joint training sessions.[95] Diplomatically, Turkey demonstrated its strong support for Saakashvili's administration when it used its influence over Muslim Adjarians to support the removal of Adjarian President Abashidze from power.[96]

Because of these bilateral accomplishments, Turkey and Georgia have had great praise for one another.[97] However, Turkey-Georgia relations appear to be on a cooling track. Primarily this has followed Ankara's rapprochement with Moscow since the end of the Cold War. Today, Turkey imports more than 70 percent of its natural gas from Russia and benefits greatly from growing trade and Russian tourism. The increasing value of the Russia-Turkey economic relationship provides Turkey with incentive to be careful in just how closely it embraces Georgia, as this is perceived negatively in Moscow.

Furthermore, since the end of the Cold War, Turkey has steadily developed a foreign policy that is no longer as deferent to the United States as it once was. Together, Turkey and Russia have opposed the war in Iraq and advocated greater ties with Iran.[98] Of more direct concern for Georgia, though, is the growing amount of unofficial trade between Turkey and Abkhazia. The Georgian navy has attempted to put an end to this trade at several times, stopping Turkish merchant ships and even making arrests. These searches of Turkish ships have created some tension.[99]

The Russia-Georgia War has further complicated Ankara-Tbilisi relations. Because of tensions in August of 2008, Russia increased its inspections of Turkish goods crossing the Russian Caucasus border. These searches could cost Turkey almost $3 billion in the short term. Some have interpreted the increasing Russian customs searches as a warning that Turkey should exercise greater caution in its ties to Georgia. While Turkey has issued calls for Georgia's territory to be respected in the wake of Russian occupation, Turkish officials have avoided directly criticizing Russia. Generally, Turkey has only aided Georgia passively, allowing U.S. ships with Georgian aid to pass through the Dardanelles.[100] Although such action was considered a major political move from some perspectives, Turkey's willingness to directly aid Georgia may be waning.

Armenia

Ethnic tensions have long played a role in the Armenia-Georgia relationship, despite their shared Christian heritage. Since gaining independence Georgia has had reason to worry about the sizable Armenian minority that lives within its borders, since there is a history of Georgian-Armenian conflicts in Javakheti. In fact, some Georgians perceive their Armenian citizens as a "fifth column" that should be closely watched. When Georgia's first war with Abkhazia began, Tbilisi also accused Yerevan of backing those separatists.[101] However, Armenia has more recently attempted to alleviate such Georgian worries. Thus, a new (although hesitant) relationship was emerging before the Russia-Georgia War.

As has been explained, Georgia is vital to north-south trade routes between Armenia and Russia. Furthermore, these roots are essential to Armenia's ability to escape the economic isolation that Azerbaijan and Turkey have imposed upon Yerevan. Therefore, even Armenian nationalists realize that it would be better to avoid ethnic confrontation with Georgia in order to establish mutually beneficial economic ties with that country. There are also a number of reasons why economic ties with Armenia would be of mutual advantage to Georgia. First, the Georgian economy is still weak and benefits from any increase in international trade. Secondly, Armenia stands in the way of any connection to Iranian gas pipelines.[102]

Both sides appear to have recognized how vital greater economic cooperation would be for their countries; and their governments have committed to repairing roads between the two nations.[103] At least since Saakashvili's regime came to power, Georgia has also realized that friendly relations with Armenia could convince Yerevan to serve as an intermediary in Georgia-Russia relations. In 2004,

Saakashvili expressed that "Armenia can be of help to us, insofar as she maintains close ties of friendship with Russia."[104] And there may be some hope in this
regard. Armenia has maintained a very balanced approach to Georgia during the
turmoil of the Russia-Georgia War. Russian transportation blockades of Georgia
have endangered Armenia's trade with Russia, which means that Armenia has a
mutual interest in encouraging the cessation of Russian trade embargoes.[105] Still,
it remains to be seen how far Armenia is willing to go in a relationship with a
state that has such rocky relations with Moscow.

Azerbaijan

Although Armenia offers future benefits, Georgian-Azeri cooperation is the
most important for Georgia in the South Caucasus. Azerbaijan not only provides
the energy resources so desperately needed for consumption in Georgia, but the
BTE and BTC pipelines also offer Georgia the opportunity to realize revenues
from transit fees that are paid to move oil and gas across its territory. Furthermore, the strategic value of these pipelines has given Georgia new levels of significance for the West, though this has been accompanied by corresponding
significance for Russian security concerns.

As a result of Georgian-Azeri cooperation on the energy field, other cooperative economic projects have emerged. For example, the Baku-Tbilisi-Kars
(BTK) railway will soon be the next addition to the development of the East-
West trade corridor that these two states form.[106] On explicit security issues,
Azerbaijan and Georgia also share similar positions on the issue of ethno-
nationalism and separatism in the South Caucasus. Such conflicts have cost
both states significant amounts of territory. Together, Tbilisi and Baku have both
promoted the importance of territorial integrity.[107]

Nevertheless, Georgia realizes that Azerbaijan is also wary of upsetting
Moscow by becoming too engaged with Tbilisi. Although Georgia has repeatedly
been able to rely on Azerbaijan for emergency gas supplies when Russia has shut
off the valves (in 2006 and 2008), Tbilisi has discovered that Baku is unwilling to
lend much more aid.[108] Azerbaijan was relatively mute on the Russia-Georgia
War, although it did allow U.S. Vice President Cheney to make a visit to the
territory to express U.S. support for Georgia.[109] Ilham Aliyev has consistently
followed in the footsteps of his father, attempting to maintain a pragmatic and
more or less balanced relationship with Moscow.

SUMMARY

Georgia's history since its earliest days reveals that a high degree of demographic fragmentation has always existed in the territory it controlled as a Soviet
Republic. It is important to realize that ethnic differences alone are not a

reasonable explanation for separatist conflict. Georgian nationalism had a significant role in producing nationalistic reactions in Abkhazia and South Ossetia, as it threatened to degrade the political autonomy they had inherited under the Soviets. When Abkhazia and South Ossetia moved to break from Georgia, Moscow was their natural ally because Russia was a major power next door. Another reason for such an alliance was that the Russians were seemingly responsible for protecting national political identity since the Soviet era.

Russia obliged these separatist republics, realizing the political and security leverage this provided to facilitate Gamsakhurdia's expulsion from Georgia, to keep Shevardnadze in line, and to counter the pro-Western orientation of Saakashvili. Though Moscow did not have control of the separatist movements at their inception, there is clear evidence that it has intervened in these conflicts to preserve their separation from Georgia. The results of these conflicts have also been largely positive for the Kremlin as a result. For instance, Shevardnadze's defeat in Abkhazia forced him to seek Russian assistance in order to maintain power. As a result, Georgia was returned to the CIS and the Russian orbit. And now, President Saakashvili's strategic miscalculation and the resulting military defeat in South Ossetia have crushed Georgian ambitions for NATO membership.

NOTES

1. Thomas Goltz, *Georgia Diary: A Chronicle of War and Political Chaos in the Post-Soviet Caucasus* (London: M. E. Sharpe, 2006), 21.

2. Ibid., 21.

3. Ole Høiris and Sefa Martin Yurukel, *Contrasts and Solutions in the Caucasus* (Aarhus: Aarhus University Press, 1998), 36.

4. David Marshall Lang, "Independent Georgia (1918–1921)," excerpt from David Marshall Lang, *A Modern History of Soviet Georgia* (London: Weidenfeld and Nicolson, 1962), http://www.conflicts.rem33.com/images/Georgia/Lang_9a.htm (accessed May 21, 2009).

5. Pourchot, 68.

6. Goltz, 26, 51–52.

7. Ibid., 51–52.

8. Høiris and Yurukel, 39–40.

9. Pourchot, 68.

10. Goltz, 47.

11. UN Security Council, "Georgia-Russia Historical Chronology," UN Security Council Report, August 27, 2008, http://www.securitycouncilreport.org/site/c.glKWLeMTIsG/ b.2703511/ (accessed November 26, 2008).

12. Goltz, 48.

13. UN Security Council, "Georgia-Russia Historical Chronology."

14. Goltz, 51.

15. Ibid., 5–10.

16. Ibid., 86, 134, 141.

17. Ibid., xxi, 196.

18. Ibid., xxi.

19. UN Security Council, "Georgia-Russia Historical Chronology."

20. Vladimer Papava and Michael Tokmazishvili, "Becoming European: Georgia's Strategy for Joining the EU," *Power, Parties, and Political Development* (January/February 2006), 31.

21. Ibid., 30.

22. Svante E. Cornell, "War in Georgia, Jitters All Around," *Current History* (October 2008), 309.

23. UN Security Council, "Georgia-Russia Historical Chronology."

24. Pavel Felgenhauer, "Russian Railroad Troops Complete Mission in Abkhazia," *Eurasia Daily Monitor* 5, 146 (July 31, 2008), http://www.jamestown.org/single/?no_cache=1&tx_ttnews%5Btt_news%5D=33850 (accessed September 2, 2009).

25. SIPRI, *SIPRI Yearbook 2008: Armaments, Disarmament and International Security* (Oxford: Oxford University Press, 2008), 189.

26. Ibid., 187.

27. SIPRI, The SIPRI Military Expenditure Database, http://milexdata.sipri.org/result.php4 (accessed September 2, 2009).

28. U.S. Department of State, "Georgia: Security Assistance," Bureau of Political-Military Affairs, July 2, 2007, http://www.state.gov/t/pm/64766.htm; Dan Darling, "Azerbaijan Boosting Military Spending," *Forecast International* (May 9, 2007). http://www.forecastinginternational.com/press/release.cfm?article=110 (accessed September 2, 2009).

29. S. Perlo-Freeman and P. Stalenheim, "Military Expenditure in the South Caucasus and Central Asia," in A. J. K. Bailes et al., *Armament and Disarmament in the Caucasus and Central Asia*, SIPRI Policy Paper no. 3 (SIPRI: Stockholm, 2003).

30. SIPRI, *SIPRI Yearbook 2008*, 189.

31. Ibid., 189–190.

32. CNN, "Russian Military Dwarfs Georgia's," *CNN*, August 11, 2008, http://edition.cnn.com/2008/WORLD/europe/08/11/georgia.russia.forces/index.html (accessed September 2, 2009).

33. Koba Liklikadze, "Georgia: Funding Cuts May Jeopardise Army Recovery," *Institute for War and Peace Reporting* (February 13, 2009), http://www.unhcr.org/refworld/docid/499a6f22c.html (accessed July 6, 2009).

34. Ibid.

35. Ibid.

36. Vakhtang Maisaia, *The Caucasus-Caspian Regional and Energy Security Agendas: Past, Contemporary and Future Geopolitics: View from Georgia*, 2nd ed. (Brussels-Tbilisi, 2007), 19.

37. Papava and Tokmazishvili, 27.

38. Ibid., 27.

39. Ibid., 28.

40. Tea Gularidze, "Russian Company Seals Controversial Takeover of Tbilisi Electricity Distribution," *Civil Georgia*, August 2, 2003, http://207.218.249.154/eng/article.php?id=4694 (accessed May 23, 2009); CITOH, "Novosti: 97% aktsii GOK 'Madneuli' prodano za $51 mln" (News: 97% of Shares JSC Madneuli are Sold at US $51.1 million), CitoH, November 7, 2005.

41. Vladimir Papava, "On the Essence of Economic Reforms in Georgia, or How European is the European Choice of Post-Revolution Georgia?" *TEPAV* 4, http://www.tepav.org.tr/karadeniz/kei.html (accessed May 23, 2009); Georgian Business Week, "Millennium

Challenge Corporation Board Approves $295.3 Million Compact with Georgia," *Georgian Business Week*, August 16, 2005, http://www.mcc.gov/mcc/press/releases/release-081605 -MCCBoardApproves.shtml (accessed January 31, 2010).

42. Vladimir Socor, "Gazprom's 'Pure Commerce' in Georgia," *Eurasia Daily Monitor* 3, no. 208 (November 9, 2006), http://www.jamestown.org/single/?no_cache=1&tx_ttnews% 5Btt_news%5D=32215 (accessed May 21, 2009).

43. Radio Free Europe, "Could Russian Pressure Leave Georgia Cold?" Radio Free Europe, September 16, 2008, http://www.rferl.org/content/Russian_Pressure_Georgia_Cold/ 1200478.html (accessed May 21, 2009).

44. Molly Corso, "To Georgia, Wine War with Russia a Question of National Security," Eurasianet.org, April 13, 2006, http://www.eurasianet.org/departments/insight/articles/ eav041306.shtml (accessed May 21, 2009); BBC, "Georgia Releases Russian 'Spies'," British Broadcasting Corporation, October 2, 2006, http://news.bbc.co.uk/2/hi/europe/5398384 .stm (accessed May 21, 2009).

45. IMF, *World Economic Outlook, April 2009* (Washington, D.C.: International Monetary Fund: 2009), 86, http://www.imf.org/external/pubs/ft/weo/2009/01/pdf/text.pdf (accessed September 2, 2009).

46. Luke Harding, "Thousands Gather for Street Protests Against Georgia Presidents," *The Guardian*, April 9, 2009, http://www.guardian.co.uk/world/2009/apr/09/georgia-protests -mikheil-saakashvili (accessed September 2, 2009).

47. Ghia Nodia and Alvaro Pinto Scholtbach, eds., *The Political Landscape of Georgia* (Delft, Netherlands: Eburon Academic Publishers, 2006), 13–14.

48. Giorgi Kandelaki, "Georgia's Rose Revolution: A Participant's Perspective," *United States Institute of Peace*, Special Report No. 167 (July 2006), http://www.usip.org/resources/ georgias -rose-revolution-participants-perspective (accessed January 31, 2010).

49. Nodia and Scholtbach, 13–14.

50. David Anabel, "The Role of Georgia's Media—and Western Aid—in the Rose Revolution," *The Harvard International Journal of Press/Politics* 11, no. 3 (2006), 7–43.

51. Jonathan Wheatley, *Georgia from National Awakening to Rose Revolution: Delayed Transition in the Former Soviet Union* (Burlington, VT: Ashgate Publishing, 2005). 189–190.

52. BBC, "How the Rose Revolution Happened," *British Broadcasting Corporation*, May 10, 2005, http://news.bbc.co.uk/2/hi/europe/4532539.stm (accessed May 21, 2009).

53. Nodia and Scholtbach, 20.

54. BBC, "How the Rose Revolution Happened."

55. Charles H. Fairbanks, "Georgia's Rose Revolution," *Journal of Democracy* 15, no. 2 (2004): 110–124.

56. Freedom House, "Country Report: Georgia," *Freedom in the World Report* (Washington, D.C.: Freedom House, 2009), http://www.freedomhouse.org/template.cfm?page=22&year= 2009&country=7612 (accessed September 2, 2009).

57. Mikhail Vignansky, "Georgia Opposition Vow to Topple Saakashvili," CRS No. 484, Institute for War and Peace Reporting, March 13, 2009, http://www.unhcr.org/refworld/ docid/49c0ae622.html (accessed August 24, 2009).

58. Freedom House, "Country Report: Georgia."

59. Vignansky.

60. Freedom House, "Country Report: Georgia."

61. Ibid.

62. Ibid.

63. Ministry of Foreign Affairs (Georgia), "Relations Between Georgia and the United States of America," Ministry of Foreign Affairs, http://www.mfa.gov.ge/index.php?sec _id=337&lang_id=ENG (accessed May 22, 2009).

64. Cornell, "War in Georgia, Jitters All Around," 312.

65. Alexander Cooley, "How the West Failed Georgia," *Current History* (October 2008): 342–344; Irakly G. Areshidze, "Helping Georgia?" *Perspective* xii, no. 4 (March–April 2002), http://www.bu.edu/iscip/vol12/areshidze.html (accessed May 15, 2009).

66. Cornell, "War in Georgia, Jitters All Around," 313.

67. Ministry of Foreign Affairs (Georgia), "Relations Between Georgia and the United States of America."

68. Joshua Kucera, "NATO: Bush's Support for Georgia, Ukraine is No Pose," *Eurasianet.org*, April 2, 2008, http://www.eurasianet.org/departments/insight/articles/eav040208.shtml (accessed May 14, 2009).

69. Ministry of Foreign Affairs (Georgia), "Information on NATO-Georgia Relations," Ministry of Foreign Affairs, http://www.mfa.gov.ge/index.php?sec_id=337&lang_id=ENG (accessed May 22, 2009).

70. Alberto Priego, "NATO Cooperation Towards South Caucasus," *Caucasian Review of International Affairs* 2, no. 1 (Winter 2008): 1–2, http://www.cria-online.org/2_7.html (accessed May 13, 2009).

71. Pourchot, 114.

72. Ministry of Foreign Affairs (Georgia), "NATO Freedom Consolidation Act of 2006," Ministry of Foreign Affairs, http://www.mfa.gov.ge/index.php?lang_id=ENG&sec _id=454&info_id=9681 (accessed May 22, 2009).

73. Ministry of Foreign Affairs (Georgia), "Information on NATO-Georgia Relations."

74. Cooley, 342–344.

75. Ibid., 1181; Andrew E. Kramer, "Putin's Grasp of Energy Drives Russian Agenda," *New York Times*, January 28, 2009, http://www.nytimes.com/2009/01/29/world/europe/ 29putin.html?_r=1&scp=2&sq=putin&st=cse (accessed May 22, 2009); Johannes Rau, *The Nagorno-Karabakh Conflict Between Armenia and Azerbaijan: A Brief Historical Outline* (Berlin: Verlag Dr. Köster, 2008), 56.

76. Ministry of Foreign Affairs (Georgia), "Chronology of Basic Events in EU-Georgia Relations," Ministry of Foreign Affairs of Georgia, http://www.mfa.gov.ge/index.php?sec _id=337&lang_id=ENG (accessed May 22, 2009).

77. Ministry of Foreign Affairs (Georgia), "Chronology of Basic Events in EU-Georgia Relations."

78. OSCE, "Overview," OSCE Mission to Georgia, http://www.osce.org/georgia/ 13199.html (accessed May 22, 2009).

79. Vladimir Socor, "Moscow Pleased with OSCE's Response to Missile Drop on Georgia," *Eurasian Monitor* 4 (September 11, 2007), http://www.mod.gov.ge/?l=E&m=14&sm= 3&st=0&id=719 (accessed May 22, 2009).

80. Konstantin Preobrazhensky, "South Ossetia: KGB Backyard in the Caucasus," *Central Asia-Caucasus Analyst* (March 11, 2009): 5, http://www.cacianalyst.org/files/090311 Analyst.pdf (accessed May 22, 2009).

81. Cornell, "War in Georgia, Jitters All Around," 309–310.

82. Ibid., 310.

83. Svante E. Cornell, David J. Smith, and S. Fredrick Starr, "The August 6 Bombing Incident in Georgia: Implications for the Euro-Atlantic Region," *CA-CI SR Program* (October 2007): 6, 9–14.

84. UN Security Council, "Georgia-Russia Historical Chronology," UN Security Council Report, August 27, 2008, http://www.securitycouncilreport.org/site/c.glKWLeMTIsG/b.2703511/ (accessed November 26, 2008).

85. Georgia Update, "From Creeping to Sweeping Annexation: Implications of Russia's Establishment of Legal Links with Abkhazia & South Ossetia," Georgia Update, April 17, 2008, http://georgiaupdate.gov.ge/en/doc/10003586/20080417,%20From%20Creeping%20to%20Sweeping%20Annexation.pdf (accessed May 22, 2009).

86. Cornell, "War in Georgia, Jitters All Around," 310–311.

87. Ibid., 310–311.

88. C. J. Chivers, "Georgia Offers Fresh Evidence on War's Start," *The New York Times*, September 15, 2008, http://www.nytimes.com/2008/09/16/world/europe/16georgia.html?pagewanted=1&_r=3&ref=world (accessed September 2, 2009).

89. Cornell, "War in Georgia, Jitters All Around," 307.

90. Info-Prod Research, "Efforts to Expand Georgia-Iran Relations," Info-Prod Research (Middle East) Ltd., May 1, 2001.

91. Financial Times, "Shevardnadze Says Georgia Intends to Step Up Relations with Iran," *Financial Times*, November 26, 2002.

92. Misha Dzhindzhikhashvili, "Iran ready to supply gas to Georgia, minister says," The Associated Press, January 24, 2006.

93. Financial Times, "Georgia to Maintain Good Relations, Partnership with Iran," *Financial Times*, May 30, 2003.

94. Kaveh L. Afrasiabi, "Iran Gambles Over Georgia's Crisis," *Asia Times*, August 16, 2008, http://www.atimes.com/atimes/Middle_East/JH16Ak01.html (accessed May 23, 2009).

95. Maisaia, 42; Financial Times, "Turkey, Georgia, Improve Military Relations," *Financial Times*, June 26, 2000.

96. Fiona Hill and Omar Taspinar, "Russia and Turkey in the Caucasus: Moving Together to Preserve the Status Quo?" Russie.Nei.Visions (January 2006): 20, http://www.brookings.edu/views/papers/fellows/hilltaspinar_20060120.pdf (accessed May 22, 2009).

97. ITAR-TASS, "Turkey-Georgia Relations an Example to Follow—Necdet," *ITAR-TASS News Agency*, November 9, 2001.

98. Hill and Taspinar, 8–9.

99. Ibid., 19–20.

100. Yigal Schleifer, "Turkey: Caucasus Crisis Leaves Ankara Torn Between US and Russia," Eurasianet.org, September 11, 2008, http://www.eurasianet.org/departments/insight/articles/eav091108.shtml (accessed May 22, 2009).

101. Regnum News Agency, "Georgia is Becoming Hostage to Azeri-Turkish Alliance: Interview with Pavel Chobanyan," Regnum News Agency, July 10, 2006, http://www.gab-bn.com/juillet_06/Ge1-%20Georgia%20is%20becoming%20hostage%20to%20Azeri%20Turkish%20alliance.pdf (accessed May 21, 2009).

102. Radio Free Europe, "Caucasus: Georgia, Armenia Consider Options After Russia Pipeline Explosions," Radio Free Europe, February 1, 2006, http://www.rferl.org/content/article/1065318.html (accessed May 21, 2009).

103. UNDP, "Study of Economic Relations Between Georgia and Armenia: The Development of Regional Trade Related Growth in Samtskhe-Javakheti," UN Development

Programme, May 13, 2008, 5, http://undp.org.ge/new/files/24_248_868263_cbc-eng.pdf (accessed May 21, 2009).

104. Rosbalt, "Mikhail Saakashvili: Armenia Can Help Georgia Repair Relations with Russia," Eurasia21.com, March 12, 2004, http://www.eurasia21.com/cgi-data/news/files/149.shtml (accessed May 21, 2009).

105. Haroutiun Khachatrian, "Armenia Concentrates on Balancing Act Between Russia and Georgia," Eurasianet.org, November 8, 2006, http://www.eurasianet.org/departments/ insight/articles/eav110806a.shtml (accessed May 20, 2009).

106. Samuel Lussac, "The Baku-Tbilisi-Kars Railroad and Its Geopolitical Implications for the South Caucasus," *Caucasian Review of International Affairs* 2, no. 4 (Autumn 2008), http:// cria-online.org/5_5.html (accessed May 20, 2009).

107. Glenn E. Curtis, ed., *Georgia: A Country Study* (Washington, DC: GPO for the Library of Congress, 1994), http://countrystudies.us/georgia/68.htm (accessed May 22, 2009).

108. The Middle East Journal, "Chronology: April 16, 2006–July 15, 2006," *The Middle East Journal* 60, no. 4 (Autumn 2006): 749–775.

109. Eurasianet.org, "Azerbaijan Plays Waiting Game Following Cheney Blow Up in Baku," Eurasianet.org, September 9, 2008, http://www.eurasianet.org/departments/insight/ articles/rp090908.shtml (accessed May 22, 2009).

CHAPTER 5

Summary of Security
in the South Caucasus

The preceding chapters illustrated that challenges to the security of the three South Caucasus states are many, but they may be grouped into three main categories of concern: *separatism*, *internal instability*, and *international rivalry*. Separatism continues to be the major security issue perpetuating tensions across the region, but internal instability and international rivalry (or competition) at the global and regional levels are also continuing concerns. The total security picture of each Caucasus state is a result of both particular domestic conditions of the state and the special international security parameters that its leaders face. In terms of domestic conditions, the persistent denial of political rights and civil liberties as well as the continuing economic fragility of these states provides a foundation for domestic dissatisfaction. The territorial division caused by separatism, as well as social divisions due to ethnic, religious, and political factors, make these small states very vulnerable to regional and global powers pursuing their own national interests in the region.

In terms of international security parameters, each state enjoys (or suffers) from a particular *strategic value* from the perspective of both great and regional powers. Moreover, each Caucasus state individually faces opportunities as well as challenges that the international players (both states and organizations) offer (or expect from) it due to its *geopolitical position*. For instance, Georgia and Azerbaijan, which share common borders with Russia, are more concerned about any Russian invasion than Armenia (even if Yerevan was not a strategic ally of Moscow), because Armenia does not have a common border with Russia. The Caucasus states do not possess an equal international setting in such a crisis situations. For example, Georgia has access to the Black Sea, so it could be supplied by the West (e.g., during the 2008 war) more rapidly than Azerbaijan, which has no such direct access. Finally, it is natural for Georgia and Azerbaijan, in the Russian "sphere of influence," to seek help from the West (especially the United States) to check or balance the power of Russia in order to enjoy greater independence in their foreign relations.

Now, we turn to a summary of the three main categories of concern regarding the challenges to the security of the South Caucasus states.

SEPARATISM

The greatest security issue that continues to threaten the existence of South Caucasus states is separatism, which continues to perpetuate internal turmoil inside the Caucasus states, conflict between these states, and the power-balancing of international powers. The Nagorno-Karabakh conflict is at the heart of the current alignment of security interests among regional and global powers in the South Caucasus. When the territorial dispute pitted Azerbaijan and Armenia against each other, it also drew in Turkey, Iran, Russia, and (to a limited extent) the United States and the EU. Under the nationalist leadership of President Elchibey, Azerbaijan's emphasis on ethnic heritage made an alliance with Turkey logical. Armenia's historical ties to Russia made Moscow a logical ally for Yerevan, at the same time that Azerbaijan's nationalism was separating that nation from the Russians. The economic isolation imposed by Turkey and Azerbaijan on Armenia made it all the more essential to maintain ties with Russia.

Simultaneously, ethnic distributions in the area made Azeri separatism a potential issue for Iran. However, Tehran managed this problem by making sure that Azerbaijan was simply too involved in its war with Armenia to support any separatist action by Iranian Azeri provinces. Initially, the West, which had closer historical ties with Christian Armenia, took a sympathetic stance toward Yerevan's cause. As the conflict become increasingly one-sided, however, the United States and the EU pressed for a quick end. This development contributed to the current security alignment of states in the region, whereas Armenia, Iran, and Russia share general security interests rooted in opposition to the expansion of Western security organization (by Russia and Iran), opposition to the Azeri-Turkish alliance (by Armenia and Iran), and opposition to the Western orientation of Turkey and Azerbaijan (by Russia and Iran).

Interestingly enough, although the Georgia-Russia war captured global headlines for days, Tbilisi's separatist challenges had a different impact. Georgia's separatist conflicts with Abkhazia and South Ossetia, and the limited dispute with Adjaria, did not have as great an impact on the regional security balance, because they did not draw neighboring states into the conflict to the same extent as the Nagorno-Karabakh crisis did. However, Moscow's involvement in the

Abkhazia and South Ossetia conflicts pitted Moscow and Tbilisi against each other in a cold conflict that became hot in August of 2008. Due to its crucial position between Azerbaijan and Turkey, and Armenia and Russia, Georgia was able to maintain a balanced position vis-à-vis its South Caucasus neighbors. The intimidating geographic proximity of Russia and its continual interference in Georgian internal affairs and sovereignty provided a major incentive for President Saakashvili to seek greater integration into the EU and NATO structure in order to secure his country from Russia.

The separatist conflicts have also had other deep impacts in the South Caucasus. First, they have had crippling economic impacts. The dire economic situations have contributed to internal political instability, though less so in Armenia than in Azerbaijan and Georgia. Separatism has also entrenched ethnic tensions within the region, and the demographic fragmentation of the Caucasus means that this is an encompassing security issue. Yet despite the historical role of ethnicity and religion in the Caucasus conflicts, these factors do not appear to be as great as the concerns over state sovereignty, territorial integrity, and economic interests. For example, Azerbaijan abandoned any claim to Iranian Azeri provinces (that Baku used to call Southern Azerbaijan) in order to reinforce its own rhetoric of territorial integrity, which Baku has used against Erevan, and to materialize oil wealth by settling the conflict. The importance of ethnicity and religion can also shift over time. For instance, Azeris were culturally closer to Iranians, but these days Azerbaijan has built a much closer relationship with Turkey: the two states have supposedly built upon their shared Turkic ethnic heritage. Baku has both economic and security interests in its political orientation. Cementing the Azeri foreign policy orientation is the decision of the Islamic Republic of Iran to collaborate closely with Christian Russia and Armenia in pursuit of its own economic and security interests as opposed to its declared constitutional policy priority of protecting Muslims anywhere.

INTERNAL INSTABILITY

Political and economic instability are other major issues that serve as sources of threat to security in the South Caucasus states. As was noted, separatism certainly played a role in such instability. The Nagorno-Karabakh conflict definitely complicated political struggles in the newly independent Azerbaijan. In Georgia, the dire economic collapse that separatism induced did the same. While Armenia de facto gained territory from the conflict, it still suffered economically. War was certainly a drain on Yerevan, but the economic isolation imposed by Azerbaijan and Turkey crippled Armenia. While all three states have stabilized their economies and experienced varying degrees of recovery, their economies remain sensitive. Political conflicts remain unsolved, threatening to burst forth again, sapping these states of money and men. These conflicts also threaten to draw in external powers, as happened during the August 2008 war between Russia and Georgia. Even though Azerbaijan's incredible oil-driven economic growth has increased the state's ability to carry out a war, Baku still faces economic instability. This is produced by the uneven distributions of oil wealth, but also by the consequences of basing an economy primarily on oil exportation. Thus, internal political and economic instability are significant factors threatening the security of all three states.

The super-presidential or semi-authoritarian governments that have dominated the South Caucasus states also pose a threat to their own long-term political stability. The rising expectation along with the denial of political rights and civil liberties in these states will perpetuate civil unrest. Of the three South Caucasus states, Armenia has been the most stable one, even though Freedom House has not currently rated Yerevan as stable as Tbilisi. Armenia is the most homogenous of the South Caucasus states, both in terms of ethnicity and religion. The war with Azerbaijan provided Armenia with a unified people, and victory in that war rewarded the economic sacrifices of Armenians. In addition, Armenia has enjoyed significant external aid from Russia, some Western states, and the Armenian diaspora, especially in Iran. Contrary the to Armenian situation, both Georgia and Azerbaijan experienced defeats in their separatist conflicts, compounding the economic and political instability in their own countries. Though the Aliyev family has shown that they can bring economic prosperity to (at least some) Azeris, they still face political illegitimacy questions. In Georgia, President Saakashvili had made many promises and given Georgians hopes in the form of economic revival, political freedom, and an alliance with the West. Today, those hopes have been shattered, and President Saakashvili appears to be holding onto power by a slim margin.

INTERNATIONAL RIVALRY

As stated earlier, internal instability is significant in security calculations, but it is also complicated by regional and global rivalry among external powers in the region. Today, the geographic centrality of the South Caucasus persists, serving as the focal point of overlapping national interests of the neighboring states and global powers. As noted, global energy politics is one of the major reasons that the South Caucasus region is important for great powers (i.e., the United States and Russia) and regional powers (i.e., Iran and Turkey). The varying energy interests have generally reinforced the alignment of powers that were produced by the separatist conflicts after the independence of the Caucasus states. They are the general alignment of Russian, Iranian, and Armenian interests and the alignment of Turkish, Azeri, Georgian, U.S., and EU interests. The alignment of such diverse groups of states and cultures simply does not support the idea of the Clash of Civilizations.[1]

Azerbaijan's interest in avoiding domination of its energy distribution networks by Russia reinforces its need for cooperation with Georgia, avoids the geographically shorter pipeline route through Armenia, and cements its economic ties to Turkey as well as the EU. Tbilisi, while refusing to openly choose between Baku and Yerevan, has clearly made a choice toward the West, in a bid to benefit from the revenues it can net from Western flowing pipelines. Armenia needs Georgia in order to maintain access to Russian energy. At the same time, Armenia is seeking to lessen its dependency on that single supply route by pursuing pipelines with Iran.

In addition to energy politics, the rivalry between global security alignments and regional security organizations are shaping the parameters of South Caucasus security. Yerevan continues to have a security interest in maintaining its ties to Moscow and Russian security umbrella organizations. By doing so, it boosts its defensive position versus Baku, which has a much greater military budget. Azerbaijan also seeks the benefits from cooperation with NATO for the modernization of its forces. Baku has also avoided joining Russia's security umbrella in order to avoid increasing Russia's ability to exert leverage over it. Yet, unlike Georgia, Azerbaijan has been slow to push toward full NATO membership. That is an action that would almost surely invite a significant negative response from its Russian neighbor. Georgia has firsthand experience of how severe the Russian reaction can be to Moscow's perceived security threats and economic interests. Specifically in regard to security competition, Georgia most vigorously pursued NATO membership. For Georgia, NATO and security ties to the West were a means to possibly pull away from constant Russian domination. Thus, Georgia becomes the greatest challenge to Russian interests in the Caucasus considering Tbilisi's challenge to Moscow's security and its role in facilitating the East-West pipeline route to the EU states.

There is also political rivalry between the global and regional powers that impacts the security of the South Caucasus. The EU and the United States are supporting the development of democracy in the South Caucasus, and democratic revolutions like the Rose Revolution generally have resulted in the election of pro-Western governments. The EU also offers the South Caucasus states the possibility of political integration. These efforts threaten to undermine Russia's historical grip on the region. The alternative political structure provided by Russia is the CIS, which it has pressured all three of the South Caucasus states to join. The war against Georgia served the additional purpose of making it clear that there are limits to the expansion of Western institutions.

Georgia's "Westward" orientation provides Russia with even more incentive to strengthen its efforts to coerce Tbilisi back into Moscow's "sphere of influence." One may ask: why would Russia care so much about bringing Georgia back into its political orbit? Beyond its symbolic value in deterring other former Soviet Republics to join NATO, the answer lies in Georgia's location in the belly of mother Russia. Georgia is only miles away from the main Russian Black Sea

Naval facilities and Russia's new oil export facilities in the port of Novorossiysk, which is where the new Russian oil pipelines end. Moreover, Georgia would serve as a bridgehead for the West to penetrate deep into Russia's security sphere in its Near Abroad and the vital energy resources in that region. To understand Moscow's sensitivity to America's "too close for comfort" military relationship with Georgia, we should remember the concerns of Washington when Russian nuclear fleet visited Cuba and, more recently, Venezuela.

Since the independence of the South Caucasus republics, the regional rivals (i.e., Turkey and Iran) have resumed their competition for political influence in this geographic area as well. Their efforts overlap the most in Azerbaijan. Turkey has relied on its ethnic and linguistic ties to Azerbaijan as a foundation to pursue their converging interests in opposition to Armenia and for East-West pipeline routes. Iran, on the other hand, has seen the strength of its historical religious ties to Azerbaijan weaken. Yet, the Shia sect continues to be the predominant faith with which Azeris identify. This provides Iran with the potential opportunity to exploit religious loyalty by harnessing Islamic revival. The Iran-Armenia relationship was forged from the necessity of finding a new source of leverage. For Turkey, Georgia was an essential political partner to secure access to its Azeri ally.

This discussion of the rivalry among the great powers seems to indicate that the idea of the Clash of Civilizations may apply to the Washington-Moscow competition in the region.[2] However, the usefulness of the idea of the Clash soon disappears when we examine the rivalry between majority Muslim states of Iran and Turkey in the Caucasus. The "Clash" argument also does not stand when we consider the diverse groups of states that have established opposing alignments. Now, we turn to a closer analysis of the Caucasus from the perspective of "the Clash of Civilizations."

CLASH OF CIVILIZATION IN THE SOUTH CAUCASUS

Based on our discussion in the previous chapters, we may illustrate the nature of relations between any two pairs of states involved in the politics and security of the Caucasus region in a matrix (see Table 5.1). The analysis of paired ties should more accurately illustrate the value of the "Clash of Civilizations" idea. In the matrix, the major players in regional politics are listed (in the same order) on the first row and column. This allows us to observe different combinations of relationship between any two states in the region. Both the row and column of the table start with the three Caucasus republics, then they list the two main regional players, and finally they mention the two great powers involved in the politics of the region. The table cells that form an axis (showing ones) illustrate the pairing of each state with itself. Obviously, such pairing of states represents a perfect correlation of one. This axis divides the table into two right-angle triangles which duplicate the pairings of the states. This leads us to focus on the nature

Table 5.1 Matrix of Ties Between States

States	Armenia	Azerbaijan	Georgia	Iran	Turkey	Russia	USA
Armenia	1	Negative Expected	Neutral Unexpected	Positive Unexpected	Negative Expected	Positive Expected	Neutral Unexpected
Azerbaijan		1	Positive Unexpected	Negative Unexpected	Positive Expected	Negative Expected	Positive Unexpected
Georgia			1	Positive Unexpected	Positive Unexpected	Negative Unexpected	Positive Unexpected
Iran				1	Neutral Unexpected	Positive Unexpected	Negative Expected
Turkey					1	Positive Unexpected	Positive Unexpected
Russia						1	Negative Expected
USA							1

Note: This matrix was prepared by the author.

of pairing in only one triangle, which shows two pieces of information about each pairing.

On the top of each cell, the nature of the state-to-state relationship of each pair of states is indicated with three general possibilities: positive, neutral, or negative. Based on the Clash of Civilizations idea, the bottom section of the same cells shows the expectation of such a relationship in the form of expected or unexpected. For instance, in the first cell (which represents the pairing of Armenia and Azerbaijan), the nature of the relationship between the two neighboring states has been predominantly negative due to their territorial conflict and war, as explained in previous chapters. However, this result was expected based on the Clash of Civilizations concept, since the two states respectively represent the conflicting cultures of Orthodox Christians and Shia Muslims, according to Huntington's argument. On the contrary, the cell representing the pairing of Armenia and Iran illustrates a very different result. First of all, the nature of this relationship is surprisingly positive, despite the fact that Christian Armenia has annexed territory of a Muslim nation—Azerbaijan. According to its own constitutional provisions, the IRI is expected to assist Muslim states or groups that struggle against tyranny, invasion, and injustice, or for their survival. Secondly, such positive ties between Yerevan and Tehran are simply unexpected based on the "Clash of Civilizations" perspective.

With the explanation of the logic for these sample cells, one should be able to understand the reasoning for the results of the other cells, based on the description in previous chapters. Nevertheless, three table cells require a little more explanation for their results. One is the cell showing the U.S.-Russia relationship, which is represented by negative, because the American and Russian national interests are obviously conflicting in this region. However, such results are not an indicator of an upcoming war between these two great powers. Since the two states are natural rivals, one expects a clashing and negative relationship. However, this does not mean that they would never cooperate. In fact, despite their reservations about each other's policies, the United States and Russia have cooperated throughout their history starting with the sale of Alaska to the United States from Tsarist Russia, moving to cooperation during WWII against common enemies, and the subsequent establishment of solid lines of communication to avoid the next Cuban Missile Crisis. Moreover, Washington-Moscow ties have produced a number of famous international agreements to decrease the level of tension between the two great powers, including SALT 1 and 2, START 1 and 2, and the Intermediate-range Nuclear Forces (or the INF) Treaty, to name a few.

Despite their rocky relations at the end of the Bush Administration, in summer 2009, Presidents Obama and Medvedev signed a new agreement to further decrease the number of nuclear warheads.[3] More importantly, Russia provided the United States with the right to fly over Russian territory to supply the war in Afghanistan.[4] Interestingly enough, this agreement was signed after Washington had lost its privilege to use an airbase in Kyrgyzstan, which was a move that appeared to be backed by Moscow. Although there is evidence to show cooperation in the American-Russian relationship in general, the Washington-Moscow connection in the Caucasus can only be characterized as natural rivalry. However, this is no indication of an upcoming war between the two great powers. For our analytical purposes, the corresponding cell on U.S.-Russia ties in the matrix shows a generally negative relationship, because of their rivalry in this geographic region. Of course, such negative ties are expected based on Huntington's argument.

Another table cell that needs explanation is the one on Armenia-Georgia ties, which is listed as neutral, simply because Tbilisi has aimed to keep a balance in its relations with both Baku and Yerevan. However, Georgia has had more collaborative efforts with Azerbaijan than with Armenia. This is in part because of the pipelines connection, and also due to the fact that Tbilisi and Baku consider themselves in the Western camp and work together in their projects with the EU, NATO, and the United States. Armenia-Georgia ties have remained cordial, as Tbilisi allows Russian supplies to reach Armenia. Moreover, Tbilisi has provided Yerevan with access to Black Sea ports for trade, but their limited functional cooperation does not match the depth and extent of the ties between Georgia and Azerbaijan. Thus, the matrix cell characterizes Armenia-Georgia ties as neutral at best, and not positive.

It should also be emphasized that Azerbaijan-Iran ties are listed as negative in the matrix, although Iran was a mediator during the initial stages of the Nagorno-Karabakh Crisis. Moreover, many Azeri refugees were forced to move across the Azeri-Iran border, where Tehran provided them with food, temporary shelter, and other services without assistance from the international community.[5] Beyond such good faith efforts, however, Tehran has been concerned about the motives of Azeri nationalists, who had called for unity with South Azerbaijan (meaning the three Azeri-dominated provinces located on the northwest of Iran). In addition, Tehran has been worried about Baku's "too close for comfort" security ties with the United States and Israel. Furthermore, Azerbaijan and Iran have not resolved their dispute over their oil-rich Caspian Sea territory. This problem even led to a brief military standoff, which raised concerns beyond the borders of the two neighboring states. Thus, on the balance, Tehran-Baku ties are negative when the positive interactions are fully weighed against the negative ones.

Now, the next table (see Table 5.2) briefly summarizes the instrumentality of the Clash of Civilizations idea, since the matrix already identified and characterized all possible paired relationships among states involved in the Caucasus region. The table simply added the number of times that a relationship between a pair of states was considered expected based on the Clash of Civilizations logic, as opposed to unexpected. To have a more accurate picture of the applicability of this idea to describe and explain the paired state-to-state ties, the table clearly divides all relationships into three categories of global, regional, and neighboring

Table 5.2 Clash of Civilizations

Levels of Relationships	Clash of Civilization Concept	
	Expected	Unexpected
Global Level	4	7
Regional Level	2	5
Neighboring State-to-State Level	1	2
Total	7	14

states levels based on the role of the major players. The matrix illustrates that the great powers (i.e., the United States and Russia) were involved in 11 pairs of ties, while the regional powers (i.e., Iran and Turkey) were associated with 7 such relationships. Finally, the three neighboring states were obviously engaged in three possible paired connections.

Nevertheless, the most interesting result of this table is that at each level, there are almost twice as many times that the Clash of Civilizations concept did not hold and failed to predict state relationships in the region. This clearly undermines the explanatory power of the Clash of Civilizations theory. Thus, one must look elsewhere for more satisfactory theories or perspectives to explain the security patterns and foreign relations of the Caucasus states. Historically, the concept of the Great Game and the Balance of Powers has been applied to the region. For the meantime, however, the most prudent explanation of the causes or sources of security threat for the Caucasus states must rely on the three common factors that were presented earlier: separatism, internal instability, and international rivalry.

NOTES

1. Samuel P. Huntington, *The Clash of Civilizations and the Remaking of World Order* (New York: Simon and Schuster, 1997).

2. Houman A. Sadri and Nathan L. Burns, "The Caspian Region: Arena for Clashing Civilizations?" in D. Katsy, ed., *The Caspian Sea Region: Arena for Clashing Civilizations* (St. Petersburg, Russia: St. Petersburg State University Press, 2008), 135–163.

3. Thom Shanker and Mark Landner, "Pentagon Checks Arsenal in Race for Nuclear Treaty," *The New York Times*, September 8, 2009, http://www.nytimes.com/2009/09/09/world/09arms.html (accessed September 13, 2009).

4. Ellen Barry, "Russia offers its Own Territory for U.S.-Afghan Shipments," *The New York Times*, http://www.nytimes.com/2009/02/06/world/asia/06iht-russia.4.19994140.html (accessed September 13, 2009).

5. Minorities at Risk Project, "Chronology for Azerbaijanis in Iran," *Minorities at Risk Project*, 2004, http://www.unhcr.org/refworld/docid/469f38a21e.html (accessed September 14, 2009).

Azerbaijan Biographies

AYAZ MUTALIBOV (1938–)

Ayaz Mutalibov was born in Baku on May 12, 1938, and served as president from 1991 to 1992. He was educated as an engineer and joined the Communist Party once out of school in 1963. Mutalibov's political career started when he joined the Communist Party in 1963 and was the Second Secretary of the Azerbaijan Communist Party for the Narimanov district of Baku. In 1979, Mutalibov gained the position of Minister of Light Industry of Azerbaijan Soviet Socialist Republic. Three years later, Mutalibov was appointed vice chairman of the Council of Ministers in Azerbaijan under Gorbachev, a post at which he served from 1982 to 1989. In 1989, he became chairman of the council and retained that position until 1991. In 1990, he also became a member of the Politburo, so when Azerbaijan gained its independence, he was in a strong political position to reach for the presidency.[1]

A month after Azerbaijan's official declaration of independence, on September 8, 1991, he was elected president of the new Republic of Azerbaijan. That election, however, was boycotted by the nationalist AXC, who opposed the grip the old Soviets still held on the government. Their boycott contributed to Mutalibov's ability to maintain the presidency, but the delegitimization of his election heightened political disunity in the young Azeri state. This internal strife was added to by the economic turmoil created by the Union's collapse, weakening the Azeri state and its ability to counter Armenian separatism in Nagorno-Karabakh.

Mutalibov's political skill was no match for the crisis he faced as Azerbaijan's economy plummeted and Armenian forces dealt repeated defeats to the Azeri military in the war for Nagorno-Karabakh. The swelling of public opposition to his presidency made his situation so precarious that he resigned from the presidency on March 6, 1992.[2] Parliament still appeared to be behind him at the time, as it attempted to reinstate him on May 14, 1992, but Elchibey and the AXC moved quickly to cement their victory by seizing the presidential palace the next day. Mutalibov fled the country and reportedly sought refuge in a heart clinic in Moscow. Once the opposition solidified their hold on power, they filed criminal charges against him. Though extradition charges were filed, he was never turned over by Russian authorities.[3]

ABULFAZ ELCHIBEY (1954–2000)

Abulfaz Elchibey was born in 1954 and served as president from 1992 to 1993. He was a leading intellectual, nationalist, and anti-Communist dissident. In 1990, he became leader of the AXC, which participated in the opposition push to unseat Mutalibov. When Mutalibov attempted to have Parliament reinstate him, it was Elchibey's party that occupied the presidential palace and seized control of government to keep him out.[4] The election of Elchibey on June 7, 1992, was overwhelming, signaling the nationalist feeling of Azeris and their desire to do away with the old Communists like Mutalibov.[5]

In the post–Cold War period, Elchibey's anti-Communist position took on tones of anti-Russian feeling. In keeping with this feeling, Elchibey withdrew Azerbaijan from the CIS. During his short, 13-month term in office, Elchibey refused to deal with Russia, and his nationalist rhetoric even began to alarm other neighbors like Iran as he openly discussed possible unification with Azeris in northern Iran.[6] Elchibey's idealistic embrace of nationalism proved to be short-sighted because it left Azerbaijan with no allies among its immediate neighbors. While Turkey supported Azerbaijan in its dispute with Armenia, Turkey only shares a border with Azerbaijan's isolated Nakhichevan region, and it stopped short of direct military support for Azerbaijan. It was under this condition of self-imposed political isolation that Armenian forces soon occupied roughly 20 percent of Azerbaijan's territory.[7] This was devastating for Elchibey's popularity and perpetuated the internal political chaos in Azerbaijan.

From the continuing chaos in Azerbaijan a military insurrection emerged, led by a Colonel Husseinov. In order to quell the resulting unrest, Elchibey invited Heydar Aliyev, then serving as head of Nakhichevan, to serve as chairman of Parliament on June 15, 1993. As the military coup moved against him, he then fled on June 18, 1993, leaving the country in the hands of Heydar Aliyev.[8] Elchibey left in disgrace and dared not return due to the blame many Azeris ascribed to him for the loss of Nagorno-Karabakh. In 1997, however, Heydar Aliyev allowed Elchibey to return to Azerbaijan, at which time he was elected chairman of the Democratic Congress, an opposition alliance. He was a vocal critic of Aliyev and very critical of the 1998 elections.[9] But Elchibey's return was short-lived. He was diagnosed with prostate cancer and died in 2000, in Ankara, Turkey.

HEYDAR ALIVEV (1923–2003)

Heydar Aliyev was born on May 10, 1923, and served as elected president from 1993 to 2003. He was born in Nakhichevan and attended Azerbaijan State University. After becoming involved in the administration in Nakhichevan, he became deeply involved in the Communist Party in 1945, and by the 1960s he had distinguished himself. In 1969, he became First Secretary of the Communist Party in Azerbaijan, assuming control of the Soviet Republic. He continued to advance in standing in the Communist Party, and in 1982, he was made First Deputy Chairman of the Council of Ministers in Moscow.[10]

This steady rise would have put Aliyev in position for the presidency immediately after Azerbaijan's independence if he had not run afoul of Gorbachev and his crackdown on corruption. In 1987, Gorbachev removed Aliyev from the Politburo and forced him to resign from his position as head of the Azerbaijan Communist Party. Those years were a setback for Aliyev. His wife died shortly thereafter and he suffered a heart attack.[11] Feeling the political changes on the way, Aliyev resigned from the Communist Party and returned to Nakhichevan. In September of 1991, as Azerbaijan moved toward independence, he was elected to the parliament in Nakhichevan. After his return to political life, he also founded the YAP, the strength of which demonstrated his continuing political popularity in Azerbaijan. As Elchibey's presidency began to fall apart in 1993, he turned to Aliyev to hold the country together, inviting him to assume the role of chairman of the parliament. When Surat Huseinov's military coup forced Elchibey from office, Aliyev was left as the acting head of the government. Huseinov recognized Aliyev as the acting president, and in return, Aliyev made him prime minister.[12]

On October 3, 1993, Aliyev was officially elected president. A former Soviet party boss, Aliyev demonstrated willingness to pragmatically defer to Russia in order to bring an end to war. He made a personal visit to Moscow in 1993 and agreed to join the CIS, a move that both Mutalibov and Elchibey had refused to take.[13] In return for Aliyev's recognition of Russia's special role in the Caucasus, Russia applied pressure on Armenian forces to halt their advance. Instead of relying on purely nationalistic rhetoric, Aliyev based his opposition to Armenian separatism on arguments for the respect of territorial integrity and internationally recognized borders. By assuming this rhetorical stance, Aliyev created a viable legal argument against the legitimacy of Nagorno-Karabakh's succession. By championing territorial integrity over the determination of borders based on nationalities, Aliyev also abandoned the logic that Elchibey had employed when he discussed the possibility of unification with Iranian Azeris.[14]

Aliyev used various alleged coup attempts throughout the 1990s to steadily strengthen his position by eliminating political opponents. In 1998, he was reelected, but in a contest that was hardly fair and widely boycotted. Though heavy-handed, he also revitalized Azerbaijan's foreign relations, in particular restoring Azerbaijan's relationship with Russia through the CIS and bringing an end to the war in Nagorno-Karabakh. This allowed Azerbaijan to stabilize and begin an economic recovery, which Aliyev drove by seeking to exploit Azeri energy resources. Heydar Aliyev realized not only the economic potential of Azerbaijan's energy, but also its political implications. Once he became president, he temporarily suspended negotiations with foreign companies in order to focus on patching up relations with Russia. Once a partnership was established with Russia's Lukoil, he then focused on creating a large consortium of foreign energy companies in what was termed the Deal of the Century.[15]

As his health waned, Aliyev prepared his son, Ilham Aliyev, to assume the presidency. In mid-2003, despite health issues, he continued to insist that he would still run for the presidency, but he also had his son's name added to the ballot. In October, when his health obviously was deteriorating, he stepped down from office and his party endorsed Ilham Aliyev as their presidential candidate.[16]

ILHAM ALIYEV (1961–)

Ilham Aliyev was born on December 24, 1961 and has served as president from 2005 until now. He was born in Baku, Azerbaijan and is the son of the former president Heydar Aliyev. He graduated in 1977 from the prestigious Moscow State Institute of International Relations (MGIMO).[17] In 1985 he received a PhD in history and then lectured at MGIMO from 1985 to 1990. Initially, his first ambition was reportedly to become a Soviet diplomat, but the collapse of the Soviet Union ended that possibility.[18] Instead, after his father secured the presidency in Azerbaijan, he was made vice president of the State Oil Company of the Republic of Azerbaijan (SOCAR), a position he held from 1994 to 2003.[19]

As his father's health failed, Ilham Aliyev ran for election as president in 2003. When the final election results were revealed, they showed him as the undisputed winner, having received 77 percent of all votes. His greatest opponent, opposition Musavat Party leader Isa Gambar, was reported to have received 14 percent of the vote, while six other candidates split the remaining votes. OSCE observers criticized the election, citing widespread fraud, and the results provoked several clashes between security forces and demonstrators from opposition parties.[20]

Aliyev offered Azerbaijan continuity and stability, maintaining Azerbaijan's friendly relations with the United States and welcoming attitude to international oil interests. He established a committee to resolve the deep-rooted problem of corruption and even promised to take steps to distribute the prosperity generated by the oil industry to the public. Ilham Aliyev has also repeated his father's pragmatic rhetorical stance on the Nagorno-Karabakh conflict and maintained largely positive ties with Russia and Iran.[21]

In March 2005 he became chairman of the New Azerbaijan Party, and in 2008, he ran for reelection as president. Once again, official reports showed a large victory for him. He was reported to have received 89 percent of the vote in an election that had 75 percent turnout of registered voters. International sources indicate that most of the opposition boycotted that election in protest of media control and unfair electoral conditions.[22] Despite this, he appears to have firm control of the state of Azerbaijan and may serve a lifelong term as president, because a referendum passed in March of 2009 has abolished all presidential term limits.[23]

NOTES

1. Harris M. Lentz III, *Head of States and Governments: A Worldwide Encyclopedia of over 2,300 Leaders, 1945 through 1992* (Jefferson, NC: McFarland and Company, 1994), 64.

2. Ronald G. Suny, *Armenia, Azerbaijan, and Georgia: Country Studies* (Library of Congress, 1995), 97.

3. Lentz, 64.

4. Suny, 97.

5. Lentz, 64.

6. Emil Souleimanov and Ondrej Ditrych, "Iran and Azerbaijan: A Contested Neighborhood," *Middle East Policy* XIV, no. 2 (Summer 2007): 104.

7. Murat Gül, "Russia and Azerbaijan: Relations after 1989," *Alternatives: Turkish Journal of International Relations* 7, no. 2 and 3 (Summer and Fall 2008): 56.

8. Lentz, 64.

9. Europa Publications Limited, *Eastern Europe and the Commonwealth of Independent States*, vol. 4 (New York, NY: Routledge, 1999): 964.

10. Ibid., 955.

11. The Guardian, "Heydar Aliyev," *The Guardian*, December 15, 2003, http://www.guardian
.co.uk/news/2003/dec/15/guardianobituaries (accessed July 6, 2009).

12. Europa, 955.

13. Gül, 57.

14. Cameron S. Brown, "Wanting Their Cake and Their Neighbor's Too: Azerbaijani Attitudes towards Karabakh and Iranian Azerbaijan," *The Middle East Journal* 58, no. 4 (Autumn 2004): 572–573, http://www.jstor.org/pss/4330064 (accessed January 31, 2010).

15. Nasib Nassibli, "Azerbaijan: Oil and Politics in the Country's Future," in *Oil and Geopolitics in the Caspian Sea Region*, Michael P. Croissant and Bulent Aras, eds. (Westport, CT: Praeger, 1999), 291.

16. China Daily, "Azerbaijan's Geidar Aliev Dies at 80," *China Daily*, December 16, 2003, http://www.chinadaily.com.cn/en/doc/2003-12/16/content_290650.htm (accessed September 3, 2009).

17. MGIMO, "Doctors Honoris Causa of MGIMO-University," Moscow State Institute of International Relations, http://english.mgimo.ru/index.php?Itemid=276&id=187 &option=com_content&task=view (accessed July 7, 2009).

18. Stephen Mulvey, "Profile: Ilham Aliyev," *British Broadcasting Corporation*, October 16, 2003, http://news.bbc.co.uk/2/hi/europe/3194422.stm (accessed July 7, 2009).

19. President of Azerbaijan, "Biography," President of Azerbaijan, http://www.president.az /browse.php?sec_id=25 (accessed July 8, 2009).

20. Freedom House, "Country Report: Azerbaijan," *Freedom in the World Report* (Washington, D.C.: Freedom House, July 16, 2009), http://www.unhcr.org/refworld/docid/4a6452d2 c.html (accessed August 19, 2009).

21. Rau, 45.

22. Freedom House, "Country Report: Azerbaijan."

23. RIA Novosti, "Azerbaijan Votes to Remove Presidential Term Limit," RIA Novostri, March 19, 2009, http://en.rian.ru/world/20090319/120633154.html (accessed September 3, 2009).

Armenian Biographies

LEVON TER-PETROSSIAN (1945–)

Levon Ter-Petrossian was born on January 9, 1945 and served as president from 1991 to 1998. He was born in Syria, to an Armenian family that had survived the genocidal violence that occurred in the Ottoman Empire during WWI. He immigrated to Armenia in 1946 and attended Yerevan State University, where he graduated from the Oriental Studies Department in 1968. He then attended the Leningrad Oriental Studies Institute, where he completed his masters and PhD programs in 1972 and 1987, respectively. With this degree, he became the Science Secretary at Saint Mesrob Mashdots (previously called Matenadaran), a position he held between 1978 and 1985. An academician, Ter-Petrossian was also a prolific writer, publishing more than 70 times in the Armenian, Russian, and French languages.[1]

As Ter-Petrossian began his political career, he exhibited a commitment to the cause of Armenians in Nagorno-Karabakh, but also consistently demonstrated pragmatism that differentiated him from the more pure Armenian nationalists of his time. As a member of the Karabakh movement in 1988, he was arrested in a Soviet attempt to diffuse the territorial crisis. A year later, he went on to become the head of the Armenian National Movement. Yet, in 1990, he was elected as the chairman for the Armenian SSR, which gave him both the position in the Soviet government structure and the political popularity necessary to become the first president of Armenia.[2]

Ter-Petrossian was elected president of the Republic of Armenia on October 16, 1991, and Armenia promptly joined the CIS. Though he supported the issue of Nagorno-Karabakh's autonomy from Azerbaijan, he understood the international political dangers of open war with Azerbaijan. This led him to oppose open military engagement with Azerbaijan, which undermined his popularity with ardent nationalists. This led to a vote of no confidence against him in 1992, but he tenaciously managed to hold the presidency. Ter-Petrossian was reelected in a disputed election in 1996; his popularity continued to wane dramatically in the two following years. Economic difficulty and his willingness to seek a compromise settlement on Nagorno-Karabakh undermined his public popularity, as did his increasingly authoritarian response to the growing political opposition. This resulted in his forced resignation in 1998 and the election of his opponent, Robert Kocharian.[3]

After his resignation, he retired from political life for some time. Then, in 2007, Ter-Petrossian announced a surprising bid for the presidency in the upcoming 2008 elections. President Kocharian, facing term limits, had endorsed his prime minister, Serzh Sargsian, and appeared to face little serious opposition until Ter-Petrossian's entrance into the race. In his campaign, Ter-Petrossian accused both Kocharian and Sargsian of corruption. When official election results were reported, Sargsian appeared to have an overwhelming victory. But the election appears to have been fraught with irregularities and elicited accusations of rigging.[4]

ROBERT KOCHARIAN (1954–)

Robert Kocharian was born on August 31, 1954 and served as president from 1998 to 2008. He was born in Stepanakert, Nagorno-Karabakh and served in the Soviet Army between 1972 and 1974. His education occurred at the Electro-Technical Department of the Yerevan Polytechnic Institute, from which he graduated with honors. Afterward, Kocharian became active in the Nagorno-Karabakh Communist Youth and other Communist organizations. Eventually this led him to become one of the leading members of the Karabakh movement. By 1989, he had assumed the office of deputy of the Armenian SSR, and in the next year he was elected deputy of Nagorno-Karabakh.[5]

As the Soviet Union fell apart, he positioned himself as one of the key leaders in the coming war for Nagorno-Karabakh. In August 1992, he became Chairman of the State Defense Committee and Prime Minister of the Nagorno-Karabakh Republic (NKR). Two years later, he was elected president of the NKR. His instrumentality in the separation of Nagorno-Karabakh from Azerbaijan also translated into popularity, with all Armenians opening the door for him to seek political positions in the new Armenian Republic.[6]

Due to the reputation he earned in Nagorno-Karabakh, Kocharian was appointed Prime Minister of Armenia by Ter-Petrossian's administration in 1997. As a Prime Minister, however, Kocharian soon came to odds with Ter-Petrossian, particularly because of Ter-Petrossian's willingness to negotiate with Azerbaijan. Many nationalists like Kocharian criticized Ter-Petrossian for considering the return of Azeri territory in exchange for its recognition of Nagorno-Karabakh's independence. Harnessing Ter-Petrossian's declining popularity, Kocharian led the political opposition against Ter-Petrossian, and after his ousting, Kocharian organized his own successful run for the presidency.[7]

Kocharian was elected president again in 2003, but not without accusations of fraud and skepticism from international election monitors.[8] During his presidency, he actually held talks himself with Azeri President Heydar Aliyev to discuss the possible settlement of the Nagorno-Karabakh conflict. Yet, no substantial progress was made through these talks. He presided over the more recent years of economic growth in Armenia, and remains a major political player. He played a large role in the 2008 election of his prime minister, Serzh Sargsian, defending him against Ter-Petrossian's attempted return to politics.[9]

SERZH SARGSIAN (1954–)

Serzh Sargsian was born on June 30, 1954 and has been serving as president since his 2008 election. Like Kocharian, he too was born in Stepanakert, Nagorno-Karabakh. He attended Yerevan State University in 1971, but served in the Soviet armed force from 1972 to 1974. He then graduated in 1979 from the Philological Department of Yerevan State University. While in school, he worked for the Electrical Devices Factory in Yervan. Then, in the year of his graduation, he became the head of the Stepanakert City Communist Party Youth Association Committee.[10]

Sargsian used his position in the Communist Party Youth Association to advance within the party, moving on to hold positions as First and Second Secretary to the Nagorno-Karabakh Regional Committee Communists Organizations. During his advancement, he served as assistant to Gerinkh Poghosyan, who was the First Secretary of the Nagorno-Karabakh Regional Committee. When fighting in Nagorno-Karabakh began to increase in violence as Azerbaijan and Armenia moved toward independence, he became chairman of the Nagorno-Karabakh Republic Self-Defense Forces Committee. And in 1990, he secured a position as a member of the Armenian Supreme Council. He led military forces in the war for Nagorno-Karabakh and made a name for himself as a military leader.[11]

As it was with Kocharian, Sargsian's experience in Nagorno-Karabakh brought him popularity and political clout. He served as the Armenian Minister of Defense from 1993 to 1995, head of the Armenian State Security Department in 1995, and the Minister of National Security from 1996 to 1999. Then when Kocharian became president in 1999, he made Sargsian the Secretary of the National Security Council. He also served as the Minister of Defense between 2000 and 2007, before being appointed as Prime Minister of Armenia on April 4, 2007.[12]

Having become a close political ally of Kocharian, Sargsian made a strong choice for the next presidential candidate of the HHK. When Sargsian ran in the 2008 presidential elections, Kocharian was a strong ally of his. In that election, opposition parties appeared to be hindered in their ability to organize, and Sargsian was awarded 53 percent of the vote. Several international monitors questioned the results, citing voting irregularities, and backers of Ter-Petrossian, who claimed to have won the election, took to the streets in protest.[13]

Today, however, Sargsian's presidency, appears secure as the HHK and his political allies retain a strong hold in the Armenian government. Sargsian appears poised to pick up where Kocharian left off, continuing Armenia's economic growth. He too has shown a willingness to hold discussions with Azerbaijan on the future of Nagorno-Karabakh, as he and Ilham Aliyev met together during a CIS summit in June 2008.[14] Since then, other meeting and reports of progress have continued to appear through 2009, but there still remains little visible or substantive progress on the resolution of the frozen conflict between these two states.[15]

NOTES

1. President of the Republic of Armenia, "The First President of Armenia," The Official Site of the President of the Republic of Armenia, http://www.president.am/library/presidents/eng/?president=1 (accessed June 30, 2009).

2. Harris M. Lentz III, *Heads of States and Governments: A Worldwide Encyclopedia of over 2,300 Leaders, 1945 through 1992* (Jefferson, NC: McFarland and Company, 1994), 46.

3. Ibid., 46.

4. Freedom House, "Country Report: Armenia," *Freedom in the World Report* (Washingston, D.C.: Freedom House, 2009), http://www.freedomhouse.org/template.cfm?page=22&year=2009&country=7557 (accessed September 2, 2009).

5. President of the Republic of Armenia.

6. Ibid.

7. Stephan A. Astourian, "From Ter-Petrosian to Kocharian: Leadership Change in Armenia," *Berkeley Program in Soviet and Post-Soviet Studies Working Paper Series* (Winter 2000–2001), http://bps.berkeley.edu/publications/2000_04-asto.pdf (accessed May 18, 2009).

8. The New York Times, "Europe: Armenia: Fraud Charged After Election," *The New York Times*, March 7, 2003, http://www.nytimes.com/2003/03/07/world/world-briefing-europe-armenia-fraud-charged-after-election.html (accessed September 3, 2009).

9. Freedom House, "Country Report: Armenia."

10. President of the Republic of Armenia.

11. Ibid.

12. Ibid.

13. Freedom House, "Country Report: Armenia."

14. Alima Bissenova, "Azerbaijan, Armenian Presidents Meet on CIS Forum Sidelines," *CA-CI Analyst* (June 6, 2008), http://www.cacianalyst.org/?q=node/4884 (accessed May 24, 2009).

15. Eurasianet.net, "Armenia, Azerbaijan Presidents Meet," Eurasianet.net, May 8, 2009, http://eurasianet.net/departments/news/articles/eav050809b.shtml (accessed May 24, 2009).

Georgian Biographies

ZVIAD GAMSAKHURDIA (1939–1993)

Zviad Gamsakhurdia was born on March 31, 1939 and served as president from 1991 to 1992. He was born in Tbilisi to Konstantin Gamsakhurdia, a leading Georgian literary figure. His education occurred at Tbilisi State University, where he earned a degree in West European languages and then obtained his PhD in philology.[1] Gamsakhurdia became a political activist in the 1950s and was arrested for his dissident activities, which included his distribution of anti-Soviet literature. In the 1970s he was again arrested, convinced to apologize for his criticism of the Soviet regime on national television, and then pardoned.[2] Despite this public apology, Gamsakhurdia returned to his criticisms and became a major figure in the Georgian nationalist movement, which came to power in the Georgian parliamentary elections of 1990. In that year, his Roundtable/Free Georgia coalition won 155 of 250 seats in the parliament.[3]

On April 9, 1991, the parliament of Georgia officially declared independence, and one month later, Gamsakhurdia was elected to the presidency with 86 percent of the vote. His victory and the hold that Georgian nationalists had on the government, however, excited the fears of the large minorities that resided within Georgia.[4] The South Ossetians were the first to try to gain independence from Georgia, and Gamsakhurdia responded with force. The first round of fighting between Ossetians and Georgians was in full swing by October of 1991. Georgia appeared to have the advantage in such fighting, but Gamsakhurdia's strident nationalism also alienated Russia. Because he viewed the CIS as an attempt by Russia to continue to exert its control over Georgia, he refused to allow Georgia to become a member of the CIS. He also openly expressed his disgust with Gorbachev and Gorbachev's foreign minister, Eduard Shevardnadze, who was a native Georgian. Because of Gamsakhurdia's enmity toward Gorbachev, a reformer whom the West viewed with admiration, the West was inclined to take a dim view of Gamsakhurdia as well. So, as Georgia began to descend into chaos, Gamsakhurdia found that he had many political enemies and no external support when a Georgian opposition movement, led by several warlords, forced him from office.[5]

At that point, Shevardnadze, a native Georgian and the former Foreign Minister of the Soviet Union, returned to Georgia to seek the presidency. However, Gamsakhurdia did not give up his plans for Georgia after his ousting, but maintained a following in Georgia and planned for the opportunity to overthrow Shevardnadze.[6] While he was attempting to consolidate power against Gamsakhurdia's nationalists, Abkhazia made its own move to gain independence. Shevardnadze was forced to turn his forces to counter this threat to Georgian territorial integrity, and by August of 1992, fighting had broken out between Georgians and Abkhazians. Though Shevardnadze himself led Georgian forces and they initially appeared successful, Georgian forces were ultimately routed in the siege of Sukhumi, creating the internal turmoil Gamsakhurdia needed to stage a coup. His gamble failed, though, when a desperate Shevardnadze turned to Russia for military aid in return for his acquiescence to Russian influence in the region and Georgia's membership in the CIS. Gamsakhurdia's ill trained, ill-equipped, and undisciplined troops were quickly routed, and in six weeks his rebellion was crushed. He escaped to Grozny, Chechnya in exile and died there under suspicious circumstances in late 1993.[7]

EDUARD SHEVARDNADZE (1928–)

Eduard Shevardnadze was born on January 25, 1928 and served as president from 1993 to 2003. He was born in Mamati, Georgia to a poor family and advanced in society by steadily climbing the ranks in Soviet institutions. Educated at the state pedagogical institute at K'ut'aisi, Shevardnadze joined the Communist Youth League at the age of 18 and the Communist Party at 20. He became a member of the Supreme Soviet and, just over 10 years later, advanced to the position of Georgia's Minister of Internal Affairs.[8]

During his political career, he gained a reputation as an honest and somewhat puritanical party leader. He fought government corruption and, in one particular year, ousted at least 45 officials from the local party. They were accused of accepting bribes, dropping out of the Communist economic system, and indulging in ideological slackness. This sort of prosecution of corruption appears to have had merit, as Shevardnadze took on party members who had indulged in marble *dachas* along the Black Sea coast. His zeal gained attention in Moscow, and his connections to Gorbachev eventually led him to a position in the Politburo. In 1985, he was appointed as Minister of Foreign Affairs by Gorbachev, and together they began to transform Soviet foreign policy. His role in the reform of the Soviet Union gained him respect in the eyes of the West, which welcomed Gorbachev's leadership.[9]

In 1990, Shevardnadze resigned as Foreign Minister under the growing opposition he faced from the military and Soviet hardliners opposed to the reforms that he and Gorbachev were pushing. He was reappointed in November of 1991, after an ineffective coup attempt by hardliners who had hoped to wrest control from Gorbachev and his fellow reformers.[10] Once the Union collapsed, he turned his attention to the growing chaos in Georgia and gained election as president after Gamsakhurdia's ousting. He won huge respect for his courage under fire during the conflict in the breakaway region of Abkhazia the following year, and he was almost killed or captured. Yet, he could not stabilize Georgia without Russian aid, and so he agreed to Georgia's membership in the CIS in 1993.[11]

Shevardnadze's leadership and compromise did eventually lead to the stabilization of Georgia, and he was reelected as president in 1995 and again in 2000.[12] He exercised authoritarian control over the Georgian state, however, and the legitimacy of both elections were disputed. Due to the decimating civil wars that Georgia had experienced, economic recovery was also very slow and painful. These factors ate away at Shevardnadze's popularity, as well as his apparent unwillingness or inability to combat the corruption that the country had become entrenched in. After the apparent rigging of parliamentary elections in 2004, political opposition led by the young intellectual Mikheil Saakashvili had enough strength to force him out of office. As peaceful protests swelled in what has come to be known as the Rose Revolution, Shevardnadze attempted to remain in control, calling Parliament into session. Protesters, however, stormed the parliament and forced him to flee the building. Saying that he wished to avoid bloodshed, Shevardnadze then resigned.[13] He did not run for reelection against Saakashvili and appears unlikely to return to Georgian politics.

MIKHEIL SAAKASHVILI (1967–)

Mikheil Saakashvili was born on December 21, 1967 and has served as president from 2005 until now. He was born in Tbilisi, Georgia and attended Kiev University's Institute of International Relations. Afterwards, he attended Columbia University in the United States, where he earned a law degree in 1995. He studied a number of issues in France, including human rights and minority issues, and he practiced commercial law in New York City for roughly a year.[14]

In 1995, he was elected to the Georgian parliament and became Chair of the Parliamentary Committee on Constitutional and Legal Issues and Legal Affairs. In that position, he began to push for the reform of the Georgian judicial system based on the U.S. model. On October 12, 2000, Shevardnadze recognized Saakashvili's potential by appointing him to the position of Minister of Justice of Georgia. However, Saakashvili resigned from that position before long, citing the great obstacle of corruption and protesting Shevardnadze's failure to take harsher measures to eliminate it.[15]

The state of public dissatisfaction with Shevardnadze's presidency created a political opportunity for Saakashvili to pursue his reforms by joining with opposition parties to change the leadership of Georgia. The growth of the opposition led to the Rose Revolution of 2003, after Shevardnadze's party appeared to rig parliamentary elections in order to avoid losing control of the legislative body. The popular uproar propelled Saakashvili to the presidency. Still, he appears to have retained respect for Shevardnadze's accomplishments, saying that his resignation was a "courageous act."[16] Saakashvili proved to be as aggressive as Shevardnadze in his early years, reforming Georgia internally and in relation to its separatist regions and Russia. This included brining Adjaria back under Georgian control.[17] Saakashvili's regime also continued Georgia's compliance with the economic advice of the West and international organizations, implementing further economic reforms, and pursuing economic integration with the EU. Under Saakashvili, a new wave of privatization also began.[18]

Despite his initial popularity, in late 2007, political opposition to Saakashvili began to harden and his presidency was increasingly denigrated as authoritarian. There were several large protests against Saakashvili, and he responded by declaring January 5, 2008 for the presidential election. This left the opposition with little time to further organize, and he won reelection despite skepticism of election monitors and accusations of foul play from the opposition.[19] Today, after the disastrous war with Georgia, Saakashvili's political position has become increasingly precarious. Opposition groups are growing in number as former allies of Saakashvili have begun to abandon him. This situation may lead to Saakashvili's early resignation or a change of leadership in the next election. If neither of these events occur, it may precipitate another revolution in the Georgia.[20]

NOTES

1. Martin McCauley, "Obituary: Zviad Gamsakhurdia," *The Independent*, February 25, 1994, http://www.independent.co.uk/news/people/obituary-zviad-gamsakhurdia-1396384 .html (accessed June 30, 2009).

2. Amy Knight, "Zviad Gamsakhurdia," Microsoft Encarta Online Encyclopedia 2009, http://encarta.msn.com (accessed July 6, 2009).

3. Thomas Goltz, *Georgia Diary: A Chronicle of War and Political Chaos in the Post-Soviet Caucasus* (London: M. E Sharpe, 2006), 47.

4. Ibid., 48.

5. Ibid., 5–10.

6. McCauley.

7. Knight.

8. Microsoft Encarta, "Eduard A. Shevardnadze," Microsoft Encarta Online Encyclopedia 2009, http://encarta.msn.com (accessed July 6, 2009).

9. Time Magazine, "Southern Corruption," *Time Magazine*, December 3, 1973, http://www.time.com/time/magazine/article/0,9171,908227,00.html (accessed July 6, 2009).

10. Carolyn McGiffert Ekedahl and Melvin Allan Goodman, *The Wars of Eduard Shevardnadze* (Dulles, VA: Pennsylvania State University Press, 2001), 249, 255–256.

11. Goltz, xxi, 196.

12. BBC, "Profile: Eduard Shevardnadze," *British Broadcasting Corporation*, November 23, 2003, http://news.bbc.co.uk/2/hi/europe/3257047.stm (accessed July 1, 2009).

13. GlobalSecurity.org, "The Shevardnadze Era," GlobalSecurity.org, http://www.globalsecurity.org/military/world/georgia/politics-shevardnadze.htm (accessed July 1, 2009).

14. President of Georgia, "Biography," President of Georgia, http://www.president.gov.ge/?l=E&m=1&sm=3 (accessed July 1, 2009).

15. Ibid.

16. BBC, "Profile: Mikheil Saakashvili," *British Broadcasting Corporation*, January 25, 2004, http://news.bbc.co.uk/2/hi/europe/3231852.stm (accessed July 1, 2009).

17. Vladimer Papava and Michael Tokmazishvili, "Becoming European: Georgia's Strategy for Joining the EU," *Power, Parties, and Political Development* (January/February 2006), 30.

18. Tea Gularidze, "Russian Company Seals Controversial Takeover of Tbilisi Electricity Distribution," *Civil Georgia*, August 2, 2003, http://207.218.249.154/eng/article.php?id=4694 (accessed May 23, 2009); CITOH, "Novosti: 97% aktsii GOK 'Madneuli' prodano za $51 mln" (News: 97% of Shares JSC Madneuli are Sold at US $51.1 Million), CITOH, November 7, 2005.

19. Freedom House, "Country Report: Georgia," *Freedom in the World Report* (Freedom House, 2009), http://www.freedomhouse.org/template.cfm?page=22&year=2009&country=7612 (accessed September 2, 2009).

20. Mikhail Vignansky, "Georgia Opposition Vow to Topple Saakashvili," CRS No. 484, *Institute for War and Peace Reporting*, March 13, 2009, http://www.unhcr.org/refworld/docid/49c0ae622.html (accessed August 24, 2009).

Chronology of Azerbaijan

History of Key Political and Military Security Events in Azerbaijan

1828	Russian and Persian Empires subscribed to the Turkmenchay Treaty where the southern part of Azerbaijan became part of Persia, and the rest of Azerbaijan became part of the Russian Empire.
1848–49	The world's first oil well was drilled near Baku.
1918	Azerbaijan declared its independence.
1920	Azerbaijan was declared a Soviet Socialist Republic.
1922	Azerbaijan, as a member of the Transcaucasian Soviet Federative Republic, was considered a founding member of the Soviet Union.
1936	Once the Transcaucasian Soviet Federative Republic was dissolved, Azerbaijan became a Republic of the Soviet Union.
1967	Heydar Aliyev became head of Azerbaijani KGB, and he then became head of the Communist Party of Azerbaijan in 1969.
1982	Heydar Aliyev was elected member of Soviet Politburo and first deputy chairman of the Council of Minister of the Union of Soviet Socialist Republics.
1987	Heydar Aliyev departed from the Politburo and the Council of Ministers.
1988	Nagorno-Karabakh's conflict began; political and military hostilities between Azeri and Armenians forced Azeri ethnic to leave Karabakh and Armenians to leave Azerbaijan. BBC reported that 26 ethnic Armenians and 6 Azeris were killed in the town of Sumqayit.

1990	As a consequence of the ethnic and military conflicts between Azerbaijan and Armenia, the Nationalist Front of Azerbaijan increased its political rallies against the Azeri government.
	Soviet and Iranian authorities agreed to ease restrictions on crossing borders between both countries after military conflicts over Nakhichevan.
	Interethnic conflicts arose in Baku, and the members of the Popular Front demanded resignation of Communist authorities.
	Ayaz Mutalibov was appointed leader of the Communist Party of Azerbaijan.
	Even though the Azeri parliament had an opposition for first time, the Azeri Communist Party retained power in multiparty elections.
1991	Mutalibov became president after the Azeri parliament voted to restore Azerbaijan's independence, though the Azeri presidential election was boycotted by opposition.
	Meanwhile, Heydar Aliyev became leader of Nakhichevan.
	Nagorno-Karabakh was declared an independent republic increasing interethnic hostilities.
1992	More than 600 Azeri died in a full-scale war over Karabakh. The Armenian army broke through Azeri territory to create a corridor linking Armenia to Karabakh.
	Ayaz Mutalibov resigned as president of Azerbaijan. Abulfaz Elchibey, leader of the nationalist People's Front, was elected president in the first contested presidential election in Azerbaijan.
1993	Armenia started a military offensive over Azeri territory around Karabakh.
	Under political and military stability, the president Elchibey invited Aliyev to assume leadership of Azerbaijan while he fled. Surat Huseinov, rebel army commander, was appointed prime minister when Aliyev assumed leadership.
	Aliyev won a presidential election, which was boycotted by Elchibey's political party, People's Front, showing a massive loss of public confidence in the former president and his political party.
1994	Armenia, Azerbaijan, and Nagorno-Karabakh signed a cease-fire agreement, and Armenians remained in control of Karabakh.
	Azeri military forces mounted Karabakh counteroffensive.
	President Aliyev declared a state of emergency after the assassination of the deputy of the Azeri parliament because that incident was considered a coup attempt against the president of Azerbaijan.
1994	Both international oil companies and Azeri government signed the "Deal of the Century" for the exploration and exploitation of three offshore oil fields.

1995	The first multiparty parliamentary election took place, and the New Azerbaijan Party, led by President Aliyev, won the majority of seats. This electoral process failed to meet international standards.
	Azerbaijan approved a new constitution by referendum.
1997	The Azeri government extradited the former Prime Minister Surat Huseinov from Russia, and after a long trial he was sentenced to life imprisonment.
	The Azerbaijan president, Aliyev, and his Armenian counterpart, Levon Ter-Petrossian, agreed to OSCE proposal for staged Karabakh solution. However, Levon Ter-Petrossian was criticized at home for making significant concessions, and he resigned.
	The Azerbaijani International Operating Company signed its first oil contracts in the "Deal of the Century."
1998	International observers reported that the presidential election where Heydar Aliyev was elected as president of Azerbaijan had several irregularities.
2001	Even though human rights violations did not decrease, Azerbaijan became a full member of the Council of Europe.
	U.S.-brokered talks on Nagorno-Karabakh, held between Azerbaijani and Armenian presidents, ended without result.
	The Azeri government provided airspace and intelligence to the United States after the terrorist attacks of September 11, and the American government lifted an aid ban imposed during the Nagorno-Karabakh conflict.
	Talks between five Caspian countries on ownership of the sea continued all year but were inconclusive. Azerbaijan, Georgia, and Turkey signed an agreement on oil and gas pipelines, linking Caspian fields with Turkey.
May 2002	Pope John Paul II visited Azerbaijan and appealed for an end to religious wars.
August 2002	A referendum on amendments to the constitution were said to get strong support from voters. Critics alleged irregularities and said the poll was a ruse to allow the president to hand over power to his son.
September 2002	The pipeline that carries the Caspian oil from Azerbaijan to Turkey via Georgia started its construction at the end of 2002.
August 2003	The Azeri president, Aliyev, appointed his son, Ilham, as prime minister of Azerbaijan.
October 2003	Ilham Aliyev won the presidential election, though international observers stated that there were several electoral irregularities.
December 2003	Heydar Aliyev died in the United States.

March 2005	Journalist Elmar Huseinov, a critic of Azerbaijan's government, was mourned by thousands after being shot dead in Baku.
May 2005	Western diplomats expressed concern about the use of police force against opposition rallies held in Baku before the opening ceremony for the Baku-Tbilisi-Ceyhan pipeline.
September–October 2005	Parliamentary elections increased political demonstrations where Azeri police used force to break up the opposition demonstrations in Baku.
November 2005	The New Azeri Party won parliamentary elections, gaining several seats, but opposition protesters demanded a rerun because the vote failed to meet democratic standards.
July 2006	In Turkey, the Baku-Tbilisi-Ceyhan pipeline was formally opened.
January 2007	The price disagreement over energy between Azerbaijan and Russia forced Azerbaijan to stop pumping oil to Russia.
June 2007	Russia offered the Gabala radar station in Azerbaijan to the United States as an alternative to the initial American plan to build a missile defense system in Europe.
July 2007	Bako Sahakian was elected to replace Arkadiy Gukasian as president.
March 2008	Azerbaijan and Armenia began military attacks in Nagorno-Karabakh after years of peace. Both sides accused each other of starting the military operations.
April 2008	Russia moved nuclear heat-isolation equipment to Iran, crossing Azeri territory. The destiny of that nuclear equipment was the Bushehr nuclear plant.
October 2008	Ilham Aliyev was elected president of Azerbaijan for a second term. The presidential election did not meet democratic standards, but it represented a significant improvement in comparison to the previous electoral process, as international observers reported.
November 2008	Armenia and Azerbaijan signed an agreement to intensify efforts to resolve the territorial controversy over Nagorno-Karabakh.
March 2009	By referendum, the presidential reelection limitation was abolished, allowing any Azeri president to be reelected without constitutional restriction.

Source: BBC, "Timeline: Azerbaijan," *British Broadcasting Corporation*, February 4, 2009, http://news.bbc.co.uk/2/hi/europe/1235740.stm (accessed August 24, 2009).

APPENDIX E

Chronology of Armenia

History of Key Political and Military Security Events in Armenia

1915–1917	In what has become known as the Armenian Genocide, between 600,000 and 1.5 million Armenians were massacred or deported from their homes in the Anatolian peninsula and sent to what is now Syria.
1916	The Russian army defeated the Ottoman Empire in the Armenian region.
1918	After the fall of the Tsar, the Soviet Union ceded Ottoman Armenia and part of what was then Russian Armenia back to the Ottoman Empire.
	Once the Ottoman Empire was defeated at the end of the First World War, Armenia emerged as independent.
1920	Turkey and Bolshevik Russia invaded Armenia, but an agreement with the Bolsheviks allowed Armenia to proclaimed itself a socialist republic.
1922	Armenia officially joined the Union of Soviet Socialist Republics.
1930s	Industrial development increased under Stalin's government, and political and military purges increased as well.
1988	Predominant Armenian population in the Nagorno-Karabakh region encouraged the Armenian government to unify both Armenia and Nagorno-Karabakh in one country.
December 1988	The Armenian nuclear plant of Metsamor was closed after an earthquake highlighted safety concerns.
1989	The Nagorno-Karabakh conflict began.

1990	Armenia declared its independence even though it was not recognized by Moscow.
	In the Armenian parliamentary elections, Armenian nationalists won the election.
September 1991	By referendum, 94 percent of Armenians claimed secession from the Soviet Union.
October 1991	Levon Ter-Petrossian was elected president of Armenia.
December 1991	The United States recognized Armenia as an independent state.
	Armenia became a member of the Commonwealth of Independent States.
1992	Armenia became a member of the United Nations.
	Azerbaijan imposed an energy embargo over Armenia due to the Nagorno-Karabakh conflict.
1994	Political instability arose in Yerevan over shortages of food and energy.
	The Russian-backed Bishkek Protocol implemented a cease-fire in the Nagorno-Karabakh fighting. The region was left with de facto independence.
1995	Privatization and liberalization programs were launched by the Armenian government.
	The ruling party won the parliamentary elections, and the president's powers increased significantly.
	The Armenian nuclear plant of Metsamor was reopened for economic reasons.
1996	Ter-Petrossian was reelected president in Armenia. The army deployed tanks and soldiers on the streets of Yerevan to quell protests against electoral fraud.
1998	Robert Kocharian became the new Armenian president when Ter-Petrossian resigned due to his failed political efforts to find a compromise with Azerbaijan over Nagorno-Karabakh conflict.
1999	The prime minister, parliamentary speaker, and six other officials were killed inside the Armenian parliament.
2000	Prime Minister Andranik Markarian admitted that, even 12 years after the earthquake of 1998, many Armenians were still living in what could be called a disaster zone.
January 2001	Armenia became a full member of Council of Europe.
	France introduced a law stating that Ottoman Turks committed genocide against Armenians in 1915.
September 2001	Vladimir Putin was the first Russian president to visit Armenia since its independence.
March 2003	President Robert Kocharian was reelected president of Armenia for a second term. Several international observers argued that the presidential election in Armenia did not meet democratic standards.

May 2003	Parliamentary elections in Armenia showed short democratic standards for international observers.
	A referendum presented popular rejection of the constitutional amendments concerning the role of parliament.
December 2003	Six people were sentenced to life terms for the 1999 parliament shootings, in which the prime minister and speaker were killed.
April 2004	The political instability increased in Armenia when thousands of opposition supporters rallied against the president.
November 2005	Constitutional amendments were approved by referendum, but opposition protesters claimed fraud.
January 2006	Gas imports were disrupted after explosions in Russian territory damaged the pipeline that runs through Georgia to Armenia.
April 2006	The price of Russian gas increased twofold.
February 2007	Armenian Parliament issued a bill to allow dual citizenship in order to expand naturalization of Armenia's massive foreign diaspora.
March 2007	Serzh Sargsian was appointed Prime Minister of Armenia when Andranik Markarian died suddenly of a heart attack.
May 2007	The Republican Party, Prime Minister Sargsian's Party, won almost 33 percent of the vote in the parliamentary election. European observers stated that the parliamentary electoral process almost met international standards.
October 2007	The U.S. Congress abandoned a resolution to declare violence against Armenians in 1915 as genocide.
February 2008	Serzh Sargsian was elected president of Armenia. Several opposition manifestations took place all over Armenia.
March 2008	The Armenian government declared a state of emergency for three weeks, and the police arrested many protesters in Yerevan. Parliament passed a law to restrict public rallies.
September 2008	The president of Turkey, Abdullah Gül sited Armenia—the first time a Turkish leader had set foot in Armenia.

Source: BBC, "Timeline: Armenia," *British Broadcasting Corporation*, February 4, 2009, http://news.bbc.co.uk/2/hi/europe/1108274.stm (accessed August 24, 2009).

Chronology of Georgia

History of Key Political and Military Security Events in Georgia

1801–1804	Georgia became part of the Russian Empire.
1918	Georgia declared its independence.
1921	The Red Army invaded Georgia, and Georgia became a Soviet Socialist Republic.
1922	Georgia, as member of the Transcaucasian Soviet Federative Republic, was considered a founding member of the Soviet Union.
1936	Once the Transcaucasian Soviet Federative Republic was dissolved, Georgia became a Republic of the Soviet Union.
1972	Eduard Shevardnadze became head of the Georgian Communist Party.
April 1989	In Tbilisi, Soviet troops killed 19 pro-independence Georgian demonstrators.
1989	Russia deployed peacekeeping troops once Georgians and Ossetians began military attacks against each other. The South Ossetia region demanded more autonomy from Georgia.
1990	The Nationalists won the parliamentary elections, and former Soviet dissident Zviad Gamsakhurdia became president.
1990–1991	The South Ossetians' independence aspirations increased significantly, and Georgian military forces increased violence against Ossetian separatists.

1991	Georgian independence was overwhelmingly supported by Georgians in a referendum, and Georgian Parliament declared its secession from the Soviet Union.
January 1992	South Ossetians claimed independence by referendum, a process which was not recognized by other countries.
March 1992	Shevardnadze became head of the newly formed State Council.
August 1992	Georgian troops fought separatist troops in Abkhazia.
October 1992	Shevardnadze was appointed chairman of Parliament.
September 1993	Separatist forces defeated Georgian troops in Abkhazia.
October 1993	Pro-Gamsakhurdia forces in western Georgia were suppressed after Shevardnadze agreed to join the CIS and then received the aid of Russian troops.
1994	A cease-fire agreement was signed by Georgian government and Abkhaz separatists. It allowed Russia to deploy peacekeeping forces in the region.
	The new constitution created a strong executive presidency.
	The lari was introduced as Georgia's new currency.
November 1995	Shevardnadze won the presidential election.
April 2000	Shevardnadze was reelected president of Georgia.
March 2001	Georgia and the separatist region of Abkhazia signed an agreement not to use force against each other.
June–July 2001	Russia returned to Georgia the military base of Vaziani.
October 2001	Russia accused Georgia of helping Chechen rebels, a charge refused by Georgian government.
November 2001	Constitutional amendments concerning the parliament role by referendum were rejected by popular vote.
	Political corruption increased during Shevardnadze's government.
April–May 2002	Georgian forces were trained by U.S. special forces in counterterrorism operations.
September 2002	Russia warned Georgia of military intervention if the Georgian government failed to deal with Chechen militants.
October 2002	The Georgian government arrested many Chechens, and several others were extradited to Russia.
May 2003	The construction of the oil pipeline that runs from Baku through Georgia to Ceyhan (Turkey) began.
November 2003	The Rose Revolution took place.
	Shevardnadze was accused of irregularities in the last parliamentary election.
January 2004	Mikhail Saakashvili became the new President of Georgia.

March 2004	As a result of the political instability created by the autonomous region of Adjaria, the Georgian government imposed sanctions.
	The National Movement–Democratic Front, Saakashvili's party, won the majority of the seats in parliament in a rerun parliamentary election.
May 2004	Aslan Abashidze, leader of Adjarian, accused the Georgian government of cutting off communication between Georgia and Adjaria.
	Saakashvili warned Abashidze to follow the Georgian constitution and disarm his forces or face removal.
	Aslan Abashidze resigned and left Georgia.
May 2004	Tbilisi did not recognize the parliamentary election held in South Ossetia.
June 2004	Russia criticized Georgia's decision to beef up its anti-smuggling operation in South Ossetia.
August 2004	Georgia and South Ossetian forces clashed. However, Georgian troops pulled back.
October 2004	The Georgian government did not recognize the Abkhaz presidential elections.
	Sergei Bagapsh won the Abkhaz presidential election, but the Abkhaz court ordered the election rerun. Bagapsh won one more time.
January 2005	Sergei Bagapsh was elected president of Abkhazia after striking a deal with his rival, Raul Khadzhimba, who became vice president.
	President Saakashvili offered political autonomy to South Ossetia, but Ossetian leaders insist on their independence. Saakashvili also proposed autonomy to Abkhazian if Georgian refugees were allowed to return home.
February 2005	Zurab Noghaideli, finance minister, was appointed prime minister after Zurab Zhvania was found dead in Tbilisi.
May 2005	George W. Bush was the first American president who visited Georgia.
July 2005	Russian troops' withdrawal from two Soviet-era bases started, and it would end by late 2008.
January 2006	Russia did not supply gas and electricity to Georgia, stating technical problems, but Saakashvili, the Georgian president, accused Russia of sabotage. Georgia received gas from Iran via pipeline running through Azerbaijan.
March 2006	Russia suspended imports of Georgian products.
May 2006	Russia established a ban on imports of Georgian mineral water on health grounds.

May–June 2006	Tensions with Russia arose when Georgia demanded that Russian peacekeepers arriving on rotation in South Ossetia have visas.
July 2006	The Baku-Tbilisi-Ceyhan pipeline opened after Caspian oil started flowing through it.
	The Georgian Parliament demanded that Russia withdraw its peacekeeping forces from South Ossetia and Abkhazia, asking for them to be replaced by international forces.
September 2006	Defense Minister Irakli Okruashvili was fired upon over South Ossetia while he was flying in a Georgian military helicopter. That incident deteriorated relations between Georgia and Russia.
	Georgia reached significant agreements with NATO.
September–October 2006	Relations grew tense between Russia and Georgia after the Georgian government accused Russian army officers of spying. Russia expelled several Georgians from Russia in response to Georgia's political measures.
November 2006	South Ossetians voted in favor of independence, but it was not recognized by the international community.
August 2007	Georgia accused Russia of violating its airspace.
September 2007	Former Georgian Defense Minister Okruashvili accused Saakashvili of corruption and murder, leading to protests.
November 2007	The Georgian government established a state of emergency after hundreds of protesters demanded the president's resignation.
	Russia announced the withdrawal of its troops from Georgia, but it would retain military presence in the breakaway provinces.
December 2007	Human Rights Watch criticized the Georgian government for using "excessive" force against protesters in November.
January 2008	Saakashvili was reelected president of Georgia.
March 2008	Abkhazia asked the United Nations to recognize its independence.
April 2008	Georgia's NATO membership was kept on hold until December.
	Russia tied relationship with Abkhazia and South Ossetia. Georgia accused Moscow of planning the republics' "de facto annexation."
May 2008	The parliamentary election in Georgia was won by the ruling party.
	Russia increased its military presence in Abkhazia, sending 300 unarmed troops. Georgia accused Russia of planning military actions against Georgia.
June 2008	Abkhazia accused the Georgian government of being behind recent blasts in Abkhazia soil.

August 2008	Georgia tried to retake South Ossetia by force, but Russia launched a counter-attack, ejecting Georgian troops from both South Ossetia and Abkhazia. After more than a week of hostilities, Russia and Georgia signed a French-brokered peace agreement.
	Russia recognized Abkhazia and South Ossetia as independent states, and Russia continued maintaining a military presence in both Abkhazia and South Ossetia.
October 2008	Nino Burjanadze, a former ally of President Saakashvili, created a new opposition group, "Democratic Movement–United Georgia," and called for early presidential elections.
	Gurgenidze, the Georgian Prime Minister, was dismissed by Saakashvili.
November 2008	Grigol Mgaloblishvili was appointed Prime Minister of Georgia.
January 2009	Mgaloblishvili left his position, citing health concerns.
February 2009	Nika Gilauri became Prime Minister of Georgia.
April 2009	Opposition groups launched a "national disobedience campaign" in an effort to persuade President Saakashvili to resign.
May 2009	Russia was accused of launching a coup against President Saakashvili.
	Russia condemned NATO military exercises in Georgia.

Source: BBC, "Timeline: Georgia," *British Broadcasting Corporation*, February 4, 2009, http://news.bbc.co.uk/2/hi/europe/1102575.stm (accessed August 24, 2009).

Documents

The following are texts or excerpts of key documents related to the security of the three Caucasus states: Azerbaijan, Armenia, and Georgia. These include:

1. Constitution of the Azerbaijan Republic
2. Constitution of the Republic of Armenia
3. Constitution of Georgia
4. Section 907 of the Freedom Support Act
5. Waiver of Section 907 of the Freedom Support Act
6. Nagorno-Karabakh Ceasefire Agreement
7. Russia-Georgia Ceasefire Agreement

DOCUMENT 1

Constitution of the Azerbaijan Republic

First Section
General

Chapter I. People's power

Article 1. The source of power

I. The sole source of state power in the Azerbaijan Republic are the people of Azerbaijan.

II. People of Azerbaijan are citizens of the Azerbaijan Republic living on the territory of the Azerbaijan Republic and outside it who are subordinate to the Azerbaijan state and its laws which does not exclude standards of international legislation.

Article 2. Sovereignty of people

I. Sovereign right of the Azerbaijanian people is the right of free and independent determination of their destiny and establishment of their own form of governance.

II. The people of Azerbaijan exercise their sovereign right directly—by way of nation-wide voting—referendum, and through their representatives elected based on universal, equal and direct suffrage by way of free, secret and personal ballot.

. . . . . .

Article 5. Unity of people

I. The people of Azerbaijan are united.

II. Unity of the Azerbaijanian people constitutes the basis of the Azerbaijanian state. Azerbaijan Republic is mutual and indivisible motherland for all citizens of the Azerbaijan Republic.

. . . . . .

Article 7. Azerbaijanian state

I. Azerbaijanian state is democratic, legal, secular, unitary republic.

II. In terms of internal problems state power in the Azerbaijan Republic is limited only by law, in terms of foreign policy—by provisions resulting from international agreements, wherein the Azerbaijan Republic is one of the parties.

III. State power in the Azerbaijan Republic is based on a principle of division of powers: Milli Majlis of the Azerbaijan Republic exercises legislative power; executive power belongs to the President of the Azerbaijan Republic; law courts of the Azerbaijan Republic exercise judicial power.

IV. According to provisions of the present Constitution legislative, executive and judicial power interact and are independent within the limits of their authority.

Article 8. The Head of the Azerbaijanian state

I. The President of the Azerbaijan Republic is the Head of the Azerbaijanian state. He represents Azerbaijanian state both within the country and in its relations with foreign countries.

II. The President of the Azerbaijan Republic represents unity of Azerbaijanian people and provides continuity of the Azerbaijanian statehood.

III. The President of the Azerbaijan Republic is guarantor of independence and territorial integrity of the Azerbaijanian state, observance of international agreements wherein the Azerbaijan Republic is one of the parties.

IV. The President of the Azerbaijan Republic is guarantor of independence of judicial power.

Article 9. Military forces

I. In order to provide its safety and defend itself the Azerbaijan Republic establishes Military forces and other military troops

II. The Azerbaijan Republic rejects a war as a means of infringement on independence of other states and a way of settlement of international conflicts.

III. The President of the Azerbaijan Republic is the Supreme Commander-in-Chief of Military Forces of the Azerbaijan Republic.

Article 10. Principles of international relations

Azerbaijan Republic develops its relations with other countries based on principles recognized in international legal standards.

Article 11. Territory

I. The territory of the Azerbaijan Republic is sole, inviolable and indivisible.

II. Internal waters of the Azerbaijan Republic, sector of the Caspian Sea (lake) belonging to the Azerbaijan Republic, air space over the Azerbaijan Republic are integral parts of the territory of the Azerbaijan Republic.

III. No part of territory of the Azerbaijan Republic may be estranged. The Azerbaijan Republic will not give any part of its territory to anybody; state borders of the Azerbaijan Republic might be changed only by free decision of its peoples made by way of referendum declared by Milli Majlis of the Azerbaijan Republic.

Article 12. The highest priority objective of the state

I. The highest priority objective of the state is to provide rights and liberties of a person and citizen.

II. Rights and liberties of a person and citizen listed in the present Constitution are implemented in accordance with international treaties wherein the Azerbaijan Republic is one of the parties.

. . . . . .

Article 14. Natural resources

Without prejudice to rights and interests of any physical persons and legal entities natural resources belong to the Azerbaijan Republic.

Article 15. Economic development and state

I. Development of economy based on various forms of property in the Azerbaijan Republic is aimed toward prosperity of people.

II. Based on market relationships the Azerbaijanian state creates conditions for development of economy, guarantees free business activity, prevents monopoly and unfair competition in economic relations.

Article 16. Social development and state

I. Azerbaijanian state takes care about improvement of prosperity of all people and each citizen, their social protection and proper living conditions.

II. Azerbaijanian state participates in development of culture, education, public health, science, arts, protects environment, historical, material and spiritual heritage of people.

. . . . . .

Article 18. Religion and state

I. Religion in the Azerbaijan Republic is separated from state. All religions are equal before the law.

II. Spreading and propaganda of religions humiliating people's dignity and contradicting the principles of humanism are prohibited.

III. State educational system is secular.

. . . . . .

Article 21. Official language

I. Azerbaijanian language is official language of the Azerbaijan Republic. Azerbaijan Republic provides development of the Azerbaijanian language.

II. Azerbaijan Republic ensures free use and development of other languages spoken by the people.

. . . . . .

Second Section
Basic rights, liberties and responsibilities

Chapter III. Basic rights and liberties of a person and citizen

Article 24. Main principle of rights and liberties of a person and citizen

I. Everyone, from the moment when they are born possesses inviolable and inalienable rights and liberties.

II. Rights and liberties envisage also responsibility and obligations of everyone to the society and other persons.

Article 25. Right for equality

I. All people are equal with respect to the law and law court.

II. Men and women possess equal rights and liberties.

III. The state guarantees equality of rights and liberties of everyone, irrespective of race, nationality, religion, language, sex, origin, financial position, occupation, political convictions, membership in political parties, trade unions and other public organizations. Rights and liberties of a person, citizens cannot be restricted due to race, nationality, religion, language, sex, origin, conviction, political and social belonging.

. . . . . .

Article 35. Right to work

I. Labor is the basis of personal and public prosperity.

II. Everyone has the right to choose independently, based on his/her abilities, kind of activity, profession, occupation and place of work.

III. Nobody might be forced to work.

IV. Labor agreements are concluded voluntarily. Nobody may be forced to conclude labor agreement.

V. Based on decisions of the law court there might be cases of forced labor, terms and conditions being specified by legislation; forced labor is permissible due to orders of authorized persons during the term of army service, state of emergency or martial law.

VI. Everyone has the right to work in safe and healthy conditions, to get remuneration for his/her work without any discrimination, not less than the minimum wage rate established by the state.

VII. Unemployed persons have the right to receive social allowances from the state.

VIII. The state will do its best to liquidate unemployment.

. . . . . .

Article 40. Right to Culture

I. Everyone has the right to take part in cultural life, to use organizations and values of culture.

II. Everyone must respect historical, cultural and spiritual inheritance, take care of it, protect historical and cultural memorials.

. . . . . .

Article 44. Right for nationality

I. Everyone has the right to keep his/her nationality. II. Nobody may be forced to change his/her nationality.

Article 45. Right to use Mother Tongue

I. Everyone has the right to use his/her mother tongue. Everyone has the right to be educated, to carry out creative activity in any language, as desired.

II. Nobody may be deprived of the right to use his/her mother tongue.

. . . . . .

Article 47. Freedom of thought and speech

I. Everyone may enjoy freedom of thought and speech.

II. Nobody should be forced to promulgate his/her thoughts and convictions or to renounce his/her thoughts and convictions.

III. Propaganda provoking racial, national, religious and social discord and animosity is prohibited.

. . . . . .

Article 49. Freedom of meetings
    I. Everyone has the right for meetings.
    II. Everyone has the right, having notified respective governmental bodies in advance, peacefully and without arms, to meet with other people, organize meetings, demonstrations, processions, place pickets.

. . . . . .

Article 54. Right to take part in political life of society and state
    I. Citizens of the Azerbaijan Republic have the right to take part in political life of society and state without restrictions.
    II. Any citizen of the Azerbaijan Republic has the right himself to stand up to the attempt of rebellion against the state or state coup.

Article 55. Right to take part in governing the state
    I. Citizens of the Azerbaijan Republic have the right to take part in governing the state. They may exercise said right themselves or through their representatives.
    II. Citizens of the Azerbaijan Republic have the right to work in governmental bodies. Officials of state bodies are appointed from citizens of the Azerbaijan Republic. Foreign citizens and stateless citizens may be employed into state organizations in an established order.

Article 56. Electoral right
    I. Citizens of the Azerbaijan Republic have the right to elect and be elected to state bodies and also to take part in referendum. II. Those recognized incapable by law court have no right to take part in elections and in referendum. III. Participation in elections of military personnel, judges, state employees, religious officials, persons imprisoned by decision of law court, other persons specified in the present Constitution and laws might be restricted by law.

. . . . . .

Article 60. Guarantee of rights and liberties by law court
    I. Legal protection of rights and liberties of every citizen is ensured.
    II. Everyone may appeal to law court regarding decisions and activity (or inactivity) of state bodies, political parties, trade unions, other public organizations and officials.

Article 63. Presumption of innocence
    I. Everyone is entitled to presumption of innocence. Everyone who is accused of crime shall be considered innocent until his guilt is proved legally and if no verdict of law court has been brought into force.
    II. A person under suspicion of crime must not be considered guilty.
    III. A person accused of crime does not need to prove his/her innocence.

IV. Proofs received against the law must not be used when administering justice.

V. Nobody may be accused of crime without the verdict of law court.

. . . . . .

Article 67. Rights of detained, arrested, accused in crime

Every person, detained, arrested, accused in crime should be immediately advised by competent state bodies about his/her rights, reasons of his arrest and institution of criminal proceeding against him/her.

. . . . . .

Article 69. Right of foreign citizens and stateless persons

I. Foreign citizens and stateless persons staying in the Azerbaijan Republic may enjoy all rights and must fulfill all obligations like citizens of the Azerbaijan Republic if not specified by legislation or international agreement in which the Azerbaijan Republic is one of the parties.

II. Rights and liberties of foreign citizens and stateless persons permanently living or temporarily staying on the territory of the Azerbaijan Republic may be restricted only according to international legal standards and laws of the Azerbaijan Republic.

Article 70. Right for political refuge

I. In accordance with recognized international legal standards the Azerbaijan Republic grants political refuge to foreign citizens and stateless persons.

II. Extradition of persons persecuted for their political beliefs and also for acts which are not regarded as crime in the Azerbaijan Republic is not permitted.

. . . . . .

Chapter IV. Main responsibilities of citizens

Article 72. Main responsibilities of citizens

I. Everyone has obligations to the state and society directly resulting from his/her rights and liberties.

II. Everyone must follow provisions of the Constitution and Laws of the Azerbaijan Republic, respect rights and liberties of other persons, fulfill other obligations envisaged by the law.

III. Not knowing the law does not release citizens from responsibility.

. . . . . .

Article 74. Loyalty to motherland

I. Loyalty to motherland is sacred.

II. Persons working in legislative, executive or judicial power bodies who were elected and appointed to their posts are responsible for accurate and conscientious fulfillment of their obligations and, whenever required by the law, make an oath.

Appendix G

III. A person working in legislative, executive or judicial power bodies who was elected and appointed to his/her post and made an oath regarding the Constitution of the Azerbaijan Republic shall be considered dismissed and will not be able to take this position if he/she was accused in crime against the state, including rebellion or state coup and has been sentenced based on this accusation.

. . . . . .

Article 75. Respect for state symbols

Every citizen must respect state symbols of the Azerbaijan Republic—its banner, state emblem and hymn.

Article 76. Defense of motherland

I. Defense of motherland is the duty of any citizen. Citizens of the Republic serve in the army according to legislation.

II. If beliefs of citizens come into conflict with service in the army then in some cases envisaged by legislation alternative service instead of regular army service is permitted.

. . . . . .

Third Section
State power

Chapter V. Legislative power

Article 81. Implementation of legislative power

Legislative power in the Azerbaijan Republic is implemented by Milli Majlis of the Azerbaijan Republic.

Article 82. Number of deputies in Milli Majlis of the Azerbaijan Republic

Milli Majlis of the Azerbaijan Republic consists of 125 deputies.

Article 83. Procedure of elections of deputies of Milli Majlis of the Azerbaijan Republic

Deputies of Milli Majlis of the Azerbaijan Republic are elected based on majority voting systems and general, equal and direct elections by way of free, individual and secret voting.

Article 84. Term of authority of a calling of Milli Majlis of the Azerbaijan Republic

I. Term of authority of each calling of Milli Majlis of the Azerbaijan Republic is 5 years.

II. Elections for each calling of Milli Majlis of the Azerbaijan Republic take place every 5 years on the first Sunday of November.

III. Term of authority of deputies of Milli Majlis of the Azerbaijan Republic is restricted by term of authority of respective calling of Milli Majlis of the Azerbaijan Republic.

IV. If new elections of deputies to replace retired deputies of Milli Majlis of the Azerbaijan Republic are carried out, then term of authority of newly elected deputy corresponds to remaining term of authority of respective retired deputy.

Article 85. Requirements to candidates to the posts of deputies of Milli Majlis of the Azerbaijan Republic

I. Every citizen of the Azerbaijan Republic not younger than 25 may be elected the deputy of Milli Majlis of the Azerbaijan Republic in an established order.

II. Persons having double citizenship, those having obligations to other states, those working in the bodies of executive or judicial power, persons involved in other payable activity except scientific, pedagogical and creative activity, religious men, persons whose incapacity has been confirmed by law court, those condemned for grave crime, serving a sentence due to verdict of law court may not be elected the deputies of Milli Majlis of the Azerbaijan Republic.

. . . . . .

Article 94. General rules established by Milli Majlis of the Azerbaijan Republic

I. Milli Majlis of the Azerbaijan Republic establishes general rules concerning the following matters: 1. use of rights and liberties of a person and citizen specified in the present Constitution, state guarantees of these rights and liberties; 2. elections of the President of the Azerbaijan Republic; 3. elections to Milli Majlis of the Azerbaijan Republic and status of deputies of Milli Majlis of the Azerbaijan Republic; 4. referendum; 5. judicial system and status of judges; procurator's office, the bar and notary's offices; 6. legal proceedings, execution of court verdicts; 7. elections to municipalities and status of municipalities; 8. state of emergency; martial law; 9. state awards; 10. status of physical persons and legal entities; 11. objects of civil law; 12. transactions, civil-legal agreements, representation and inheritance; 13. right of property, including legal regime of state, private and municipal property, right of intellectual property, other proprietary rights; liability right; 14. family relationships, including guardianship and trusteeship; 15. basis of financial activity—taxes, duties and charges; 16. labor relationships and social maintenance; 17. interpretation of crime and other violations of law; establishment of responsibility for these acts; 18. defence and military service; 19. governmental employment; 20. basis of security; 21. territorial arrangement; regime of state borders; 22. ratification and denunciation of international treaties; 23. communications and transport; 24. statistics; metrology and standards; 25. customs; 26. commerce and stock exchange activity; 27. banking business, accounting, insurance.

II. As per questions specified in paragraphs 2, 3, 4 of the present Article the laws are approved by majority of 83 votes, as per other questions—by majority of 63 votes.

III. The first part of the present Article might be supplemented with the Constitutional law.

Article 95. Competence of Milli Majlis of the Azerbaijan Republic

I. The following questions fall under the competence of Milli Majlis of the Azerbaijan Republic: 1. organization of work of Milli Majlis of the Azerbaijan Republic; 2. based on recommendation by the President of the Azerbaijan Republic establishment of diplomatic representations of the Azerbaijan Republic; 3. administrative-territorial division; 4. ratification and denunciation of international agreements; 5. based on recommendation by the President of the Azerbaijan Republic approval of state budget of the Azerbaijan Republic and control over its execution; 6. election of Ombudsman of Azerbaijan Republic upon recommendation of the President of the Azerbaijan Republic; 7. based on recommendation by the President of the Azerbaijan Republic approval of military doctrine of the Azerbaijan Republic; 8. in cases specified in the present Constitution approval of decrees of the President of the Azerbaijan Republic; 9. based on recommendation by the President of the Azerbaijan Republic giving consent for appointment of Prime-minister of the Azerbaijan Republic; 10. based on recommendation by the President of the Azerbaijan Republic appointment of judges of Constitutional Court of the Azerbaijan Republic, Supreme Court of the Azerbaijan Republic and the Courts of Appeal of the Azerbaijan Republic; 11. based on recommendation by the President of the Azerbaijan Republic giving consent for appointment and dismissal of General Procurator of the Azerbaijan Republic; 12. dismissal of the President of the Azerbaijan Republic by way of impeachment based on recommendation of Constitutional Court of the Azerbaijan Republic; 13. based on recommendation by the President of the Azerbaijan Republic dismissal of judges; 14. taking decision regarding a vote of confidence in the Cabinet of Ministers of the Azerbaijan Republic; 15. based on recommendation by the President of the Azerbaijan Republic appointment and dismissal of members of Administration Board of National Bank of the Azerbaijan Republic; 16. based on recommendation by the President of the Azerbaijan Republic giving consent for enlistment of Military Forces of the Azerbaijan Republic to operations other than their normal duties; 17. based on request of the President of the Azerbaijan Republic giving consent for announcement of war and conclusion of peace treaty; 18. announcement of referendum; 19. amnesty.

II. As per questions specified in paragraphs 1–5 of the present Article the laws are approved by majority of 63 votes, as per other questions decrees are approved in the same order if not specified otherwise by the present Constitution.

III. Resolutions shall be also adopted with respect to other issues which, according to the present Constitution, fall within the competence of Milli Majlis of Azerbaijan Republic, the issues connected with the organization of the activity of Milli Majlis of Azerbaijan Republic as well as the issues where the opinions of Milli Majlis of Azerbaijan Republic are required.

IV. The first part of the present Article may be supplemented with the Constitutional law.

. . . . . .

Chapter VI. Executive power

Article 99. Belonging of executive power

Executive power in the Azerbaijan Republic belongs to the President of the Azerbaijan Republic.

Article 100. Requirements to candidates to the post of the President of the Azerbaijan Republic

Citizens of the Azerbaijan Republic not younger than 35, permanently living on the territory of the Azerbaijan Republic longer than 10 years, possessing voting rights, without previous conviction, having no liabilities in other states, with university degree, not having double citizenship may be elected the President of the Azerbaijan Republic.

Article 101. Procedure of elections of the President of the Azerbaijan Republic

I. The President of the Azerbaijan Republic is elected for a 5-year term by way of general, direct and equal elections, with free, personal and secret ballot.

II. The President of the Azerbaijan Republic is elected by the majority of more than the half of votes.

III. If required majority has not achieved in the first round of voting, then second round will be held on second Sunday after the first round. Only two candidates who gained more votes than others in the first round, or two candidates following closely the first ones, should they recall their candidatures, will take part in the second round of elections.

IV. The candidate having collected the majority of votes in the second round of elections is considered elected the President of the Azerbaijan Republic.

V. No one may be elected the President of the Azerbaijan Republic repeatedly, more than two times.

. . . . . .

Article 106. Immunity of the President of the Azerbaijan Republic

The President of the Azerbaijan Republic enjoys the right of personal immunity. Honor and dignity of the President of the Azerbaijan Republic are protected by law.

Article 107. Dismissal of the President of the Azerbaijan Republic from his post

I. In case of grave crime done by the President of the Azerbaijan Republic the question of dismissal of the President may be submitted to Milli Majlis of the Azerbaijan Republic on initiative of Constitutional Court of the Azerbaijan Republic based on conclusions of Supreme Court of the Azerbaijan Republic presented within 30 days.

II. The President of the Azerbaijan Republic may be dismissed from his post by decree of Milli Majlis of the Azerbaijan Republic taken by majority of 95 votes of deputies. This decree is signed by the Chairman of Constitutional Court of the Azerbaijan Republic. If Constitutional Court of the Azerbaijan Republic fails to sign said decree within one week it shall not come into force.

III. Decree about dismissal of the President of the Azerbaijan Republic from his post must be accepted within 2 months from the date of application of Constitutional Court of the Azerbaijan Republic to Milli Majlis of the Azerbaijan Republic. If said decree is not taken within said term, then accusation against the President of the Azerbaijan Republic is considered rejected.

. . . . . .

Article 109. Competence of the President of the Azerbaijan Republic

The President of the Azerbaijan Republic: 1. announces elections to Milli Majlis of the Azerbaijan Republic; 2. submits for approval by Milli Majlis of the Azerbaijan Republic state budget of the Azerbaijan Republic; 3. approves state economic and social programs; 4. by consent of Milli Majlis of the Azerbaijan Republic appoints Prime-minister of the Azerbaijan Republic, dismisses Prime-minister of the Azerbaijan Republic; 5. appoints and dismisses members of Cabinet of Ministers of the Azerbaijan Republic; whenever necessary takes chair at the meetings of Cabinet of Ministers of the Azerbaijan Republic; 6. takes decision about resignation of Cabinet of Ministers of the Azerbaijan Republic; 7. establishes central and local executive power bodies within the limits of sums allotted in state budget of the Azerbaijan Republic; 8. cancels decrees and orders of Cabinet of Ministers of the Azerbaijan Republic and Cabinet of Ministers of Nakhichevan Autonomous Republic, acts of central and local executive power bodies; 9. submits proposals to Milli Majlis of the Azerbaijan Republic about appointment of judges of Constitutional Court of the Azerbaijan Republic, Supreme Court of the Azerbaijan Republic and the Courts of Appeal of the

Azerbaijan Republic; appoints judges of other courts of the Azerbaijan Republic; by consent of Milli Majlis of the Azerbaijan Republic appoints and dismisses General procurator of the Azerbaijan Republic; 10. submits recommendations to Milli Majlis of the Azerbaijan Republic about appointment and dismissal of members of Administration Board of National Bank of the Azerbaijan Republic; 11. submits to Milli Majlis of the Azerbaijan Republic for approval military doctrine of the Azerbaijan Republic; 12. appoints and dismisses officers of higher rank to Military Forces of the Azerbaijan Republic; 13. forms the executive office of the President of the Azerbaijan Republic, appoints its head; 14. shall recommend to the Milli Majlis of Azerbaijan Republic as regards the election of the Ombudsman of Azerbaijan Republic; 15. submits recommendations to Milli Majlis of the Azerbaijan Republic about establishment of diplomatic representations of the Azerbaijan Republic in foreign countries and under international organizations, appoints and dismisses diplomatic representatives of the Azerbaijan Republic in foreign countries and in international organizations; 16. receives credential papers and letters of recall from diplomatic representatives of foreign countries; 17. concludes interstate and intergovernmental agreements, presents interstate agreements to Milli Majlis of the Azerbaijan Republic for ratification and denunciation; signs decrees on ratification of international agreements; 18. announces referendum; 19. signs and issues laws; 20. settles questions concerning citizenship; 21. settles questions concerning granting political refuge; 22. grants pardon; 23. gives state awards; 24. assigns higher military and higher special ranks; 25. announces total or partial mobilization and also demobilization; 26. takes decision about calling up citizens of the Azerbaijan Republic to urgent military service and transfer to the reserve of soldiers of urgent military service; 27. forms Security Council of the Azerbaijan Republic; 28. submits recommendation to Milli Majlis of the Azerbaijan Republic about consent for use of Military Forces of the Azerbaijan Republic in implementation of duties other than their normal duties; 29. announces state of emergency and martial law; 30. on consent of Milli Majlis of the Azerbaijan Republic announces a war and concludes peace agreements; 31. forms special security bodies within the limits of sums allotted from state budget of the Azerbaijan Republic; 32. settles other questions which under the present Constitution do not pertain to the competence of Milli Majlis of the Azerbaijan Republic and law courts of the Azerbaijan Republic.

. . . . . .

Article 111. Declaration of martial law

In cases of actual occupation of some part of the territory of the Azerbaijan Republic, announcement of war by foreign country or countries against the Azerbaijan Republic, blockade of the territory of the Azerbaijan Republic and also whenever there is real danger of armed attack against the Azerbaijan

Republic, blockade of the territory of the Azerbaijan Republic and also in case of real threat of such blockade the President of the Azerbaijan Republic announces martial law all over the territory of the Azerbaijan Republic or in individual areas, and within 24 hours submits respective decree for approval by Milli Majlis of the Azerbaijan Republic.

. . . . . .

Article 118. Procedure of appointment of Prime-minister of the Azerbaijan Republic

I. Prime-minister of Azerbaijan Republic is appointed by the President of the Azerbaijan Republic on consent of Milli Majlis of the Azerbaijan Republic.

II. Proposed candidature for the post of Prime-minister of the Azerbaijan Republic is submitted for consideration to Milli Majlis of the Azerbaijan Republic by the President of the Azerbaijan Republic not later than one month from the day when the President begins carrying out his powers, or not later than two weeks from the day of resignation of Cabinet of Ministers of the Azerbaijan Republic.

III. Milli Majlis of the Azerbaijan Republic make decision concerning the candidate to the post of Prime-minister of the Azerbaijan Republic not later than within one week from the day when such candidature has been proposed. Should said procedure be violated, or candidatures proposed by the President of the Azerbaijan Republic for the post of Prime-minister of the Azerbaijan Republic be rejected three times, then the President of the Azerbaijan Republic may appoint Prime-minister of the Azerbaijan Republic without consent of Milli Majlis of the Azerbaijan Republic.

. . . . . .

Article 123. Immunity of Prime-minister of the Azerbaijan Republic

I. Prime-minister of the Azerbaijan Republic enjoys immunity during the whole term of his powers.

II. Prime-minister of the Azerbaijan Republic may not be arrested, called to criminal responsibility except cases when he has been caught in the act of crime, disciplinary measures may not be applied to him by law court, he may not be searched.

III. Prime-minister of the Azerbaijan Republic may be arrested if he has been caught in the act of crime. In such case body detained the deputy of Milli Majlis of the Azerbaijan Republic must immediately notify General Procurator of the Azerbaijan Republic about the fact.

IV. Immunity of Prime-minister of the Azerbaijan Republic might be stopped only by the President of the Azerbaijan Republic, based on application of General Procurator of the Azerbaijan Republic.

Chapter VII. Judicial power

Article 125. Judicial power

I. Judicial power in Azerbaijan is implemented by law courts.

II. Judicial power is implemented through the Constitutional Court of the Azerbaijan Republic, Supreme Court of the Azerbaijan Republic, Courts of Appeal of the Azerbaijan Republic, ordinary and specialized law courts of the Azerbaijan Republic.

III. Judicial power is implemented by way of constitutional, civil and criminal legal proceedings and other forms of legislation provided for by law.

IV. In criminal legal proceedings, Procurator's Office of the Azerbaijan Republic and lawyers take part.

V. Judicial system and legal proceedings in the Azerbaijan Republic are determined by law.

VI. Use of legal means aimed to change authority of law courts and establishment of extraordinary law courts which are not envisaged by the law are prohibited.

Article 126. Requirements to candidates to judges posts

I. Judges shall be citizens of the Azerbaijan Republic not younger than 30, having voting right, higher juridical education and at least 5-year working experience in the sphere of law.

II. Judges may not occupy any other posts, irrespective of the procedure—elections or appointment, may not be involved in business, commercial and other payable activity, except scientific, pedagogical and creative activity, may not be involved in political activity and join political parties, may not get remuneration other than their wages and money for scientific, pedagogical and creative activity.

Article 127. Independence of judges, main principles and conditions of implementation of justice

I. Judges are independent, they are subordinate only to Constitution and laws of the Azerbaijan Republic, they cannot be replaced during the term of their authority.

II. In consideration of legal cases judges must be impartial, fair, they should provide juridical equality of parties, act based on facts and according to the law.

III. Direct and indirect restriction of legal proceedings from somebody's part and due to some reason, illegal influence, threats and interference are not allowed.

IV. Justice shall be implemented based on equality of citizens before the law and law court.

V. In all law courts hearing of legal cases shall be open.

VI. It is allowed to have closed hearing of legal cases only if the law court decides that open hearings may result in disclosure of state, professional or commercial secrets, or that it is necessary to keep confidentiality with respect to personal or family life.

VII. Except cases envisaged by law it is prohibited to carry out legal proceedings by correspondence.

VIII. Law proceedings are carried out based on the principle of contest.

IX. Everyone has the right for defense at all stages of legal proceedings.

X. Justice is based on presumption of innocence.

XI. In the Azerbaijan Republic legal proceedings are carried out in state language of the Azerbaijan Republic or in a language of majority of population in specific area. Persons—participants of legal proceedings not knowing the language of proceedings—have the right to be acquainted with materials of proceedings, to take part in legal proceedings using interpreter, to make statements in the law court in their native language.

Article 128. Immunity of judges

I. Judges are immune.

II. A judge may be called to criminal responsibility only in accordance with law.

III. Authority of judges might be stopped only based on reasons and rules envisaged by the law.

IV. Whenever judges commit crime, the President of the Azerbaijan Republic, based on conclusions of Supreme Court of the Azerbaijan Republic, may make statement in Milli Majlis of the Azerbaijan Republic with the initiative to dismiss judges from their posts. Respective conclusions of Supreme Court of the Azerbaijan Republic must be presented to the President of the Azerbaijan Republic within 30 days after his request.

V. Decision about dismissal of judges of Constitutional Court of the Azerbaijan Republic, Supreme Court of the Azerbaijan Republic and Economic Court of the Azerbaijan Republic is taken by Milli Majlis of the Azerbaijan Republic with majority of 83 votes; decision about dismissal of other judges is taken by Milli Majlis of the Azerbaijan Republic with majority of 63 votes.

. . . . . .

Article 130. Constitutional Court of the Azerbaijan Republic

I. Constitutional Court of the Azerbaijan Republic consists of 9 judges.

II. Judges of Constitutional Court of the Azerbaijan Republic are appointed by Milli Majlis of the Azerbaijan Republic on recommendation by the President of the Azerbaijan Republic.

III. Constitutional Court of the Azerbaijan Republic based on inquiry of the President of the Azerbaijan Republic, Milli Majlis of the Azerbaijan

Republic, Cabinet of Ministers of the Azerbaijan Republic, Supreme Court of the Azerbaijan Republic, Procurator's Office of the Azerbaijan Republic, Ali Majlis of Nakhichevan Autonomous Republic takes decisions regarding the following:

- correspondence of laws of the Azerbaijan Republic, decrees and orders of the President of the Azerbaijan Republic, decrees of Milli Majlis of the Azerbaijan Republic, decrees and orders of Cabinet of Ministers of the Azerbaijan Republic, normative-legal acts of central bodies of executive power to Constitution of the Azerbaijan Republic;
- correspondence of decrees of the President of the Azerbaijan Republic, decrees of Cabinet of Ministers of the Azerbaijan Republic, normative-legal acts of central bodies of executive power to the laws of the Azerbaijan Republic;
- correspondence of decrees of Cabinet of Ministers of the Azerbaijan Republic and normative-legal acts of central bodies of executive power to decrees of the President of the Azerbaijan Republic;
- in cases envisaged by law, correspondence of decisions of Supreme Court of the Azerbaijan Republic to Constitution and laws of the Azerbaijan Republic;
- correspondence of acts of municipalities to Constitution of the Azerbaijan Republic, laws of the Azerbaijan Republic, decrees of the President of the Azerbaijan Republic, decrees of Cabinet of Ministers of the Azerbaijan Republic (in Nakhichevan Autonomous Republic—also to Constitution and laws of Nakhichevan Autonomous Republic and decrees of Cabinet of Ministers of Nakhichevan Autonomous Republic);
- correspondence of interstate agreements of the Azerbaijan Republic, which have not yet become valid, to Constitution of the Azerbaijan Republic; correspondence of intergovernmental agreements of the Azerbaijan Republic to Constitution and laws of the Azerbaijan Republic;
- correspondence of Constitution and laws of Nakhichevan Autonomous Republic, decrees of Ali Majlis of Nakhichevan Autonomous Republic, decrees of Cabinet of Ministers of Nakhichevan Autonomous Republic to Constitution of the Azerbaijan Republic; correspondence of laws of Nakhichevan Autonomous Republic, decrees of Cabinet of Ministers of Nakhichevan Autonomous Republic to laws of the Azerbaijan Republic; correspondence of decrees of Cabinet of Ministers of Nakhichevan Autonomous Republic to decrees of the President of the Azerbaijan Republic and decrees of Cabinet of Ministers of the Azerbaijan Republic;
- settlement of disputes connected with division of authority between legislative, executive and judicial powers.

IV. Constitutional Court of the Azerbaijan Republic gives interpretation of the Constitution and laws of the Azerbaijan Republic based on inquiries of the President of the Azerbaijan Republic, Milli Majlis of the Azerbaijan Republic, Cabinet of Ministers of the Azerbaijan Republic, Supreme Court of the Azerbaijan Republic, Procurator's Office of the Azerbaijan Republic and Ali Majlis of Nakhichevan Autonomous Republic.

V. Everyone claiming to be the victim of a violation of his/her rights and freedoms by the decisions of legislative, executive and judiciary, municipal acts set forth in the items 1–7 of the Para III of this Article may appeal, in accordance with the procedure provided for by law, to the Constitutional Court of the Republic of Azerbaijan with the view of the restoration of violated human rights and freedoms.

VI. In accordance with the procedure provided for by the laws of Azerbaijan Republic the courts may file the Constitutional Court of Azerbaijan Republic a request on interpretation of the Constitution and the laws of Azerbaijan Republic as regards the matters concerning the implementation of human rights and freedoms.

VII. Ombudsman of Azerbaijan Republic in accordance with the procedure provided for by the laws of the Republic of Azerbaijan for solving the matters indicated in items 1–7, para III of the given Article shall apply to the Constitutional Court of the Republic of Azerbaijan in cases where the rights and freedoms of a person had been violated by legislative acts in force, normative acts of executive power, municipalities as well as the court decisions.

VIII. Constitutional Court of the Azerbaijan Republic exercises also other authorities envisaged in the present Constitution.

IX. Constitutional Court of the Azerbaijan Republic takes decisions as regards the questions of its competence. Decisions of Constitutional Court of the Azerbaijan Republic are obligatory all over the territory of the Azerbaijan Republic.

X. Laws and other acts, individual provisions of these documents, intergovernmental agreements of the Azerbaijan Republic cease to be valid in term specified in the decision of Constitutional Court of the Azerbaijan Republic, and interstate agreements of the Azerbaijan Republic do not come into force.

Article 131. Supreme Court of the Azerbaijan Republic

I. Supreme Court of the Azerbaijan Republic is the highest judicial body on civil, criminal, administrative and other cases directed to general and specialized law courts; it, via the cassation procedure, shall administer the justice; gives explanations as per practices in activity of law courts in an order envisaged by legislation.

II. Judges of Supreme Court of the Azerbaijan Republic are appointed by Milli Majlis of the Azerbaijan Republic on recommendation of the President of the Azerbaijan Republic.

. . . . . .

Chapter VIII. Nakhichevan Autonomous Republic

Article 134. Status of Nakhichevan Autonomous Republic

  I. Nakhichevan Autonomous Republic is autonomous state within the Azerbaijan Republic.
 II. Status of Nakhichevan Autonomous Republic is defined in the present Constitution.
III. Nakhichevan Autonomous Republic is an integral part of the Azerbaijan Republic.
 IV. Constitution of the Azerbaijan Republic, laws of the Azerbaijan Republic, decrees of the President of the Azerbaijan Republic and decrees of Cabinet of Ministers of the Azerbaijan Republic are obligatory on the territory of Nakhichevan Autonomous Republic.
  V. Constitution and laws of Nakhichevan Autonomous Republic accepted by Ali Majlis of Nakhichevan Autonomous Republic shall not contradict respectively to Constitution and laws of the Azerbaijan Republic; decrees accepted by Cabinet of Ministers of Nakhichevan Autonomous Republic—to Constitution and laws of the Azerbaijan Republic, decrees of the President of the Azerbaijan Republic and decrees of Cabinet of Ministers of the Azerbaijan Republic.
 VI. The Constitution of Nakhchivan Autonomous Republic shall be submitted to the Milli Majlis of Azerbaijan Republic by the President of Azerbaijan Republic and shall by approved by the Constitutional Law.

Article 135. Division of powers in Nakhichevan Autonomous Republic

  I. Legislative power in Nakhichevan Autonomous Republic is implemented by Ali Majlis of Nakhichevan Autonomous Republic, executive power— by the Cabinet of Ministers of Nakhichevan Autonomous Republic, judicial power—by law courts of Nakhichevan Autonomous Republic.
 II. Ali Majlis of Nakhichevan Autonomous Republic independently settle questions which according to Constitution and laws of the Azerbaijan Republic fall under its competence; Cabinet of Ministers of Nakhichevan Autonomous Republic independently settles questions which according to Constitution and laws of the Azerbaijan Republic, decrees of the President of the Azerbaijan Republic fall under its competence; law courts of Nakhichevan Autonomous Republic independently settle questions which according to Constitution and laws of the Azerbaijan Republic fall under their competence.

Article 136. The highest official of Nakhichevan Autonomous Republic

Chairman of Ali Majlis of Nakhichevan Autonomous Republic is the highest official of Nakhichevan Autonomous Republic.

Article 137. Ali Majlis of Nakhichevan Autonomous Republic

I. Ali Majlis of Nakhichevan Autonomous Republic consists of 45 members.

II. Term of authority of Ali Majlis of Nakhichevan Autonomous Republic is 5 years.

III. Ali Majlis of Nakhichevan Autonomous Republic elects chairman of Ali Majlis of Nakhichevan Autonomous Republic and his deputies, establishes permanent and other commissions.

Article 138. Competence of Ali Majlis of Nakhichevan Autonomous Republic

I. Ali Majlis of Nakhichevan Autonomous Republic establishes general procedures concerning the following:
- elections to Ali Majlis of Nakhichevan Autonomous Republic;
- taxes;
- routes of economic development of Nakhichevan Autonomous Republic;
- social maintenance;
- protection of environment;
- tourism;
- protection of health, science, culture.

II. Ali Majlis of Nakhichevan Autonomous Republic accepts laws related to questions specified in the present Article.

Article 139. Questions solved by the Ali Majlis of Nakhichevan Autonomous Republic

I. Ali Majlis of Nakhichevan Autonomous Republic takes decisions concerning the following questions:
- organization of work in Ali Majlis of Nakhichevan Autonomous Republic;
- approval of the budget of Nakhichevan Autonomous Republic;
- approval of economic and social programs of Nakhichevan Autonomous Republic;
- appointment and dismissal of Prime-minister of Nakhichevan Autonomous Republic;
- approval of composition of Cabinet of Ministers of Nakhichevan Autonomous Republic;
- decisions concerning vote of confidence in Cabinet of Ministers of Nakhichevan Autonomous Republic.

II. Ali Majlis of Nakhichevan Autonomous Republic issues decree concerning questions specified in the present Article.

Article 140. Cabinet of Ministers of Nakhichevan Autonomous Republic

   I. Composition of Cabinet of Ministers of Nakhichevan Autonomous Republic recommended by Prime-minister of Nakhichevan Autonomous Republic is approved by Ali Majlis of Nakhichevan Autonomous Republic.
  II. Prime-minister of Nakhichevan Autonomous Republic is appointed by Ali Majlis of Nakhichevan Autonomous Republic on recommendation by the President of the Azerbaijan Republic.
 III. Cabinet of Ministers of Nakhichevan Autonomous Republic:
   • prepares draft of budget of Autonomous Republic and presents it for approval by Ali Majlis of Nakhichevan Autonomous Republic;
   • implements the budget of Autonomous Republic;
   • provides implementation of economic programs of Autonomous Republic;
   • provides implementation of social programs of Autonomous Republic;
   • settles other questions delegated to it by the President of the Azerbaijan Republic.
  IV. Cabinet of Ministers of Nakhichevan Autonomous Republic issues orders and decrees.

Article 141. Local executive power in Nakhichevan Autonomous Republic

In Nakhichevan Autonomous Republic heads of local executive power bodies are appointed by the President of the Azerbaijan Republic on recommendation of the Chairman of Ali Majlis of Nakhichevan Autonomous Republic.

Fourth Section
Local self-government

Chapter IX. Municipalities

Article 142. Organization of local self-government

   I. Local self-government is carried out by municipalities.
  II. Municipalities are formed based on elections.
 III. The foundations of the status of municipalities shall be determined by given Constitution. The regulations of elections to the municipalities shall be determined by law.

. . . . . .

Article 146. Guarantee of inviolability of municipalities

Legal protection of municipalities, compensation of additional expenditures resulted from decisions made by state bodies are guaranteed.

Fifth Section
The right and the law

Chapter X. Legislative system

Article 147. Legal force of Constitution of the Azerbaijan Republic
  I.   Constitution of the Azerbaijan Republic possesses highest legal power.
  II. Constitution of the Azerbaijan Republic possesses direct legal power.
  III. Constitution of the Azerbaijan Republic is the basis of legislative system of the Azerbaijan Republic.

Article 148. Acts constituting legislative system of the Azerbaijan Republic
  I.   Legislative system consists of the following normative-legal acts:
    • Constitution;
    • acts accepted by referendum;
    • laws;
    • orders;
    • decrees of Cabinet of Ministers of the Azerbaijan Republic; normative acts of central executive power bodies.
  II. International agreements wherein the Azerbaijan Republic is one of the parties constitute an integral part of legislative system of the Azerbaijan Republic.
  III. In Nakhichevan Autonomous Republic Constitution and laws of Nakhichevan Autonomous Republic, decrees of the Cabinet of Ministers of Nakhichevan Autonomous Republic also possess legal power.
  IV. Legislative system of Nakhichevan Autonomous Republic should conform to legislative system of the Azerbaijan Republic.
  V.   Within the limits of their authority local bodies of executive power may accept normative acts not contradicting acts constituting the legislative system.

Article 149. Normative-legal acts
  I.   Normative-legal acts should be based on law and justice (same attitude to equal interests).
  II. Use and implementation of acts taken by referendum is obligatory for citizens, legislative, executive and judicial power bodies, legal entities and municipalities only after their publication.
  III. The laws should not contradict the Constitution. Use and implementation of published laws is obligatory for all citizens, legislative, executive and judicial power bodies, legal entities and municipalities.
  IV. Decrees of the President of the Azerbaijan Republic should not contradict the Constitution and laws of the Azerbaijan Republic. Use and implementation of published decrees is obligatory for all citizens, executive power bodies, legal entities.

V. Decrees of Cabinet of Ministers of the Azerbaijan Republic should not contradict the Constitution, laws of the Azerbaijan Republic and decrees of the President of the Azerbaijan Republic. Use and implementation of published decrees of the Cabinet of Ministers is obligatory for citizens, central and local executive power bodies, legal entities.

VI. Acts of central bodies of executive power should not contradict the Constitution, laws of the Azerbaijan Republic, decrees of the President of the Azerbaijan Republic, decrees of Cabinet of Ministers of the Azerbaijan Republic.

VII. Normative-legal acts improving legal situation of physical persons and legal entities, eliminating or mitigating their legal responsibility have reverse power. Other normative-legal acts have no reverse power.

. . . . . .

Article 151. Legal value of international acts

Whenever there is disagreement between normative-legal acts in legislative system of the Azerbaijan Republic (except Constitution of the Azerbaijan Republic and acts accepted by way of referendum) and international agreements wherein the Azerbaijan Republic is one of the parties, provisions of international agreements shall dominate.

Chapter XI. Changes in Constitution of the Azerbaijan Republic

Article 152. Procedure of introduction of changes into Constitution of the Azerbaijan Republic.

Changes in the text of the Constitution of the Azerbaijan Republic may be made only by way of referendum.

. . . . . .

Chapter XII. Amendments to the Constitution of the Azerbaijan Republic

Article 156. Procedure of introduction of amendments to the Constitution of the Azerbaijan Republic

I. Amendments to the Constitution of the Azerbaijan Republic are taken in the form of Constitutional laws in Milli Majlis of the Azerbaijan Republic, by majority of 95 votes.

II. Constitutional laws on amendments to Constitution of the Azerbaijan Republic are put to the vote in Milli Majlis of the Azerbaijan Republic twice. The second voting shall be held 6 months after the first one.

III. Constitutional laws on amendments to Constitution of the Azerbaijan Republic are submitted to the President of the Azerbaijan Republic for signing in an order envisaged in the present Constitution for laws, both after the first and after the second voting.

IV. Constitutional laws and amendments to the Constitution of the Azerbaijan Republic become valid after they have been signed by the President of the Azerbaijan Republic after the second voting.

V. Constitutional laws on amendments are an integral part of Constitution of the Azerbaijan Republic and should not contradict main text of Constitution of the Azerbaijan Republic.

Article 157. Initiative on introduction of amendments to Constitution of the Azerbaijan Republic

Amendments to Constitution of the Azerbaijan Republic may be proposed by the President of the Azerbaijan Republic or at least by 63 deputies of Milli Majlis of the Azerbaijan Republic.

Article 158. Limitation on initiative on introduction of additions to the Constitution of Azerbaijan Republic

There cannot be proposed the introduction of additions to the Constitution of Azerbaijan Republic with respect to provisions envisaged in Chapter I of the present Constitution.

. . . . . .

With modifications introduced to the Constitution as a result of Referendum held on 24 August 24, 2002.

DOCUMENT 2

Constitution of the Republic of Armenia

The Armenian People, Recognizing as a basis the fundamental principles of Armenian statehood and the national aspirations engraved in the Declaration of Independence of Armenia, Having fulfilled the sacred message of its freedom loving ancestors for the restoration of the sovereign state, Committed to the strengthening and prosperity of the fatherland. In order to ensure the freedom, general well being and civic harmony of future generations, Declaring their faithfulness to universal values, Hereby adopts the Constitution of the Republic of Armenia.

Chapter 1. The foundations of constitutional order

Article 1

The Republic of Armenia is a sovereign, democratic state, based on social justice and the rule of law.

Article 2

In the Republic of Armenia power lies with the people. The people exercise their power through free elections and referenda, as well as through state and local self-governing bodies and public officials as provided by the Constitution. The usurpation of power by any organization or individual constitutes a crime.

Article 3
The elections of the President, the National Assembly and local self-governing bodies of the Republic of Armenia, as well as referenda, are held based on the right to universal, equal and direct suffrage by secret ballot.

Article 4
The state guarantees the protection of human rights and freedoms based on the Constitution and the laws, in accordance with the principles and norms of international law.

Article 5
State power shall be exercised in accordance with the Constitution and the laws based on the principle of the separation of the legislative, executive and judicial powers. State bodies and public officials may execute only such acts as authorized by legislation.

Article 6
The supremacy of the law shall be guaranteed in the Republic of Armenia. The Constitution of the Republic has supreme juridical force, and its norms are applicable directly. Laws found to contradict the Constitution as well as other juridical acts found to contradict the Constitution and the law shall have no legal force. Laws shall take effect only after official publication. Unpublished juridical acts pertaining to human rights, freedoms, and duties shall have no juridical force. International treaties that have been ratified are a constituent part of the legal system of the Republic. If norms are provided in these treaties other than those provided by laws of the Republic, then the norms provided in the treaty shall prevail. International treaties that contradict the Constitution may be ratified after making a corresponding amendment to the Constitution.

Article 7
The multiparty system is recognized in the Republic of Armenia. Parties are formed freely and promote the formulation and expression of the political will of the people. Their activities may not contravene the Constitution and the laws, nor may their structure and practice contravene the principles of democracy. Parties shall ensure the openness of their financial activities.

Article 8
The right to property is recognized and protected in the Republic of Armenia. The owner of property may dispose of, use and manage the property at his or her discretion. The right to property may not be exercised so as to cause damage to the environment or infringe on the rights and lawful interests of other persons,

society, or the state. The state shall guarantee the free development and equal
legal protection of all forms of property, the freedom of economic activity and
free economic competition.

Article 9
The foreign policy of the Republic of Armenia shall be conducted in accordance
with the norms of international law, with the aim of establishing good neighborly
and mutually beneficial relations with all states.

Article 10
The state shall ensure the protection and reproduction of the environment and
the rational utilization of natural resources.

Article 11
Historical and cultural monuments and other cultural values are under the care
and protection of the state. Within the framework of principles and norms
of international law, the Republic of Armenia shall promote the protection of
Armenian historical and cultural values located in other countries, and shall support the development of Armenian educational and cultural life.

. . . . . .

Chapter 2. Fundamental human and civil rights and freedoms

Article 14
The procedures for acquiring and terminating citizenship of the Republic of
Armenia are determined by law. Individuals of Armenian origin shall acquire citizenship of the Republic of Armenia through a simplified procedure. A citizen of
the Republic of Armenia may not be a citizen of another state simultaneously.

Article 15
Citizens, regardless of national origin, race, sex, language, creed, political or other
persuasion, social origin, wealth or other status, are entitled to all the rights and
freedoms, and subject to the duties determined by the Constitution and the laws.

Article 16
All are equal before the law and shall be given equal protection of the law without
discrimination.

Article 17
Everyone has the right to life. Until such time as it is abolished, the death pen-
alty may be prescribed by law for particular capital crimes, as an exceptional
punishment.

Article 18
Everyone is entitled to freedom and the right to be secure in their person. No
one may be arrested or searched except as prescribed by law. A person may be

detained only by court order and in accordance with legally prescribed procedures.

Article 19

No one may be subjected to torture and to treatment and punishment that are cruel or degrading to the individual's dignity. No one may be subjected to medical or scientific experimentation without his or her consent.

Article 20

Everyone is entitled to defend his or her private and family life from unlawful interference and defend his or her honor and reputation from attack. The gathering, maintenance, use and dissemination of illegally obtained information about a person's private and family life are prohibited. Everyone has the right to confidentiality in his or her correspondence, telephone conversations, mail, telegraph and other communications, which may only be restricted by court order.

Article 21

Everyone is entitled to privacy in his or her own dwelling. It is prohibited to enter a person's dwelling against his or her own will except under cases prescribed by law. A dwelling may be searched only by court order and in accordance with legal procedures.

Article 22

Every citizen is entitled to freedom of movement and residence within the territory of the Republic. Everyone has the right to leave the Republic. Every citizen is entitled to return to the Republic.

Article 23

Everyone is entitled to freedom of thought, conscience and religion. The freedom to exercise one's religion and beliefs may only be restricted by law on the grounds prescribed in Article 45 of the Constitution.

Article 24

Everyone is entitled to assert his or her opinion. No one shall be forced to retract or change his or her opinion. Everyone is entitled to freedom of speech, including the freedom to seek, receive and disseminate information and ideas through any medium of information, regardless of state borders.

Article 25

Everyone has the right to form associations with other persons, including the right to form or join trade unions. Every citizen is entitled to form political parties with other citizens and join such parties. These rights may be restricted for persons belonging to the armed forces and law enforcement organizations. No one shall be forced to join a political party or association.

Article 26

Citizens are entitled to hold peaceful and unarmed meetings, rallies, demonstrations and processions.

Article 27

Citizens of the Republic of Armenia who have attained the age of eighteen years are entitled to participate in the government of the state directly or through their freely elected representatives. Citizens found to be incompetent by a court ruling, or duly convicted of a crime and serving a sentence may not vote or be elected.

. . . . . .

Article 36

Everyone is entitled to freedom of literary, artistic, scientific and technical creation, to benefit from the achievements of scientific progress and to participate in the cultural life of society. Intellectual property shall be protected by law.

Article 37

Citizens belonging to national minorities are entitled to the preservation of their traditions and the development of their language and culture.

Article 38

Everyone is entitled to defend his or her rights and freedoms by all means not otherwise prescribed by law. Everyone is entitled to defend in court the rights and freedoms engraved in the Constitution and the laws.

Article 39

Everyone is entitled to restore any rights which may have been violated, as well as to a public hearing by an independent and impartial court, under the equal protection of the law and fulfilling all the demands of justice, to clear himself or herself of any accusations. The presence of the news media and representatives of the public at a judicial hearing may be prohibited by law wholly or in part, for the purpose of safeguarding public morality, the social order, national security, the safety of the parties and the interests of justice.

Article 40

Everyone is entitled to receive legal assistance. Legal assistance may be provided free of charge in cases prescribed for by law. Everyone is entitled to legal counsel from the moment he or she is arrested, detained, or charged. Every convicted person is entitled to have his or her conviction reviewed by a higher court, in a manner prescribed by law. Every convicted person is entitled to request a pardon or mitigation of any given punishment. Compensation for the harm caused to the wronged party shall be provided in a manner prescribed by law.

Article 41

A person accused of a crime shall be presumed innocent until proven guilty in a manner prescribed by law, and by a court sentence properly entered

into force. The defendant does not have the burden to prove his or her innocence. Accusations not proven beyond a doubt shall be resolved in favor of
the defendant.

Article 42

A person shall not be compelled to be a witness against himself or herself or against
his or her spouse, or against a close relative. The law may foresee other circumstances
relieving a person from the obligation to testify. Illegally obtained evidence shall not
be used. A punishment may not exceed that which could have been met by the law
in effect when the crime was committed. A person shall not be considered to be
guilty for a crime if at the time of its commission the act was not legally considered
a crime. Laws limiting or increasing liability shall not have retroactive effect.

Article 43

The rights and freedoms set forth in the Constitution are not exhaustive and shall
not be construed to exclude other universally accepted human and civil rights
and freedoms.

Article 44

The fundamental human and civil rights and freedoms established under Articles
23 and 27 of the Constitution may only be restricted by law, if necessary for the
protection of state and public security, public order, public health and morality,
and the rights, freedoms, honor and reputation of others.

Article 45

Some human and civil rights and freedoms, except for those provided under
Articles 17, 20, 39 and 41, 43 of the Constitution, may be temporarily in a manner prescribed by law, in the event of martial law, or in cases prescribed under
paragraph 4 of Article 55 of the Constitution.

. . . . . .

Article 47

Every citizen shall participate in the defense of the Republic of Armenia in a
manner prescribed by law.

Article 48

Everyone shall uphold the Constitution and the laws, and respect the rights, freedoms and dignity of others. The exercise of rights and freedoms shall not serve
toward the violent overthrow of the Constitutional order, for the instigation of
national, racial, or religious hatred or for the incitement to violence and war.

Chapter 3. The President of the Republic

Article 49

The President of the Republic of Armenia shall uphold the Constitution, and
ensure the normal functioning of the legislative, executive and judicial

authorities. The President of the Republic shall be the guarantor of the independence, territorial integrity and security of' the Republic.

Article 50
The President of the Republic shall be elected by the citizens of the Republic of Armenia for a five-year term of office. Every person having attained the age of thirty-five, having been a citizen of the Republic of Armenia for the preceding ten years, having permanently resided in the Republic for the preceding ten years, and having the right to vote is eligible for the Presidency. The same person may not be elected for the post of the President of the Republic for more than two consecutive terms.

Article 51
Elections for the post of President of the Republic shall be held fifty days prior to the expiration of the term of office of the President in office and in accordance with procedures set by the Constitution and the laws. The candidate who received more than half of the votes cast for the presidential candidates shall be considered as having been elected President of the Republic. If the election involved more than two candidates and none received the necessary votes, a second round of elections shall be held on the fourteenth day following the first round of the election, at which time the two candidates having received the highest number of votes in the first round shall participate. The candidate who receives the highest number of votes during this second round shall be considered to have been elected. In the event only one candidate is presented, the candidate shall be considered as having been elected if he or she has received more than half of the votes cast. If a President is not elected, there shall be new elections on the fortieth day after the first round of elections. The President-elect of the Republic shall assume office on the day when the term of the previous President expires. A President who shall be elected by new or extraordinary elections shall assume office within ten days of such elections.

. . . . . .

Article 54
The President of the Republic shall assume office by pledging an oath to the people during a special sitting of the National Assembly.

Article 55
The President of the Republic:
   1) shall address the people and the National Assembly;
   2) shall sign and promulgate within twenty-one days of receipt, laws passed by the National Assembly; during this period, the President may remand a law to the National Assembly with objections and recommendations requesting new deliberations. The President shall sign and publish the law within five days of the second passing of such law by the National Assembly;

3) may dissolve the National Assembly and designate special elections after consultations with the President of the National Assembly and the Prime Minister. Special elections shall be held no sooner than thirty and no later than forty days after the dissolution of the National Assembly. The President may not dissolve the National Assembly during the last six months of his or her term of office;

4) shall appoint and remove the Prime Minister. The President shall appoint and remove the members of the Government upon the recommendation of the Prime Minister. In the event that the National Assembly adopts a vote of no confidence against the Government, the President shall, within twenty one days accept the resignation of the Government, appoint a Prime Minister and form a Government;

5) shall make appointments to civilian positions in cases prescribed by law;

6) may establish advisory bodies.

7) shall represent the Republic of Armenia in international relations, conduct and oversee foreign policy, make international treaties, sign international treaties that are ratified by the National Assembly, ratify intergovernmental agreements;

8) shall appoint and recall the diplomatic representatives of the Republic of Armenia to foreign countries and international organizations, and receive the credentials and letters of recall of diplomatic representatives of foreign countries;

9) shall appoint and remove the Prosecutor General upon the recommendation of the Prime Minister;

10) shall appoint members and the President of the Constitutional Court. He may, on the basis of a determination by the Constitutional Court, remove from office any of his or her appointees to the Court or sanction the arrest of such a member of the Court, and through the judicial process authorize the initiation of administrative or criminal proceedings against that member;

11) shall appoint, in accordance with the procedure provided in Article 95 of the Constitution, the president and judges of the Court of Appeals and its chambers, the courts of review, the courts of first instance and other courts, the deputy prosecutors general and prosecutors heading the organizational subdivisions of the office of the Prosecutor General; may remove from office any judge, sanction the arrest of a judge and through the judicial process, authorize the initiation of administrative or criminal proceedings against a judge and remove the prosecutors that he or she has appointed;

12) is the Commander in Chief of the armed forces and shall appoint the staff of the highest command of the armed forces;

13) shall decide on the use of the armed forces. In the vent of an armed attack against or of an immediate anger to the Republic, or a declaration of war

by the National Assembly, the President shall declare a state of martial law and may call for a general or partial mobilization. Upon the declaration of martial law, a special sitting of the National Assembly shall be held;

14) in the event of an imminent danger to the constitutional order, and upon consultations with the President of the National Assembly and the Prime Minister, shall take measures appropriate to the situation and address the people on the subject;

15) shall grant citizenship of the Republic of Armenia and decide on the granting of political asylum;

16) shall award the orders and medals of the Republic of Armenia and grant the highest military and honorary titles and diplomatic and other titles;

17) may grant pardons to convicted individuals.

Article 56

The President of the Republic may issue orders and decrees which shall be executed throughout the Republic. The orders and decrees of the President of the Republic shall not contravene the Constitution and the laws.

Article 57

The President may be removed from office for state treason or other high crimes. In order to request a determination on questions pertaining to the removal of the President of the Republic from office, the National Assembly must appeal to the Constitutional Court by a resolution adopted by the majority of the deputies. A decision to remove the President of the Republic from office must be reached by the National Assembly by a minimum two thirds majority vote of the total number of deputies, based on the determination of the Constitutional Court.

. . . . . .

Chapter 4. The National Assembly

Article 62

Legislative power in the Republic of Armenia: shall be vested in the National Assembly. Under cases provided by Articles 59, 66, 73, 74, 78, 81, 83, 84, 111, 112 of the Constitution, as well as for purposes of organizing its own activities, the National Assembly shall adopt resolutions which shall be signed and published by its President. The powers of the National Assembly are determined by the Constitution. The National Assembly shall operate in accordance with its rules of procedure.

Article 63

The National Assembly shall have one hundred and thirty one deputies. The authority of the National Assembly shall expire in June of the fourth year following its election, on the opening day of the first session of the newly elected National Assembly, on which day the newly elected National Assembly shall assume its powers. The National Assembly may be dissolved in accordance with the Constitution. A newly elected National Assembly may not be dissolved during a one year period following its election. The National Assembly may not be dissolved during a state of martial law, or under the cases foreseen under paragraph 14 of Article 55 of the Constitution, or when the removal of the President of the Republic from office is being deliberated.

Article 64

Any person having attained the age of twenty five, having been a citizen of the Republic of Armenia for the preceding five years, having permanently resided in the Republic for the preceding five years, and who has the right to vote, may be elected as a Deputy.

. . . . . .

Article 68

Regular elections to the National Assembly shall be held within sixty days prior to the expiration of the term of the current Assembly. Procedures for elections to the National Assembly shall be prescribed by law. The date of elections shall be fixed by Presidential decree. The first session of a newly elected National Assembly shall convene on the second Thursday following the election of at least two-thirds of the total number of Deputies. Until the election of the President of the National Assembly, its meetings shall be chaired by the Deputy who is most senior in age.

. . . . . .

Article 71

Laws and resolutions of the National Assembly shall be passed by the majority vote of the Deputies present at a given sitting, if more than half of the total number of Deputies participate in the voting, except for cases covered under Articles 57, 58, 59, 72, 74, 84, 111 of the Constitution, and paragraph 4 of Article 75, the first paragraph of Article 79, and Section 3 of Article 83 of the Constitution.

Article 72

The National Assembly shall deliberate on a priority basis any law which has been remanded by the President. Should the National Assembly decline to accept the recommendations and objections presented by the President of the Republic, it shall pass the remanded law, again with a majority vote of the number of Deputies.

. . . . . .

Article 74

Within twenty days of the formation of a newly elected National Assembly or of its own formation, the Government shall present its program to the National Assembly for its approval, thus raising the question of a vote of confidence before the National Assembly. A draft resolution expressing a vote of no confidence toward the Government may be proposed within twenty-four hours of the Government's raising of the question of the vote of confidence by not less than one third of the total number of Deputies. The proposal for a vote of no confidence shall be voted on no sooner than forty-eight hours and no later than seventy-two hours from its initial submittal. The proposal must be passed by a majority vote of the total number of Deputies. If a vote of no confidence toward the Government is not proposed, or such proposal is not passed, the Government's program shall be considered to have been approved by the National Assembly. If a vote of no confidence is passed, the Prime Minister shall submit the resignation of the Government to the President of the Republic.

Article 75
The right to initiate legislation in the National Assembly shall belong to the Deputies and the Government. The Government shall stipulate the sequence for debate of its proposed draft legislation and may request that they be voted on only with amendments acceptable to it. Any draft legislation which is considered urgent by a Government resolution shall be debated and voted on by the National Assembly within a one month period. The National Assembly shall consider all draft legislation reducing state revenues or increasing state expenditures only upon the agreement of the Government and shall pass such legislation by a majority vote of the total number of Deputies. The Government may raise the question of a vote of confidence in conjunction with its proposed legislation. If the National Assembly does not adopt a vote of no confidence against the Government as provided by Article 74 of the Constitution, then the Government's proposed legislation will be considered to have been adopted. The Government may not raise the issue of a vote of confidence in conjunction with a proposed legislation more than twice during any single session.

. . . . . .

Article 78
In order to ensure the legislative basis of the Government's program, the National Assembly may authorize the Government to adopt resolutions that have the effect of law that do not contravene any laws in force during a period specified by the National Assembly. Such resolutions must be signed by the President of the Republic.

Article 79
The National Assembly shall elect its President for the duration of its full term by a majority vote of the total number of Deputies. The President of the National Assembly shall chair the sittings, manage its material and financial resources, and shall ensure its normal functioning. The National Assembly shall elect two Vice Presidents of the National Assembly.

. . . . . .

Article 81

Upon the recommendation of the President of the Republic, the National Assembly:
1) may declare an amnesty;
2) shall ratify or revoke the international treaties signed by the Republic of Armenia. The range of international agreements which are subject to ratification by the National Assembly shall be prescribed by law;
3) may declare war.

The National Assembly, upon the determination of the Constitutional Court, may suspend the execution of the provisions of Sections 13 and 14 of Article 55 of the Constitution.

Article 82

The National Assembly, upon the recommendation of the Government, shall determine the administrative territorial divisions of the Republic.

Article 83

The National Assembly:
1) shall appoint the Chairman of the Central Bank upon the recommendation of the President of the Republic;
2) shall appoint the Chairman of the National Assembly's Oversight Office upon the recommendation of the President of the National Assembly and members and the President of the Constitutional Court from among the members of the Court. If within thirty days of the formation of the Constitutional Court the National Assembly fails to appoint the President of the Constitutional Court, the President of the Constitutional Court shall then be appointed by the President of the Republic;
3) may, upon the determination of the Constitutional Court, terminate the powers of a member of the Constitutional Court the Assembly has appointed, approve such member's arrest, and authorize the initiation of administrative or criminal proceedings against such member through the judicial process.

Article 84

The National Assembly may adopt a vote of no confidence toward the Government by a majority vote of the total number of Deputies. The National Assembly may not exercise this right in situations of martial law or under circumstances provided by Section 14 of Article 55 of the Constitution.

Chapter 5. The government

Article 85

Executive power in the Republic of Armenia shall be vested in the Government of the Republic of Armenia. The Government shall be composed of the Prime

Minister and the Ministers. The powers of the Government shall be determined by the Constitution and by laws. The organization and rules of operation of the Government shall be determined by a decree of the President of the Republic, upon the recommendation of the Prime Minister.

Article 86
The meetings of the Government shall be chaired by the President of the Republic, or upon his or her recommendation, by the Prime Minister. Government decisions shall be signed by the Prime Minister and approved by the President. The Prime Minister shall convene and chair a Government meeting when requested by the majority of Government members under the circumstances foreseen in Article 59 of the Constitution.

Article 87
The Prime Minister shall oversee the Government's regular activities and shall coordinate the work of the Ministers. The Prime Minister may adopt resolutions. In cases prescribed by the rules of operations of the Government, resolutions approved by the Prime Minister may also be signed by the Minister responsible for the implementation of the resolution.

Article 88
A member of the Government may not be a member of any representative body, hold any other public office, or engage in any other paid occupation.

Article 89
The Government:
1) shall submit its program to the National Assembly for approval in accordance with Article 74 of the Constitution;
2) shall submit the draft state budget to the National Assembly for approval, guarantee the implementation of the budget and submit financial reports on the budget to the National Assembly;
3) shall manage state property;
4) shall ensure the implementation of unified state policies in the areas of finances, economy, taxation and loans and credits;
5) shall ensure the implementation of state policies in the areas of science, education, culture, health, social security and environmental protection;
6) shall ensure the implementation of the defense, national security and foreign policies of the Republic;
7) shall take measures toward the strengthening of legality, the protection of the rights and freedoms of citizens and the protection of property and public order.

. . . . . .

Chapter 6. Judicial power

Article 91

In the Republic of Armenia justice shall be administered solely by the courts in accordance with the Constitution and the laws. In cases prescribed by law, trials are held with the participation of a jury.

Article 92

The Courts of general jurisdiction in the Republic of Armenia shall be the courts of first instance, the review courts and the court of appeals. In the Republic of Armenia, there shall also be economic, military and other courts as may be provided by law. The establishment of extraordinary courts is prohibited.

Article 93

Sentences, verdicts and decisions entered into legal force may be reviewed by the court of appeals based on appeals filed by the Prosecutor General, his or her deputies, or specially licensed lawyers registered with the court of appeals.

Article 94

The President of the Republic shall be the guarantor of the independence of the judicial bodies. He or she shall preside over the Judicial Council. The Minister of Justice and the Prosecutor General shall be the vice presidents of the Council. The Council shall include fourteen members appointed by the President of the Republic for a period of five years, including two legal scholars, nine judges and three prosecutors. Three Council members shall be appointed each from among the judges of the courts of first instance, the courts of review and the court of appeals. The general assembly of judges shall submit three candidates by secret ballot for each seat allocated to judges. The Prosecutor General shall submit the names of candidates for the prosecutors' seats in the Council.

Article 95

The Judicial Council:
1) shall, upon the recommendation of the Minister of Justice, draft and submit for the approval of the President of the Republic the annual list of judges, in view of their competence and professional advancement, which shall be used as the basis for appointments.
2) shall, upon the recommendation of the Prosecutor General, draft and submit for the approval of the President of the Republic the annual list of prosecutors, in view of their competence and professional advancement, which shall be used as the basis for appointments.
3) shall propose candidates for the presidency of the court of appeals, the presidency and judgeship positions of its chambers, the presidency of the courts of review, courts of first instance and other courts. It shall make

recommendations about the other judicial candidates proposed by the
Ministry of Justice;

4) shall make recommendations regarding the candidates for Deputy Prosecutor proposed by the Prosecutor General, and the candidates for prosecutors heading operational divisions in the Office of the Prosecutor;

5) shall make recommendations regarding training programs for judges and
   prosecutors;

6) shall make recommendations regarding the removal from office of a judge,
   the arrest of a judge, and the initiation of administrative or criminal proceedings through the judicial process against a judge;

7) shall take disciplinary action against judges. The president of the court of
   appeals shall chair the meetings of the Judicial Council when the Council
   is considering disciplinary action against a judge. The President of the
   Republic, the Minister of Justice and the Prosecutor General shall not take
   part in these meetings;

8) shall express its opinion on issues of pardons when requested by the
   President of the Republic. The operational procedures of the Judicial
   Council shall be prescribed by law.

Article 96

Judges and members of the Constitutional Court are appointed for life. A judge
may hold office until the age of 65, while a member of the Constitutional Court
may do so until the age of 70. They may be removed from office only in accordance with the Constitution and the laws.

. . . . . .

Article 98

Judges and members of the Constitutional Court may not hold any other public
office, nor engage in any other paid occupation, except for scientific, educational
and creative work. Judges and members of the Constitutional Court may not be
members of any political party nor engage in any political activity.

Article 99

The Constitutional Court shall be composed of nine members, five of whom
shall be appointed by the National Assembly and four by the President of the
Republic.

Article 100

The Constitutional Court, in accordance with the law:

1) shall decide on whether the laws, the resolutions of the National Assembly,
   the orders and decrees of the President of the Republic and the resolutions
   of Government are in conformity with the Constitution;

2) shall decide, prior to the ratification of an international treaty, whether the
   obligations assumed therein are in conformity with the Constitution;

3) shall rule on disputes concerning referenda and the results of presidential and parliamentary elections;

4) shall ascertain the existence of insurmountable obstacles facing a presidential candidate or the elimination of such obstacles;

5) shall determine whether there are grounds for the removal of the President of the Republic;

6) shall determine whether there are grounds for the application of Sections 13 and 14 of Article 55 of the Constitution;

7) shall determine whether the President of the Republic is incapable of continuing to perform his or her functions;

8) shall determine whether there are grounds for the removal of a member of the Constitutional Court, his or her arrest or initiation of administrative or criminal proceedings through the judicial process;

9) shall decide on the suspension or prohibition of a political party in cases prescribed by law.

. . . . . .

Article 102

The Constitutional Court shall render its decisions and findings no later than thirty days after a case has been filed. The decisions of the Constitutional Court shall be final, may not be subject to review and shall enter into legal force upon their publication. The Constitutional Court shall decide with a majority vote of its total number of members on matters pertaining to Sections I through 4 of Article 100 of the Constitution, and with a vote of two-thirds of its members on matters pertaining to Sections 5 through 9 of Article 100.

. . . . . .

Chapter 7. Territorial administration and local self-government

Article 104

The administrative territorial units of the Republic of Armenia shall be the provinces and districts. Provinces shall include urban and rural districts.

Article 105

Districts shall have local self-government. To manage the property of the district and to solve problems of local significance, self governing local bodies shall be elected for a period of three years: a Council of Elders, composed of five to fifteen members, and a District Administrator: a City Mayor or Village Mayor. The District Administrator shall organize his or her staff.

. . . . . .

Article 107

The provinces shall be governed by the state Government. The Government shall appoint and remove the Governors of the provinces, who shall implement the

Government's regional policy and coordinate the regional activities of republican executive bodies.

. . . . . .

Article 110
The election procedure of local self-governing bodies and their powers shall be determined by the Constitution and the laws.

Chapter 8. Adoption of the Constitution, amendments and referendum

Article 111
The Constitution shall be adopted or amended by referendum which may be initiated by the President of the Republic or the National Assembly. The President of the Republic shall call a referendum upon the request or agreement of the majority of the Deputies of the National Assembly. The President of the Republic may remand the Draft Constitution or the draft of constitutional amendments, within twenty-one days following their submittal back to the National Assembly, with his or her objections and suggestions, requesting a reexamination. The President of the Republic will submit to a referendum within the period prescribed by the National Assembly a draft Constitution or draft constitutional amendments, when they are reintroduced by at least two-thirds of the total number of Deputies of the National Assembly.

Article 112
Laws may be submitted to a referendum upon the request of the National Assembly or the Government in accordance with Article 111 of the Constitution. Laws passed by referendum may only be amended by referendum.

Article 113
A proposed legislation submitted to a referendum shall be considered to have been passed if it receives more than fifty percent of the votes, but not less than one-third of the number of registered voters.

Article 114
Articles 1, 2 and 114 of the Constitution may not be amended.

Chapter 9. Provisions for the transitional period

Article 115
Referendum results and upon its publication.

Article 116
From the moment the Constitution enters into force:
   1) The 1978 Constitution, its subsequent amendments and supplements, as well as related constitutional laws shall become inoperative;

2) Laws and other legal acts of the Republic of Armenia shall have the force of law to the extent they do not contravene this Constitution;

3) The President of the Republic shall exercise the powers reserved to him or her by the Constitution. Until the expiration of his powers, the Vice-President of the Republic shall carry out the instructions of the President of the Republic;

4) The National Assembly shall exercise the powers reserved to it by the Constitution. The provisions of Section I of Article 63, Article 64 and Section I of Article 65 of the Constitution shall apply to the sessions of the next National Assembly. Until that time, Articles 4 and 5 of the Constitutional Law dated March 27, 1995, shall be effective;

5) Until the formation of the Constitutional Court, international treaties shall be ratified without its determination;

6) Until the adoption of legislation pertaining to regional governments and local self-governing bodies in conformity with the Constitution, current village, town, city and regional councils of deputies and their executive bodies shall continue to exercise their powers as prescribed by law. Until legislation on territorial government and local self-government is adopted, the right to adopt a vote of no confidence toward the chairmen of deputies to the city and regional councils belongs to the National Assembly;

7) Until the adoption of legislation pertaining to court systems and procedures and the establishment of the new judicial system in conformance with the Constitution, the regional (city) people's courts and the Supreme Court shall continue to operate in accordance with their previous authorities;

8) Until the establishment of economic courts, the State Arbitrage shall continue to operate in accordance to their previous prerogatives;

9) The authority of the judges of the regional (city) people's court shall be extended for a maximum period of six months, during which the President of the Republic, upon the recommendation of the Judicial Council, shall appoint new judges for these courts for a period of three years;

10) The authority of the members of the Supreme Court shall be extended until the establishment of the court of appeals, but not for a period to exceed three years;

11) Until the institution of the new judicial system, the Judicial Council shall consist of eleven members appointed by the President of the Republic, composed of two legal scholars, six judges and three public prosecutors. Three Council members shall be appointed from among the judges of the regional (city) people's courts and three from the Supreme Court, in accordance with the provisions of Article 94 of the Constitution. The Council shall be headed by the President of the Republic. The Minister of Justice and the Prosecutor General shall serve as its Council's Vice Presidents. The Judicial Council shall exercise the powers reserved to it by the Constitution;

12) Until the passage of the law on the Office of the Persecutor General, the latter shall exercise the powers reserved for to it by the Constitution in accordance with current legislation;
13) The Supreme Court shall review court verdicts, judgments and decisions which have the force of law, when these are appealed by the Prosecutor General, his or her deputies and specially licensed lawyers registered with the Supreme Court;
14) Until the Criminal Code is made to conform with the Constitution, current procedures for searches and arrests shall remain in effect.

Article 117
The day the Constitution is adopted shall be proclaimed a holiday known as Constitution Day.

DOCUMENT 3

Constitution of Georgia

Adopted on August 24, 1995

Last amendment December 27, 2006

The citizens of Georgia,
Whose firm will is to establish a democratic social order, economic freedom, a rule-of-law based social State,
To secure universally recognized human rights and freedoms,
To enhance the state independence and peaceful relations with other people,
bearing in mind the centuries-old traditions of the Statehood of the Georgian Nation and the basic principles of the Constitution of Georgia of 1921,
Proclaim nation-wide the present Constitution.

Chapter 1
General Provisions

Article 1
1. Georgia shall be an independent, unified and indivisible state, as confirmed by the Referendum of 31 March 1991, held throughout the territory of the country, including the Autonomous Soviet Socialist Republic of Abkhazia and the Former Autonomous Region of South Ossetia and by the Act of Restoration of the State Independence of Georgia of 9 April 1991.
2. The form of political structure of the state of Georgia shall be a democratic republic.
3. "Georgia" shall be the name of the state of Georgia.

Article 2

1. The territory of the state of Georgia shall be determined as of 21 December 1991. The territorial integrity of Georgia and the inviolability of the state frontiers, being recognized by the world community of nations and international organizations, shall be confirmed by the Constitution and laws of Georgia.
2. The alienation of the territory of Georgia shall be prohibited. The state frontiers shall be changed only by a bilateral agreement concluded with the neighbouring State.
3. The territorial state structure of Georgia shall be determined by a Constitutional Law on the basis of the principle of circumscription of authorisation after the complete restoration of the jurisdiction of Georgia over the whole territory of the country.
4. The citizens of Georgia shall regulate the matters of local importance through local self-government without the prejudice to the state sovereignty. The office of the superiors of the executive bodies and a representative office of local self-government shall be electoral. The procedure of the creation of the bodies of local self- government, their authority and relation with state bodies shall be determined by the Organic Law. (6.02.2004, # 3272)

Article 3

1. The following shall fall within the exclusive competence of higher state bodies of Georgia:
   a) legislation on Georgian citizenship, human rights and freedoms, emigration and immigration, entrance and leaving the country, temporary or permanent residence of citizens of foreign states and stateless persons in Georgia;
   b) the status, boundary regime and defense of the state frontiers; the status and defense of territorial waters, airspace, the continental shelf and Exclusive Economic Zone;
   c) state defense and security, armed forces, military industry and trade in arms;
   d) the issues of war and peace, the determination of a legal regime of the state of emergency and the martial law and their introduction;
   e) foreign policy and international relations;
   f) foreign trade, customs and tariff regimes;
   g) state finances and state loan; issuing money; legislation on banking, credit, insurance and taxes;
   h) standards and models; geodesy and cartography; determination of the exact time; state statistics;
   i) a unified energetic system and regime; communications; merchant fleet; ensigns; harbours of general state importance; airports and

aerodromes; control of airspace, transit and air transport, registration of
air transport; meteorological service; environmental observation system;

j) railways and motor roads of state importance;

k) fishing in ocean and high seas;

l) frontier-sanitary cordon;

m) legislation on pharmaceutical medicines;

n) legislation on accreditation of educational institutions and academic
degrees; (27.12.06)

o) legislation on intellectual property;

p) legislation on trade law, criminal law, civil law, administrative law and
labour law, penitentiary and procedures legislation;

q) criminal police and investigation;

r) legislation on land, subsoil and natural resources;

2. Issues falling within the joint competence shall be determined separately.

3. The status of the Autonomous Republic of Ajara shall be determined by
the Constitutional Law of Georgia "On the Status of the Autonomous
Republic of Ajara". (added by the Constitutional Law of Georgia of
20 April 2000)

Article 4

1. After the creation of appropriate conditions and formation of the bodies
of local self-government throughout the whole territory of Georgia two
chambers shall be set up within the Parliament of Georgia: the Council
of Republic and the Senate.

2. The Council of Republic shall consist of members elected after a proportional system.

3. The Senate shall consist of members elected from Abkhazia, the Autonomous Republic of Ajara and other territorial units of Georgia and five
members appointed by the President of Georgia. (Added by the Constitutional Law of Georgia of 20 April 2000.)

4. The composition, authority and election procedure of the chambers shall
be determined By the Organic Law.

Article 5

1. The people shall be the source of state authority in Georgia. The state
authority shall be exercised within the framework established by the
Constitution.

2. The people shall exercise their authority through referendum, other forms
of direct democracy and their representatives.

3. No one shall have the right to seize the authority or usurp it.

4. State authority shall be exercised on the basis of the principle of separation
of powers.

Article 6
1. The Constitution of Georgia shall be the supreme law of the state. All other legal acts shall correspond to the Constitution.
2. The legislation of Georgia shall correspond to universally recognized principles and rules of international law. An international treaty or agreement of Georgia unless it contradicts the Constitution of Georgia, the Constitutional Agreement, shall take precedence over domestic normative acts. (Change is added by the Constitutional Law of Georgia of 30 March 2001.)

Article 7
The state shall recognize and protect universally recognized human rights and freedoms as eternal and supreme human values. While exercising authority, the people and the state shall be bound by these rights and freedoms as directly acting law.

Article 8
The state language of Georgia shall be Georgian, and in Abkhazia—also Abkhazian. (Change is added by the Constitutional Law of Georgia of 10 October 2002.)

Article 9
1. The state shall declare complete freedom of belief and religion, as well as shall recognize the special role of the Apostle Autocephalous Orthodox Church of Georgia in the history of Georgia and its independence from the state.
2. The relations between the state of Georgia and the Apostle Autocephalous Orthodox Church of Georgia shall be determined by the Constitutional Agreement. The Constitutional Agreement shall correspond completely to universally recognized principles and norms of international law, in particular, in the field of human rights and fundamental freedoms. (change is added by the Constitutional Law of Georgia of 30 March 2001.)

. . . . . .

Chapter 2
Georgian Citizenship. Basic Rights and Freedoms of Individual

Article 12
1. Georgian citizenship shall be acquired by birth and naturalization.
2. A citizen of Georgia shall not at the same time be a citizen of another state, save in cases established by this paragraph. Citizenship of Georgia shall be granted by the President of Georgia to a citizen of foreign country, who has a special merit before Georgia or grant the citizenship of Georgia to him/her is due to State interests. (6.02.2004.N3272)

3. The procedure for the acquisition and loss of citizenship shall be determined by the Organic Law.

Article 13

1. Georgia shall protect its citizen regardless of his/her whereabouts.
2. No one shall be deprived of his/her citizenship.
3. The expulsion of a citizen of Georgia from Georgia shall be impermissible.
4. The extradition/transfer of a citizen of Georgia to the foreign state shall be impermissible,
   except for the cases prescribed by international treaty. A decision on extradition/transfer may be appealed in a court.

Article 14

Everyone is free by birth and is equal before law regardless of race, colour, language, sex, religion, political and other opinions, national, ethnic and social belonging, origin, property and title, place of residence.

Article 15

1. Everyone has the inviolable right to life and this right shall be protected by law.
2. Capital punishment is prohibited. (27.12.06)
3. Physical or mental coercion of a person detained or otherwise restricted in his/her liberty is impermissible. (27.12.06)

. . . . . .

Article 17

1. Honor and dignity of an individual is inviolable.
2. Torture, inhuman, cruel treatment and punishment or treatment and punishment infringing upon honor and dignity shall be impermissible.

Article 18

1. Liberty of an individual is inviolable.
2. Deprivation of liberty or other restriction of personal liberty without a court decision shall be impermissible.
3. An arrest of an individual shall be permissible by a specially authorized official in the cases determined by law. Everyone arrested or otherwise restricted in his/her liberty shall be brought before a competent court not later than 48 hours. If, within next 24 hours, the court fails to adjudicate upon the detention or another type of restriction of liberty, the individual shall immediately be released.
4. Deleted (27.12.06)
5. An arrested or detained person shall be informed about his/her rights and the grounds for restriction of his/her liberty upon his/her arrest or detention. The arrested or detained person may request for the assistance of a defender upon his/her arrest or detention, the request shall be met.

6. The term of arrest of a suspect in the commission of a crime shall not exceed 72 hours and the term of detention on remand of an accused shall not exceed 9 months.
7. The violation of the requirements of the present Article shall be punishable by law. A person arrested or detained illegally shall have the right to receive a compensation.

Article 19

1. Everyone has the right to freedom of speech, thought, conscience, religion and belief.
2. The persecution of a person on the account of his/her speech, thought, religion or belief as well as the compulsion to express his/her opinion about them shall be impermissible.
3. The restriction of the freedoms enumerated in the present Article shall be impermissible unless their manifestation infringes upon the rights of others.

Article 20

1. Everyone's private life, place of personal activity, personal records, correspondence, communication by telephone or other technical means, as well as messages received through technical means shall be inviolable. Restriction of the aforementioned rights shall be permissible by a court decision or also without such decision in the case of the urgent necessity provided for by law.
2. No one shall have the right to enter the house and other possessions against the will of possessors, or conduct search unless there is a court decision or the urgent necessity provided for by law.

. . . . . .

Article 22

1. Everyone legally within the territory of Georgia shall, within throughout the territory of the country, have the right to liberty of movement and freedom to choose his/her residence.
2. Everyone legally within the territory of Georgia shall be free to leave Georgia. A citizen of Georgia may freely enter Georgia.
3. These rights may be restricted only in accordance with law, in the interests of securing national security or public safety, protection of health, prevention of crime or administration of justice that is necessary for maintaining a democratic society.

. . . . . .

Article 24

1. Everyone has the right to freely receive and impart information, to express and impart his/her opinion orally, in writing or by in any other means.
2. Mass media shall be free. The censorship shall be impermissible.

3. Neither the state nor particular individuals shall have the right to monopolize mass media or means of dissemination of information.

4. The exercise of the rights enumerated in the first and second paragraphs of the present Article may be restricted by law on such conditions which are necessary in a democratic society in the interests of ensuring state security, territorial integrity or public safety, for preventing of crime, for the protection of the rights and dignity of others, for prevention of the disclosure of information acknowledged as confidential or for ensuring the independence and impartiality of justice.

Article 25

1. Everyone, except members of the armed forces and Ministry of Internal Affairs, has the right to public assembly without arms either indoors or outdoors without prior permission. (23.12.2005, # 2494)

2. The necessity of prior notification of the authorities may be established by law in the case where a public assembly or manifestation is held on a public thoroughfare.

3. Only the authorities shall have the right to brake up a public assembly or manifestation in case it assumes an illegal character.

Article 26

1. Everyone shall have the right to form and to join public associations, including trade unions.

2. Citizens of Georgia shall have the right to form a political party or other political association and participate in its activity in accordance with the Organic Law.

3. The formation and activity of such public and political associations aiming at overthrowing or forcibly changing the constitutional structure of Georgia, infringing upon the independence and territorial integrity of the country or propagandising war or violence, provoking national, local, religious or social animosity, shall be impermissible.

4. The creation of armed formations by public and political associations shall be impermissible.

5. A person who is enrolled in the personnel of the armed forces or the forces of the bodies o internal affairs or a person having been designated as a judge or a prosecutor shall cease his/her membership of any political association. (23.12.2005, # 2494)

6. Suspension or prohibition of the activity of public or political associations shall be possible only under a court decision, in the cases determined by the Organic Law and in accordance with a procedure prescribed by law.

Article 27

The state shall be entitled to impose restriction on the political activity of citizens of a foreign country and stateless persons.

Article 28

1. Every citizen of Georgia who has attained the age of 18 shall have the right to participate in referendum or elections of state and self-government bodies. Free expression of the will of electors shall be guaranteed.
2. A citizen, who is recognized as legally incapable by a court or who is detained in a penitentiary institution following a conviction by a court, shall have no right to participate in elections and referendum.

Article 29

1. Every citizen of Georgia shall have the right to hold any state position if he/she meets the requirements established by legislation.
2. The conditions of public office shall be determined by law.

. . . . . .

Article 31

The state shall take care for the equal socioeconomic development of the whole territory of the country. With the view of ensuring the socioeconomic progress of the high mountain regions special privileges shall be determined by law.

. . . . . .

Article 34

1. The state shall promote the development of culture, the unrestricted participation of citizens in cultural life, expression and enrichment of cultural originality, recognition of national and common values and deepening of international cultural relations.
2. Every citizen of Georgia shall be obliged to care for the protection and preservation of the cultural heritage. The state shall protect the cultural heritage by law.

. . . . . .

Article 38

1. Citizens of Georgia shall be equal in social, economic, cultural and political life irrespective of their national, ethnic, religious or linguistic belonging. In accordance with universally recognized principles and rules of international law, they shall have the right to develop freely, without any discrimination and interference, their culture, to use their mother tongue in private and in public.
2. In accordance with universally recognized principles and rules of international law, the exercise of minority rights shall not oppose the sovereignty, state structure, territorial integrity and political independence of Georgia.

Article 39

The Constitution of Georgia shall not deny other universally recognized rights, freedoms and guarantees of an individual and a citizen, which are not referred to herein but stem inherently from the principles of the Constitution.

Article 40

1. An individual shall be presumed innocent until the commission of an offense by him/her is proved in accordance with the procedure prescribed by law and under a final judgment of conviction.
2. No one shall be obliged to prove his innocence. A burden of proof shall rest with the prosecutor.
3. A resolution on preceding a person as an accused, a bill of indictment and a judgment of conviction shall be based only on the evidence beyond a reasonable doubt. An accused shall be given the benefit of doubt in any event.

. . . . . .

Article 42

1. Everyone has the right to apply to a court for the protection of his/her rights and freedoms.
2. Everyone shall be tried only by a court under jurisdiction of which his/her case is.
3. The right to defense shall be guaranteed.
4. No one shall be convicted twice for the same crime.
5. No one shall be held responsible on account of an action, which did not constitute a criminal offense at the time it was committed. The law that neither mitigate nor abrogate responsibility shall have no retroactive force.
6. The accused shall have the right to request summonsing and interrogation of his/her witnesses under the same conditions as witnesses of the prosecution.
7. Evidence obtained in contravention of law shall have no legal force.
8. No one shall be obliged to testify against himself/herself or those relatives whose circle shall be determined by law.
9. Everyone having sustained illegally a damage by the state, self-government bodies and officials shall be guaranteed to receive complete compensation from state funds through the court proceedings.

Article 43

1. The protection of human rights and fundamental freedoms within the territory of Georgia shall be supervised by the Public Defender of Georgia who shall be elected for a term of five years by the majority of the total number of the members of the Parliament of Georgia.
2. The Public Defender shall be authorized to reveal facts of the violation of human rights and freedoms and to report on them to corresponding

bodies and officials. The creation of impediments to the activity of the
Public Defender shall be punishable by law.

3. The authority of the Public Defender shall be determined by the
   Organic Law.

Article 44

1. Everyone residing in Georgia shall be obliged to observe the requirements
   of the Constitution and legislation of Georgia.
2. The exercise of the rights and freedoms of an individual shall not infringe
   upon the rights and freedoms of others.

. . . .

Article 46

1. In case of a state emergency or martial law, the President of Georgia shall
   be authorized to restrict the rights and freedoms enumerated in Articles
   18, 20, 21, 22, 24, 25, 30, 33 and 41 of the Constitution either throughout the whole country or a certain part thereof. The President shall be
   obliged to submit the decision to the Parliament for approval within
   48 hours.
2. In case of introduction of a state of emergency or martial law throughout
   the whole territory of the state, elections of the President of Georgia, the
   Parliament of Georgia or other representative bodies of Georgia shall be
   held upon the cancellation of the state. In case of introduction of a state
   of emergency in a certain part of the state the Parliament of Georgia shall
   adopt a decision on holding the elections throughout the other territories
   of the state. (6.02.2004.N3272)

Article 47

1. Foreign citizens and stateless persons residing in Georgia shall have the
   rights and obligations equal to the rights and obligations of citizens of
   Georgia with exceptions envisaged by the Constitution and law.
2. In accordance with universally recognized rules of international law, the
   procedure established by law, Georgia shall grant asylum to foreign citizens and stateless persons.
3. It shall be inadmissible to extradite/transfer an individual seeking a shelter,
   being persecuted for political creed or prosecuted for an action not
   regarded as a crime under the legislation of Georgia.

Chapter 3
The Parliament of Georgia

Article 48

The Parliament of Georgia shall be the supreme representative body of the country, which shall exercise legislative power, determine the principal directions of

domestic and foreign policy, exercise control over the activity of the Government within the framework determined by the Constitution and discharge other powers.

Article 49

1. The Parliament of Georgia shall consist of 100 members of the Parliament elected by a proportional system and 50 members of Parliament elected by a majority system for a term of four years on the basis of universal, equal and direct suffrage by secret ballot. (23.02.2005 # 1010)
2. A citizen, who has attained the age of 25, having the right to vote, may be elected a member of the Parliament.
3. The internal structure of the Parliament and procedure of its activity shall be determined by the Regulations of the Parliament.
4. The current expenditure for the Parliament of Georgia in the State Budget comparatively to the amount of budgetary means of the previous year may be reduced only by the prior consent of the Parliament. The Parliament shall adopt a decision itself on the distribution of the budgetary means of the Parliament in the State Budget. (6.02.2004.N3272)

. . . . . .

Article 51

The Parliament shall be dissolved by the President only in cases determined by the Constitution, save for:
   a. within six months from the holding of the elections of the Parliament;
   b. discharging of an authority determined by Article 63 of the Constitution by the Parliament;
   c. in time of a state of emergency or martial law;
   d. within the last 6 months of the term of office of the President of Georgia. (6.02.2004.N3272)

Article 52

1. A member of the Parliament of Georgia shall be a representative of the whole of Georgia. He/she shall enjoy a free mandate and his/her recall shall be impermissible.
2. Arrest or detention of a member of the Parliament, the search of his/her apartment, car, workplace or his/her person shall be permissible only by the consent of the Parliament, except in the cases when he/she is caught flagrante delicto which shall immediately be notified to the Parliament. Unless the Parliament gives the consent, the arrested or detained member of the Parliament shall immediately be released. (23.04.2004, # 6)
3. A member of the Parliament shall have the right not to testify on the fact disclosed to him/her as to a member of the Parliament. Seizure of written materials connected with this matter shall be impermissible. The right

shall also be reserved to a member of the Parliament after the termination of his/her office.

4. A member of the Parliament shall not be proceeded on the account of the ideas and opinions expressed by him/her in and outside the Parliament while performing his/her duties.

5. The conditions of unimpeded exercise of the authority by a member of the Parliament shall be guaranteed. On the basis of the application of a member of the Parliament the state bodies shall ensure his/her personal security.

6. The creation of impediments to the discharge of the duties by a member of the Parliament shall be punishable by law.

. . . . . .

Article 55

1. The Parliament of Georgia for the term of its authority, in accordance with a procedure established by the Regulations of the Parliament shall elect the President and the Vice-Presidents of the Parliament by a secret ballot, inter alia, one from the members of the Parliament elected respectively in Abkhazia and the Autonomous Republic of Ajara upon the submission of the latter. (The change is added by the Constitutional Law of Georgia of 20 April 2000)

2. The President of the Parliament shall lead the work of the Parliament, ensure free expression of opinions, sign acts adopted by the Parliament, perform other authorities provided for by the Regulations of the Parliament.

3. A Vice-President shall perform the responsibilities of the President under the instructions of the latter, in case of inability of the President to discharge his/her authority or his/her dismissal.

4. The President of the Parliament shall exercise all administrative functions in the House of the Parliament in accordance with a procedure provided for by the Regulations of the Parliament.

. . . . . .

Article 58

1. The members of the Parliament shall be entitled to unite in a Parliamentary Faction. The number of the members of the Parliamentary Faction shall be not less than seven. (23.02.2005, # 1010)

2. The formation and functioning procedure of a faction and its authority shall be determined by law and the Regulations of the Parliament.

. . . . . .

Article 62

Decision of the Parliament on the issues of war and peace, state of emergency or martial law and issues determined by Article 46 of the Constitution shall be adopted by the majority of the total number of the members of the Parliament.

Article 63

1. Under the circumstances defined in the second paragraph of Article 75, not less than one-third of the total number of the members of the Parliament shall be entitled to raise the question of the dismissal of the President of Georgia in accordance with impeachment procedure. The case shall be submitted to the Supreme Court or Constitutional Court for a conclusion.

2. If, by its conclusion, the Supreme Court confirmed corpus delicti in the act of the President or the Constitutional Court confirmed the violation of the Constitution, after having discussed the conclusion the Parliament shall adopt a decision by the majority of votes of the total number of the members of the Parliament on putting the issue of impeachment of the President to the vote.

3. The President shall be deemed to be dismissed from office in accordance with impeachment procedure, if not less than two thirds of the total number of the members of the Parliament supported the decision.

4. The issue shall be deemed stricken off if the Parliament fails to adopt the decision within a term of 30 days. Bringing of the same charge against the President shall be impermissible during the following one year.

5. Discussion of the charge brought against the President and the adoption of the decision in the Parliament shall be impermissible during war, a state of emergency or martial law.

Article 64

1. In case of the violation of the Constitution, commission of high treason and other criminal offenses, not less than one-third of the total number of the members of the Parliament shall be entitled to raise the question about the dismissal in accordance with impeachment procedure of the President of the Supreme Court, members of the Government, the Prosecutor General, the President of the Chamber of Control and members of the Council of National Bank.

2. After having received the conclusion in accordance with a procedure envisaged in the second paragraph of Article 63, the Parliament shall be authorized to dismiss the officials listed in the first paragraph of the present Article by the majority of the total number of the members of the Parliament. The requirements of the fourth paragraph of Article 63 shall apply to such cases as well.

Article 65

1. The Parliament of Georgia by the majority of the total number of the members of the Parliament shall ratify, denounce and annul the international treaties and agreements.

2. Apart from the international treaties and agreements providing for ratification, it shall also be obligatory to ratify an international treaty and agreement which:
   a. provides for accession of Georgia to an international organization or intergovernmental union;
   b. is of a military character;
   c. pertains to the territorial integrity of the state or change of the state frontiers;
   d. is related to borrowing or lending loans by the state;
   e. requires a change of domestic legislation, adoption of necessary laws and acts with force of law with the view of honoring the undertaken international obligations.
3. The Parliament shall be notified about the conclusion of other international treaties and agreements.
4. In case of lodging a constitutional claim or a submission with the Constitutional Court, ratification of the respective international treaty or agreement shall be impermissible before adjudication by the Constitutional Court.

. . . . . .

Article 67

1. The President of Georgia only in the exclusive cases, the Government, a member of the Parliament, a Parliamentary Faction, a Parliamentary Committee, the higher representative bodies of the Autonomous Republic of Abkhazia, the Autonomous Republic of Ajara, not less than 30,000 electors shall have the right to legislative initiative.
2. At the request of the President of Georgia, the Parliament shall give the priority to the discussion of a draft law submitted by the former.
3. In case the Government does not submit the remarks with regard to a draft law considering in the Parliament within a term provided for by law, the draft law shall be deemed approved. (6.02.2004.N3272)

. . . . . .

Chapter 4
The President of Georgia

Article 69

1. The President of Georgia shall be the Head of State of Georgia. (6.02.2004.N3272)
2. The President of Georgia shall lead and exercise the internal and foreign policy of the state. He/she shall ensure the unity and integrity of the country and the activity of the state bodies in accordance with the Constitution.
3. The President of Georgia shall be the higher representative of Georgia in foreign relations.

Article 70

1. The President of Georgia shall be elected on the basis of universal, equal and direct suffrage by secret ballot for a term of five years. The same person may be elected the President only for two consecutive terms.

2. Any person may be elected the President of Georgia if he/she is a native-born citizen of Georgia, having the right to vote, has attained the age of 35, has lived in Georgia for at least fifteen years and lives in Georgia by the day on which the election is scheduled.

3. The right to nominate a candidate to the office of the President shall be vested with a political association of citizens or a stirring group. The nomination shall be confirmed by the signatures of not less than 50,000 electors.

4. A candidate shall be deemed to be elected if he/she has obtained more than half of the votes of participants. (6.02.2004.N3272)

5. If no candidate has received the required number of votes in the first round, a second round of elections shall be held in two weeks after an official announcement of the first round results. (27.12.06)

6. Two candidates having the best results in the first round shall be put to the vote in the second round. The candidate who received more votes shall be deemed to be elected. (6.02.2004.N3272)

7. If only one candidate took part in the first round, who did not receive the necessary number of votes, or if no President was elected in the second round, new elections shall be held within two months from the date of elections. (27.12.06)

8. No election shall be held in case of a state of emergency or martial law.

9. Regular elections for Presidency shall be held in October of the calendar year when the presidential authority expires. The President of Georgia shall fix the date of the elections not later than within 60 days before the elections. (27.12.06)

10. The procedure and conditions of the election of the President as well as the inadmissibility to participate in election as a candidate shall be determined by the Constitution and the Organic Law.

(Added by the Constitutional Law of Georgia of 20 July 1999)

. . . . . .

Article 73

1. The President of Georgia shall:

   a) conclude international agreements and treaties, negotiate with foreign states; appoint and dismiss ambassadors and other diplomatic representatives of Georgia with the consent of the Parliament; accredit ambassadors and other diplomatic representatives of foreign states and international organizations; (27.12.06) a1) conclude a constitutional agreement with the Apostle Autocephalous Orthodox Church of Georgia on behalf of the state of Georgia; (30.03.2001, # 826)

b) appoint the Prime Minister, give the Prime Minister consent to appoint a member of the Government—a Minister; (6.02.2004. N3272)

c) be entitled, on his/her own initiative or in other cases envisaged by the Constitution, to dissolve the Government, dismiss the Ministers of Internal Affairs and Defense of Georgia (23.12.2005, # 2494)

d) accept the resignation of the Government, a member of the Government and other officials as determined by law, shall be entitled to require the Government, a member of the Government to perform their official duties until the appointment of a new composition of the Government or a new member of the Government; (6.02.2004. N3272)

e) give the Government consent to submit the State Budget of Georgia to the Parliament; (6.02.2004.N3272)

f) submit the Parliament the officials, appoint and dismiss them in the cases and in accordance with the procedure defined in the Constitution and law;

g) declare a martial law in the case of armed attack on Georgia, make peace when appropriate conditions exist and submit the decisions to the Parliament within 48 hours for approval;

h) in the case of war or mass disorder, infringement upon the territorial integrity of the country, coup d'etat, armed insurrection, ecological disasters, epidemics or in other cases, when state bodies are unable to normally exercise their Constitutional powers, shall declare a state of emergency throughout the whole territory of the country or a certain part thereof and submit this decision to the Parliament within 48 hours for approval. In the case of a state of emergency issue the decrees having the force of law, which shall remain in force until the end of the state of emergency, shall take emergency measures. The decrees shall be submitted to the Parliament when it is assembled. Emergency authorities shall apply only to the territory where the state of emergency is declared for the reasons mentioned in the present paragraph;

i) with the consent of the Parliament, be entitled to suspend the activity of the institutions of self-government or other representative bodies of territorial units or dismiss them if their activity endangers the sovereignty, territorial integrity of the country or the exercise of constitutional authority of state bodies;

j) issue decrees and orders on the basis of the Constitution and law;

     k) sign and promulgate laws in accordance with the procedure prescribed by the Constitution;

     l) decide about the matters of citizenship, granting asylum;

     m) award state honors, higher military ranks, special and honorary titles and higher diplomatic ranks;

     n) grant pardon to convicted persons;

     o) dissolve the Parliament in accordance with a procedure and in the cases established by the Constitution. (6.02.2004.N3272)

     p) Deleted (27.12.06)

     q) from the dissolution of the Parliament to the first convocation of the newly elected Parliament, in the exclusive cases, be entitled to issue a decree having the force of law on tax and budgetary issues, which shall be invalid in case it is not approved by the newly elected Parliament within a month from the first convocation; (6.02.2004.N3272)

     r) be entitled to appoint the Prime Minister and give his/her consent for the appointment of the ministers under the circumstances defined in subparagraphs "a"–"d" of Article 511 in case of non-declaration of confidence to the composition of the Government by the Parliament within a term established by the Constitution. Within a month from the end of the above mentioned circumstances the President shall re-submit the composition of the Government to the Parliament for confidence. (6.02.2004.N3272)

2. The President shall schedule the date of elections of the Parliament and representative bodies in accordance with the procedure prescribed by law.

3. The President of Georgia shall be authorized to suspend or abrogate acts of the Government and the bodies of the executive power, if they are in contradiction with the Constitution of Georgia, international treaties and agreements, laws and the normative acts of the President. (6.02.2004.N3272)

4. The President is the Supreme Commander-in-Chief of the Armed Forces of Georgia. He/she appoints members of the National Security Council, and appoints and dismisses the Chief of the General Staff of the Armed Forces of Georgia, other commanders; (6.02.2004.N3272)

5. The President shall be authorized to address the people and the Parliament. Once a year he/she shall submit a report to the Parliament on the most important state issues.

6. The President shall exercise other powers determined by the Constitution and law.

. . . . . .

Article 75

1. The President of Georgia shall enjoy personal immunity. While holding his/her position, his/her detention or proceeding shall be impermissible.

2. In case of the violation of the Constitution, commission of high treason and other criminal offense, the Parliament shall be authorized to dismiss the President in accordance with a procedures of Article 63 of the Constitution and in accordance with a procedures determined by the Organic Law if:
   a. the violation of the Constitution is confirmed by a judgment of the Constitutional Court;
   b. corpus delicti of high treason and other criminal offense is confirmed by a conclusion of the Supreme Court.

. . . . . .

Chapter 4.1
The Government of Georgia
(6.02.2004.N3272)

Article 78
1. The Government shall ensure the exercise of the executive power, the internal and foreign policy of the state in accordance with the legislation of Georgia. The Government shall be responsible before the President and the Parliament of Georgia.
2. The Government shall be composed by the Prime Minister and the Ministers. The State Minister (the State Ministers) may be in the composition of the Government. The Prime Minister shall charge one of the members of the Government with the exercise of the responsibilities of the Vice Prime Minister. The Government and the members of the Government shall withdraw the authority before the President of Georgia.
3. The Government shall adopt a decree and a resolution on the basis of the constitution, laws and the normative acts of the President and for their realisation thereof, which shall be signed by the Prime Minister.
4. The President of Georgia shall be authorized to convene and preside over the sittings of the Government with regard to the issues of exclusive state importance. Decision adopted at the sitting shall be formed by the act of the President.
5. The structure, authority, and a procedure of the activity of the Government shall be determined by the Constitution and law, the draft of which shall be submitted to the Parliament by the Government by the consent of the President.
6. The Government shall be authorized to retire by its own decision.
7. The authority of the Government shall begin upon the appointment of the members of the Government in accordance with a procedure and in cases established by the Constitution. (6.02.2004.N3272)

Article 79

1. The Prime Minister shall be the head of the Government.
2. The Prime Minister shall determine the directions of the activity of the Government, organize the activity of the Government, exercise co-ordination and control over the activity of the members of the Government, submit report on the activity of the Government to the President and be responsible for the activity of the Government before the President and the Parliament of Georgia.
3. At the request of the Parliament the Prime Minister shall submit an account to it on the realisation of the governmental program.
4. The Prime Minister within his/her authority shall issue an individual legal act- an order, exercise full administrative functions in the building of the Government as well.
5. The Prime Minister shall appoint other members of the Government by the consent of the President, be authorized to dismiss the members of the Government.
6. The Prime Minister shall appoint and dismiss other officials in accordance with a procedure and in cases envisaged by law.
7. Resignation of the Prime Minister or termination of his/her authority shall result in termination of the authority of the other members of the Government. In case of resignation or dismissal of the other member of the Government the Prime minister shall appoint a new member of the Government within two weeks by the consent of the President of Georgia. (6.02.2004.N3272)

Article 80

1. After taking the oath by the President of Georgia, the Government shall withdraw the authority before the President of Georgia. The President shall uphold the withdrawal of the authority of the Government and be entitled to charge the Government with the exercise of the responsibilities until the appointment of a new composition.
2. The President of Georgia within 7 days from the resignation, dismissal and withdrawal of the authority of the Government after the consultations with the Parliamentary Factions shall choose a candidate of the Prime Minister, whereas the candidate of the Prime Minister—the candidates of the members of the Government by the consent of the President within a term of 10 days. Within 3 days from the end of the procedure envisaged by the first sentence of this paragraph the President of Georgia shall submit the composition of the Government to the Parliament for confidence.
3. Within a week from the submission of the composition of the Government by the President of Georgia the Parliament shall consider and vote the issue of declaration of confidence to the composition of the Government and the

Governmental program. The confidence of the Parliament shall be gained by the majority of the total number of the members of the Parliament. The members of the Government shall be appointed within a term of three days from the declaration of confidence. The Parliament shall be entitled to declare non-confidence to the composition of the Government and raise a question of recusal of a particular member of the Government in the same decision. In case of approval of the decision of the Parliament on the recusal by the President the recused person shall not be appointed in the same composition of the Government instead of a dismissed or resigned member.

4. In case a composition of the Government and its governmental program do not gain the confidence of the Parliament, the President of Georgia shall submit the same or a new composition of the Government to the Parliament within a term of a week. The Parliament shall exercise the procedure provided for by paragraph 3 of this Article.

5. In case a composition of the Government and the program of the Governmental thereof do not gain the confidence of the Parliament for three times, the President of Georgia shall nominate a new candidate of the Prime Minister within a term of 5 days or appoint the Prime Minister without consent of the Parliament, whereas the Prime Minister shall appoint the Ministers by the consent of the President of Georgia within a term of 5 days as well. In such a case the President of Georgia shall dissolve the Parliament and schedule extraordinary elections.

6. It shall be impermissible to put the issue of dismissal of the President of Georgia in accordance with impeachment procedure during the procedures envisaged by this Article. (6.02.2004.N3272)

Article 81

1. The Parliament shall be entitled to declare non-confidence to the Government by the majority of the total number. Not less than one third of the total number of the members of the Parliament shall be entitled to raise a question of declaration of non- confidence. After the declaration of non-confidence to the Government the President of Georgia shall dismiss the Government or not approve the decision of the Parliament. In case the Parliament declares non-confidence to the Government again not earlier than 90 days ant not later than 100 days, the President of Georgia shall dismiss the Government or dissolve the Parliament and schedule extraordinary elections. In case of circumstances provided for by subparagraphs "a"–"d" of Article 511 re-voting of non-confidence shall be held within 15 days from the end of these circumstances.

2. The Parliament shall be entitled to raise the question of declaration of unconditional non-confidence to the Government by a resolution. In case the Parliament declares non-confidence to the Government by the majority of three-fifths of the total number of the members of the Parliament not earlier

than 15 days and not later than 20 days from the adoption of the resolution, the President shall dismiss the Government. In case the Parliament does not declare non-confidence to the Government, it shall be impermissible to put the question of non-confidence to the Government within next 6 months.

3. In case of dismissal of the Government in accordance with a procedure provided for by paragraph 2 of this Article the President of Georgia shall not be entitled to appoint the same person as a Prime Minister in the next composition of the Government or nominate the same candidate of the Prime Minister.

4. The Prime Minister shall be entitled to put the question of confidence of the Government on the draft laws on the State Budget, Tax Code and a procedure of the structure, authority and activity of the Government considering at the Parliament. The Parliament shall declare the confidence to the Government by the majority of the total number. In case the Parliament does not declare the confidence to the Government, the President of Georgia shall dismiss the Government or dissolve the Parliament within a week and schedule extraordinary elections.

5. Voting the declaration of confidence shall be held within 15 days from the putting of the question. Failure of voting during this term shall mean the declaration of confidence.

6. A relevant draft law shall be deemed adopted upon the declaration of confidence to the Government by the Parliament.

7. It shall be impermissible to put the question of dismissal of the President of Georgia in accordance with impeachment procedure during the procedures provided for by this Article. (6.02.2004.N3272)

. . . . . .

Chapter 5
Judicial Power

Article 82

1. Judicial power shall be exercised by means of constitutional control, justice and other forms determined by law.

2. Acts of courts shall be obligatory for all state bodies and persons throughout the whole territory of the country.

3. The judiciary shall be independent and exercised exclusively by courts.

4. A court shall adopt a judgment in the name of Georgia.

5. The cases shall be considered by juries before the courts of general jurisdiction in accordance with a procedure and in cases prescribed by law. (6.02.2004.N3272)

Article 83

1. The Constitutional Court of Georgia shall be the judicial body of Constitutional review. Its authority, the procedures of its creation and activity shall be determined by the Constitution and the Organic Law.
2. Justice shall be administered by general courts. Their system shall be determined by an organic law. (27.12.06)
3. Introduction of a court martial shall be permissible at war and exclusively within the system of the courts of general jurisdiction.
4. Creation of either extraordinary or special courts shall be prohibited.

. . . . . .

Article 86

1. A judge shall be a citizen of Georgia who has attained the age of 28, and has the highest legal education and at least five years experience in the practice of law. (27.12.2005, # 2496)
2. A judge shall be designated on the position for a period of not less than ten years. The selection, appointment or dismissal procedure of a judge shall be determined by law.
3. The position of a judge shall be incompatible with any other occupation and remunerative activity, except for pedagogical and scientific activities. A judge shall not be a member of a political party or participate in a political activity. (27.12.2005, # 2496)

. . . . . .

Article 87

1. A judge shall enjoy personal immunity. Criminal proceeding of a judge, his/her arrest or detention, the search of his/her apartment, car, workplace or his/her person shall be permissible by the consent of the President of the Supreme Court of Georgia, except when he/she is caught flagrante delicto, which shall immediately be notified to the President of the Supreme Court of Georgia. Unless the President of the Supreme Court gives his/her consent to the arrest or detention, the arrested or detained judge shall immediately be released.
2. The state shall ensure the security of a judge and his/her family.

Article 88

1. The Constitutional Court of Georgia shall exercise the judicial power by virtue of the constitutional legal proceedings.
2. The Constitutional Court of Georgia shall consist of nine judges— the members of the Constitutional Court. Three members of the Constitutional Court shall be appointed by the President of Georgia, three members shall be elected by the Parliament by not less than three fifths of the

number of the members of the Parliament on the current nominal list, three members shall be appointed by the Supreme Court. The term of office of the members of the Constitutional Court shall be ten years. The Constitutional Court shall elect the President of the Constitutional Court among its members for a period of five years. The President shall not be re-elected.

3. A member of the Constitutional Court shall not be a person who has held this position before.

4. A member of the Constitutional Court may be a citizen of Georgia who has attained the age of 30 and has the highest legal education. The selection, appointment and election procedure and the issue of termination of the office of the members of the Constitutional Court as well as other issues of the constitutional legal proceeding and the activity of the Constitutional Court shall be determined by law. (27.12.2005, # 2496)

5. A member of the Constitutional Court shall enjoy personal immunity. A member of the Constitutional Court shall not be proceeded, arrested or detained, nor shall his/her apartment, car, workplace or his/her person be subject to search without the consent of the Constitutional Court, except when he/she is caught flagrante delicto, which shall immediately be notified to the Constitutional Court. Unless the Constitutional Court gives its consent to the arrest or detention, an arrested or detained member shall immediately be released.

Article 89

1. The Constitutional Court of Georgia on the basis of a constitutional claim or a submission of the President of Georgia, the Government, not less than one fifth of the members of the Parliament, a court, the higher representative bodies the Autonomous Republic of Abkhazia and the Autonomous Republic of Ajara, the Public Defender or a citizen in accordance with a procedure established by the Organic Law: (6.02.2004.N3272)

   a. adjudicate upon the constitutionality of a Constitutional Agreement, law, normative acts of the President and the Government, the normative acts of the higher state bodies of the Autonomous Republic Abkhazia and the Autonomous Republic of Ajara (6.02.2004.N3272)

   b. consider dispute on competence between state bodies;

   c. consider constitutionality of formation and activity of political associations of citizens;

   d. consider dispute on constitutionality of provisions on referenda and elections as well as dispute on constitutionality of referenda and elections held on the basis of these provisions; (27.12.2005, # 2496)

   e. consider constitutionality of international treaties and agreements;

    f. consider, on the basis of a claim of a person, constitutionality of normative acts in relation to fundamental human rights and freedoms enshrined in Chapter Two of the Constitution; (27.12.2005, # 2496)

    f1. consider dispute on violation of the Constitutional Law of Georgia on the Status of the Autonomous Republic of Ajara; (01.07.2004, # 306)

    g. exercise other powers determined by the Constitution and the Organic Law of Georgia.

2. The judgment of the Constitutional Court shall be final. A normative act or a part thereof recognized as unconstitutional shall cease to have legal effect from the moment of the promulgation of the respective judgment of the Constitutional Court.

Article 90

1. The Supreme Court of Georgia is the highest cassation court. (27.12.2005, # 2496)
2. The President and the judges of the Supreme Court of Georgia shall be elected for a period of not less than ten years by the Parliament by the majority of the number of the members of Parliament on the current nominal list upon the submission of the President of Georgia.
3. The authority, organization of the Supreme Court of Georgia and the procedure of activity and of the preterm termination of the office of the judges of the Supreme Court shall be determined by law.
4. The President and the members of the Supreme Court of Georgia shall enjoy personal immunity. Criminal proceeding of the President or a judge of the Supreme Court, their arrest or detention, the search of their apartment, car, workplace or person shall be permissible only by the consent of the Parliament, except when the President or a judge is caught flagrante delicto, which shall immediately be notified to the Parliament. Unless the Parliament gives its consent, the arrested or detained shall immediately be released.

. . . . . .

Chapter 6
State Finances and Control

Article 92

1. The Parliament of Georgia by the majority of the number of the members of the Parliament on the current nominal list shall annually adopt the Law on the State Budget, which shall be signed by the President of Georgia.
2. The procedure of the drafting and adoption of the State Budget shall be determined by law.

. . . . . .

Chapter 7
State Defense

Article 98
1. Defensive war shall be a sovereign right of Georgia.
2. Georgia shall have the armed forces for the defense of the independence, sovereignty and territorial integrity of the country, as well as for the honoring of its international obligations.
3. The types and the composition of the armed forces shall be determined by law. The structure of the armed forces shall be approved by the President of Georgia, while the strength thereof shall be approved by the Parliament by the majority of the number of the members of the Parliament on the current nominal list upon the submission of the Council of National Security.

Article 99
1. With the view of organizing the military construction and defense of the country, the Council of National Security shall be set up which shall be guided by the President of Georgia.
2. The composition, authority and procedure activity of the Council of National Security shall be determined by the Organic Law.

Article 100
1. The President of Georgia shall adopt a decision on the use of the armed forces and submit it to the Parliament within 48 hours for approval. In addition the use of the armed forces for the honoring international obligations shall be impermissible without the consent of the Parliament of Georgia.
2. For the purpose of state defense in the exclusive cases and in cases envisaged by law, the decision about the entrance, use and movement of the armed forces of another state on the territory of Georgia shall be adopted by the President of Georgia. The decision shall immediately be submitted to the Parliament for approval and shall be enforced after the consent of the Parliament. (6.02.2004.N3272)

Article 101
1. Defense of Georgia shall be an obligation of every citizen of Georgia.
2. Defense of the country and discharge of military service shall be a duty of every citizen being fit thereupon. The form of the discharge of military service shall be determined by law.

Chapter 8
Revision of the Constitution

Article 102
1. The following shall be entitled to submit a draft law on general or partial revision of the Constitution:
   a. the President;
   b. more than half of the total number of the members of the Parliament;
   c. not less than 200,000 electors.
2. A draft law on the revision of the Constitution shall be submitted to the Parliament, which shall promulgate the former for the public discussion. The Parliament shall begin the discussion of the draft law after a month from its promulgation.
3. The draft law on the revision of the Constitution shall be deemed to be adopted if it is supported by at least two thirds of the total number of the members of the Parliament of Georgia.
4. The law on the revision of the Constitution shall be signed and promulgated by the President of Georgia in accordance with a procedure provided for by Article 68 of the Constitution.

Article 103
The announcement of a state of emergency or martial law shall lead to the suspension of the revision of the Constitution until the cancellation of the state of emergency or martial law.

Chapter 9
Transitional Provisions

Article 104
1. The Constitution of Georgia shall enter into force from the day of the recognition of the authority of the newly elected President and the Parliament of Georgia.
2. Articles 49, 50 and 70 of the Constitution shall enter into force upon the promulgation of the Constitution.

. . . . . .

Article 109
1. The Constitution adopted in accordance with the established procedure shall be signed and promulgated by the Head of State of Georgia.
2. The members of the Parliament of Georgia and the members of the Constitutional Commission shall sign the text of the Constitution. After the

enforcement of the Constitution, at least within a year, the text of the Constitution shall publicly be displayed in the buildings of all local bodies of Georgia in order the population become familiar with its contents.

DOCUMENT 4

Section 907 of the Freedom Support Act

S.2532

FREEDOM Support Act (Enrolled as Agreed to or Passed by Both House and Senate)

SEC. 907. RESTRICTION ON ASSISTANCE TO AZERBAIJAN.

United States assistance under this or any other ACT (other than assistance under title V of this Act) may not be provided to the Government of Azerbaijan until the President determines, and so reports to the Congress, that the Government of Azerbaijan is taking demonstrable steps to cease all blockades and other offensive uses of force against Armenia and Nagorno-Karabakh.

DOCUMENT 5

Waiver of Section 907 of the Freedom Support Act

THE WHITE HOUSE
Office of the Press Secretary
January 28, 2002

January 25, 2002
PRESIDENTIAL DETERMINATION NO. 2002-06
MEMORANDUM FOR THE SECRETARY OF STATE

SUBJECT: Waiver of Section 907 of the FREEDOM Support Act with Respect to Assistance to the Government of Azerbaijan

Pursuant to the authority contained in Title II of the "Kenneth M. Ludden Foreign Operations, Export Financing, and Related Programs Appropriations Act, 2002" (Public Law 107–115), I hereby determine and certify that a waiver of section 907 of the FREEDOM Support Act of 1992 (Public Law 102–511):
— is necessary to support U.S. efforts to counter international terrorism;
— is necessary to support the operational readiness of U.S. Armed Forces or coalition partners to counter international terrorism;

— is important to Azerbaijan's border security; and

— will not undermine or hamper ongoing efforts to negotiate a peaceful settlement between Armenia and Azerbaijan or be used for offensive purposes against Armenia.

Accordingly, I hereby waive section 907 of the FREEDOM Support Act.

You are authorized and directed to notify the Congress of this determination and to arrange for its publication in the Federal Register.

GEORGE W. BUSH

DOCUMENT 6

Nagorno-Karabakh Ceasefire Agreement

The Bishkek Protocol
Bishkek, 5 May 1994

Participants of the meeting held in May 4–5 in Bishkek on the initiative of the CIS Inter-Parliamentary Assembly, Parliament of Kyrgyz Republic, Federal Congress and Ministry of Foreign Affairs of the Russian Federation:

express determination to assist in all possible ways to the cessation of armed conflict in and around Nagorno Karabakh, which does not only cause irretrievable losses to Azerbaijani and Armenian people, but also significantly affects the interests of other countries in the region and seriously complicates the international situation;

supporting the April 15, 1994 Statement by the CIS Council of heads of states, express readiness to fully support the efforts by heads and representatives of executive power on cessation of the armed conflict and liquidation of its consequences by reaching an appropriate agreement as soon as possible;

advocate a naturally active role of the Commonwealth and Inter-Parliamentary Assembly in cessation of the conflict, in realization of thereupon principles, goals and the UN and OSCE certain decisions (first of all the UN Security Council resolutions 822, 853, 874, 884);

call upon the conflicting sides to come to common senses: cease to fire at the midnight of May 8 to 9, guided by the February 18, 1994 Protocol (including the part on allocating observers), and work intensively to confirm this as soon as possible by signing a reliable, legally binding agreement envisaging a mechanism, ensuring the non-resumption of military and hostile activities, withdrawal of troops from occupied territories and restoration of communication, return of refugees;

agree to suggest Parliaments of the CIS member-states to discuss the initiative by Chairman of Council of the Inter-Parliamentary Assembly V. Shumeyko and Head of the Assembly's Peacemaking Group on Nagorno Karabakh M. Sherimkulov on creating a CIS peacemaking force;

consider appropriate to continue such meetings for peaceful resolution of the armed conflict;

express gratitude to the people and leadership of Kyrgyzstan for creating excellent working conditions, cordiality and hospitality.

ON BEHALF OF DELEGATIONS:

A. Jalilov
(signed by R. Guliyev, Chairman of the Azerbaijani Supreme Soviet)

K. Babourian
(Chairman of the Nagorno Karabakh Republic Supreme Soviet)

B. Ararktsian
(Chairman of the Supreme Soviet of Armenia)

V. Shumeyko
(Chairman of the Council of Federation of Russia)

M. Sherimkulov
(Chairman of the Supreme Soviet of Kyrgyzstan)

V. Kazimirov
(Plenipotentiary Representative of the President of the Russian Federation, Head of the Russian Mediation Mission)

M. Krotov
(Head of the Secretariat of the Council of the Inter-Parliamentary Assembly of member states)

DOCUMENT 7

Russia-Georgia Ceasefire Agreement

Translation of Text

The President of the Federation of Russia D. A. Medvedev and the President of the French Republic N.Sarcozy underline the following principles for resolving the conflict and call on the parties in question to adhere to these principles:

1. No recourse to the use of force
2. Definitive cessation of hostilities
3. Free access to humanitarian aid (and to allow the return of refugees)

4. Georgian military forces must withdraw to their normal bases of encampment

5. Russian military forces must withdraw to the lines prior to the start of hostilities. While awaiting an international mechanism, Russia peace-keeping forces will implement additional security measures (six months)

6. Opening of international discussions on the modalities of lasting security in Abkhazia and South Ossetia (based on the decisions of the U.N. and the O.S.C.E.)

Glossary

Armenian diaspora — The 7–8 million Armenians residing outside of the territory of the modern state of Armenia.

Armenian Genocide — Refers to ethnic violence against Armenians in 1915, during WWI, when the Ottoman Empire relocated its Armenian population. At that time, an estimated one-third to one-half of the Armenian population was killed.

Ayatollah — Literally means, "the sign of God." This title is bestowed on high-ranking clerics in Shia Islam who have been distinguished through scholarship, popularity, and fundraising.

Bolsheviks — Members of the majority group in the Russian Social Democratic Workers' Party that seized power in Russia in 1917.

Caucasus — The geographic region the Black and Caspian Seas. Politically, the Caucasus includes southwest Russia, Armenia, Azerbaijan, and Georgia; the northeast of Turkey; and the north of Iran.

Christianization — Conversion of populations to Christianity. In the Caucasus, Christianization was brought about by the Tsarist Russian Empire, as it encouraged Russians to settle in the Caucasus and developed its ties with the Christian Armenians in the newly conquered parts of the Caucasus.

Current Account Balance (CAB) — The difference between a state's exports and its imports.

Diaspora — The movement or scattering of a population away from their established or ancestral homeland.

Duma — The Russian parliament.

Dutch disease — As profits from natural resources (like oil) increase, this can drive up the value of a state's national currency which can make the price of that state's exports rise, lowering export sales as foreign consumers buy less of the more costly exports. This can then lead to the economic slowdown of that state's industries.

Foreign Direct Investment (FDI) — Foreign direct investment is a measure of the amount of foreign ownership of a state's assets (i.e., factories, businesses, etc.).

Genocide — A deliberate and systematic attempt to destroy a specific ethnic, religious, linguistic, cultural, or political group.

Geopolitics — The study of the relationship between geography, demography, politics and economics.

Glasnost — Literally means, "publicity." Used to describe Gorbachev's commitment to the opening of Soviet society.

Gross Domestic Product (GDP) — The total market value of all goods and services produced within the borders of a state.

Imam — This title is used to refer to a teacher of Muslims as well as Muslim leaders.

Intermediate-range Nuclear Forces (INF) Treaty — A 1987 agreement between the United States and the USSR, eliminating intermediate range (300–3,400 miles) ground-launched ballistic and cruise missiles.

Islam — Literally means, "submission." One of the three major, monotheistic religions of the world, in addition to Christianity and Judaism.

Madrasa — A building or institution for teaching Islamic theology and religious law.

Mullah — A male religious teacher in the Islamic faith.

Near Abroad — A term used in Russia to describe the post-Soviet states, which Russia views as its special sphere of influence.

North Caucasus — The geographic region of the Caucasus that is north of the Caucasus Mountains, which is politically a part of Russia.

Orthodox Christianity — An eastern division of Christianity. Eastern Orthodox is the largest Christian denomination after Catholicism, which is the largest western division of Christianity.

Perestroika — Literally means, "restructuring." Used to describe Gorbachev's commitment to the restructuring of the Soviet economy and government.

Pogrom — Riot or violence against a particular group of people.

Putsch — A coup or violent attempt to overthrow a government.

Rose Revolution — The popular and peaceful protest of voter fraud in Georgia that led to President Shevardnadze's resignation in 2003.

Russification — Pressure on local populations in the Caucasus to learn Russian and abandon their cultural heritage under the Soviet Union.

SALT 1 & 2 (Strategic Arms Limitation Talks 1 & 2) — Two rounds of bilateral talks and treaties between the United States and the Soviet Union that focused on limiting the stockpiles of nuclear weapons.

Separatism — A movement by a distinct group of people to gain political autonomy.

Shah — Means, "king." This title was bestowed upon hereditary monarchs in Iran.

Shia Islam — The second largest sect of Islam after Sunni Islam. This sect believes that religious authority should belong to the descendents of the Prophet Mohammad.

South Caucasus — The geographic region of the Caucasus that is south of the Caucasus Mountains, primarily occupied by the states of Armenia, Azerbaijan, and Georgia.

START 1 & 2 (Strategic Arms Reduction Treaty 1 & 2) — Two rounds of bilateral talks and treaties between the United States and the USSR that focused on limiting strategic, offensive arms.

Sufism — An umbrella term for mystical movements within Islam.

Sunni Islam — The largest sect of Islam. This sect accepts the authority of a broad range of leaders, including political, if they are protectors of the Islamic community.

Tsar — The title of male emperors of the Russian Empire.

Bibliography

Abbasov, Shahin. "Azerbaijan: Russian Arms Scandal Feeds Baku's Support for Nabucco." Eurasianet.org, February 2, 2009, http://eurasianet.org/departments/insightb/articles/eav020409b_pr.shtml (accessed April 10, 2009).

Abdullayeva, Sevindzh and Viktor Shulman. "Iran Wants Wider Relations with Azerbaijan: Foreign Minister." *ITAR-TASS News Agency*, November 28, 2005.

Abrahamyan, Gayane. "Armenian Village Plans for Turkish Border Openings." Eurasianet.org, April 16, 2009, http://www.eurasianet.org/departments/insightb/articles/eav041609.shtml (accessed May 23, 2009).

Afrasiabi, Kaveh L. "Iran Gambles Over Georgia's Crisis." *Asia Times*, August 16, 2008, http://www.atimes.com/atimes/Middle_East/JH16Ak01.html (accessed May 23, 2009).

AFX News Limited. "Turkmenistan, Iran Discuss Caspian Sea Status; Armenia Seeks 3-Way Union." *AFX News Limited*, November 28, 2000.

Aksin, Sina. *Turkey: From Empire to Revolutionary Republic*. New York, NY: New York University Press, 2007).

Alan, Ray. "The Great Game." *The New Leader* 76, no. 4 (March 8, 1993).

Anabel, David. "The Role of Georgia's Media—and Western Aid—in the Rose Revolution." *The Harvard International Journal of Press/Politics* 11, no. 3 (2006): 7–43.

Ansari, Ali M. *Confronting Iran: The Failure of American Foreign Policy the Next Great Crisis in the Middle East*. New York, NY: Basic Books, 2006.

Antidze, Margarita and Hasmik Mkrtchyan. "PM Forecast to Win Armenian Presidential Election." Reuters, February 19, 2008, http://www.reuters.com/article/latestCrisis/idUSL1842327 (accessed May 24, 2009).

Areshidze, Irakly G. "Helping Georgia?" *Perspective* xii, no. 4 (March–April 2002), http://www.bu.edu/iscip/vol12/areshidze.html (accessed May 15, 2009).

Armenian Foreign Ministry. "European Neighborhood Policy—ARMENIA." Armenian Foreign Ministry, April 3, 2008, http://www.armeniaforeignministry.am/doc/id/memo_eu.pdf (accessed May 23, 2009).

Arminfo News Agency. "Azerbaijan FM: Problem with Opening of Boundary Connected Not Only with Armenian-Azerbaijani Conflict, but also with Relations Between Turkey and Armenia." Arminfo News Agency, May 31, 2004.

———. "Development of Armenia-Turkey Relations Suspended." Arminfo News Agency, May 31, 2004.

———. "EU Interested in Normalization of Armenia-Turkey Relations." Arminfo News Agency, April 5, 2006.

———. "RA FM: Turkey is Not Ready to Establish Diplomatic Relations with Armenia." Arminfo News Agency, June 9, 2006.

———. "Armenian Defense Chief Unfazed by Bigger Military Spending in Azerbaijan." Arminfo, November 6, 2006. (Translation from Russian, World News Connection, National Technical Information Service, NTIS, U.S. Department of Commerce.)

Aron, Raymond, Daniel J. Mahoney, and Brian C. Anderson. *Peace & War: A Theory of International Relations*. Brunswick, NJ: Transaction Publishers, 2003.

Asbarez.com. "CSTO Rubez War Games Begin in Armenia." Asbarez.com, July 22, 2008, http://www.asbarez.com/2008/07/22/csto-rubezh-war-games-begin-in-armenia/ (accessed May 24, 2009).

Astourian, Stephan A. "From Ter-Petrosian to Kocharian: Leadership Change in Armenia." *Berkeley Program in Soviet and Post-Soviet Studies Working Paper Series* (Winter 2000–2001), http://bps.berkeley.edu/publications/2000_04-asto.pdf (accessed May 18, 2009).

Atabaki, Touraj, ed. *The State and the Subaltern: Modernization, Society and the State in Turkey and Iran*. New York, NY: I. B.Tauris & Co. Ltd., 2007.

Badawi, Ibrahim El and Samir Makdisi. "Explaining the Democracy Deficit in the Arab World." *The Quarterly Review of Economics and Finance* 46, no. 5 (February 2007).

Baer, Robert. *The Devil We Know: Dealing with the New Iranian Superpower*. Carlton North: Scribe Publications, 2008.

Bahrampour, Tara, and Phillip P. Pan. "Military Ship Delivers Aid to Georgia; Vessel Shifts Course, Avoids Port Where Russians are Posted." *Washington Post*, August 28, 2008.

Bailes, Alyson J. K., et al. "The Shanghai Cooperation Organization." *SIPRI Policy Paper*, no. 17, May 2007, 24, http://books.sipri.org/files/PP/SIPRIPP17.pdf (accessed September 2, 2009).

Balgov, Sergei. "Armenia and Russia Reassert Bonds Amid Georgia's Crisis." Eurasianet.org, November 17, 2003, http://www.eurasianet.org/departments/insight/articles/eav111703.shtml (accessed May 24, 2009).

Barber, Benjamin R. *Jihad vs. McWorld*. New York, NY: Times Books, 1995.

Barry, Ellen. "Russia offers its Own Territory for U.S.-Afghan Shipments." *The New York Times*, http://www.nytimes.com/2009/02/06/world/asia/06iht-russia.4.19994140.html (accessed September 13, 2009).

Baser, Bahar and Ashok Swain. "Diaspora Design Versus Homeland Realities: Case Study of the Armenian Diaspora." *Caucasian Review of International Affairs* 3, no. 1 (Winter 2009).

BBC. "Georgia Releases Russian 'Spies'." British Broadcasting Corporation, October 2, 2006, http://news.bbc.co.uk/2/hi/europe/5398384.stm (accessed May 21, 2009).

———. "How the Rose Revolution Happened." British Broadcasting Corporation, May 10, 2005, http://news.bbc.co.uk/2/hi/europe/4532539.stm (accessed May 21, 2009).

———. "Plan to Improve Turkey's Relations with Armenia Said Shelved." *British Broadcasting Corporation*, January 16, 2001.

————. "Profile: Eduard Shevardnadze." British Broadcasting Corporation, November 23, 2003, http://news.bbc.co.uk/2/hi/europe/3257047.stm (accessed July 1, 2009).

————. "Profile: Mikheil Saakashvili." British Broadcasting Corporation, January 25, 2004, http://news.bbc.co.uk/2/hi/europe/3231852.stm (accessed July 1, 2009).

————. "Russian Tanks Enter South Ossetia." British Broadcasting Corporation, August 8, 2008, http://news.bbc.co.uk/2/hi/europe/7548715.stm (accessed April 10, 2009).

Bissenova, Alima. "Azerbaijan, Armenian Presidents Meet on CIS Forum Sidelines." *CA-CI Analyst* (June 6, 2008), http://www.cacianalyst.org/?q=node/4884 (accessed May 24, 2009).

————. "Gazprom to Invest $200 Mln in Iran-Armenia Pipeline." *CA-CI Analyst* (June 11, 2008), http://www.cacianalyst.org/?q=node/4884 (accessed May 23, 2009).

Bohdan, Nahaylo and Victor Svoboda, *Soviet Disunion: A History of the Nationality Problem in the USSR*. New York, NY: Macmillan, 1990.

Bournoutian, George. "Eastern Armenia from the Seventeenth century to the Russian Annexation." In Richard Hovannisian, ed. *The Armenian People from Ancient to Modern Times*, vol. II. New York, NY: St. Martin's Press, 1997.

British Petroleum. *BP Statistical Review of World Energy June 2008*. British Petroleum, 2008, http://www.bp.com/statisticalreview (accessed Jan. 29, 2009).

Brown, Cameron S. "Wanting Their Cake and Their Neighbor's Too: Azerbaijani Attitudes Towards Karabakh and Iranian Azerbaijan." *The Middle East Journal* 58, no. 4 (Autumn 2004).

Brown, Michael Edward. *Rational Choice and Security Studies: Stephen Walt and His Critics*, Cambridge, MA: MIT Press, 2000.

Brzeziński, Zbigniew. *The Grand Chessboard: American Primacy and Its Geostrategic Imperatives*, New York, NY: Basic Books, 1998.

Burns, Nathan L. "Iran Carrying Out Policy in the Caspian Sea Region." In H. Sadri & D. Katsy, eds. *Trends, Prospects and Challenges of Globalization*. St. Petersburg, Russia: St. Petersburg State University Press, 2009.

Caucaz Europenews. "Georgia, Armenia Discuss Border Delimination." *Caucaz Europenews*, February 21, 2007, http://caucaz.com/home_eng/depeches.php?idp=1536&PHPSESSID =5fa14f0afa45094e55c33cce6e13f542 (accessed May 24, 2009).

CA-CI. "Azeri Military Budget to Equal Total Armenian State Budget." *Central Asia-Caucasus Institute* (March 22, 2006).

China Daily. "Azerbaijan's Geidar Aliev Dies at 80." ChinaDaily.com, December 16, 2003, http://www.chinadaily.com.cn/en/doc/2003-12/16/content_290650.htm (accessed September 3, 2009).

Chivers, C. J. "Georgia Offers Fresh Evidence on War's Start." *The New York Times*, September 15, 2008, http://www.nytimes.com/2008/09/16/world/europe/16georgia.html?pagewanted =1&_r=3&ref=world (accessed September 2, 2009).

CIA. "Armenia," *The World Factbook*. Central Intelligence Agency, 2009, https://www.cia.gov/ library/publications/the-world-factbook/geos/am.html (accessed May 18, 2009).

————. "Georgia," *The World Factbook*. Central Intelligence Agency, 2009, https:// www.cia.gov/library/publications/the-world-factbook/geos/gg.html (accessed May 18, 2009).

————. "Azerbaijan," *The World Factbook*, Central Intelligence Agency, 2009, https:// www.cia.gov/library/publications/the-world-factbook/geos/aj.html (accessed May 18, 2009).

CITOH. "Novosti: 97% aktsii GOK 'Madneuli' prodano za $51 mln" (News: 97% of Shares
    JSC Madneuli are Sold at US $51.1 Million). *CITOH*, November 7, 2005.
CNN. "Russian Military Dwarfs Georgia's." CNN, August 11, 2008, http://edition.cnn.com/
    2008/WORLD/europe/08/11/gerogia.russia.forces/index.html (accessed September 2,
    2009).
Collier, Paul, and Anke Hoeffler. "Greed and Grievance in Civil War." *Oxford Economic Papers*
    56, no. 4 (2004): 563–595.
Commission of the European Communities. "Country Report: Azerbaijan." *Commission Staff
    Working Paper* (February 3, 2005), http://ec.europa.eu/world/enp/pdf/country/azerbaijan
    _country_report_2005_en.pdf (accessed April 10, 2009).
Commonwealth Secretariat. *Small States: Economic Review and Basic Statistics*. Commonwealth
    Secretariat, 2008.
Cooley, Alexander. "How the West Failed Georgia." *Current History* (October 2008): 342–344.
———. "Principles in the Pipeline: Managing Transatlantic Values and Interests in Central
    Asia." *International Affairs* 84, no. 6 (2008): 1174–1188.
Cornell, Svante E. "The Politization of Islam in Azerbaijan." *CA-CI SR Paper* (October 2006).
Cornell, Svante E., David J. Smith, and S. Fredrick Starr. "The August 6 Bombing Incident in
    Georgia: Implications for the Euro-Atlantic Region." *CA-CI SR Paper* (October 2007).
Corso, Molly. "To Georgia, Wine War with Russia a Question of National Security."
    Eurasianet.org, April 13, 2006, http://www.eurasianet.org/departments/insight/articles/
    eav041306.shtml (accessed May 21, 2009).
Croissant, Michael P. *The Armenia-Azerbaijan Conflict: Causes and Implications*. Westport, CT:
    Greenwood Publishing Group, 1998.
CSIS. "Russia Report." *Center for Strategic and International Studies*, no. 1 (May 2007, 24),
    http://www.csis.ro/docs/CSIS.ro_Russia_Report.pdf (accessed August 14, 2009).
Curtis, Glenn E., ed. *Azerbaijan: A Country Study*. Washington, D.C.: GPO for the Library of
    Congress, 1995, http://countrystudies.us/azerbaijan/10.htm (accessed May 22, 2009).
———. *Georgia: A Country Study*. Washington, D.C.: GPO for the Library of Congress,
    1994, http://countrystudies.us/georgia/68.htm (accessed May 22, 2009).
Danielyan, Emil. "Georgian Transit Ban Hinders Russian Military Presence in Armenia."
    Eurasianet.org, October 10, 2008, http://www.eurasianet.org/departments/insight/
    articles/eav101008a.shtml (accessed May 24, 2009).
Darling, Dan. "Azerbaijan Boosting Military Spending." *Forecast International* (May 9, 2007),
    http://www.forecastinginternational.com/press/release.cfm?article=110 (accessed Septem-
    ber 2, 2009).
de Waal, Thomas. *Black Garden: Armenia and Azerbaijan through War and Peace*. New York,
    NY: New York University Press, 2003.
Dinmore, Guy, and David Stern. "Azeri Leader Criticizes Iran Over Oil Claim in Caspian."
    Financial Times, August 30, 2001, http://proquest.umi.com.ucfproxy.fcla.edu (accessed
    October 16, 2006).
Dodds, Klaus. *Geopolitics: A Very Short Introduction*. Oxford: Oxford University Press, 2007.
Donaldson, Robert H., and Joseph L. Nogee. *The Foreign Policy of Russia: Changing Systems,
    Enduring Interests*, 4th ed. Armonk, NY: M.E. Sharpe, 2009, 419 pp.
Dougherty, James E., and Robert L. Pfaltzgraff. *Contending Theories of International Relations*,
    5th ed. New York, NY: Addison Wesley Longman, Inc., 2001.
Dzhindzhikhashvili, Misha. "Iran Ready to Supply Gas to Georgia, Minister Says." *The Asso-
    ciated Press*, January 24, 2006.

EC. "European Neighborhood Policy: Strategy Paper." European Commission, May 12, 2004, http://ec.europa.eu/world/enp/pdf/strategy/strategy_paper_en.pdf (September 2, 2009).

EIA. "Azerbaijan Energy Profile." Energy Information Administration, May 15, 2009, http://tonto.eia.doe.gov/country/country_energy_data.cfm?fips=AJ (accessed May 18, 2009).

———. "Armenia Energy Profile." Energy Information Administration, May 15, 2009, http://tonto.eia.doe.gov/country/country_energy_data.cfm?fips=AM (accessed March 24, 2009).

———. "Country Analysis Briefs: Azerbaijan." Energy Information Agency, November 2007, http://www.eia.doe.gov/emeu/cabs/Azerbaijan/pdf.pdf (accessed June 10, 2009).

———. "Country Analysis Briefs: Central Asia." Energy Information Administration, February 2008, http://www.eia.doe.gov/emeu/cabs/Centasia/pdf.pdf (accessed January 20, 2008).

Ekedahl, Carolyn McGiffert and Melvin Allan Goodman. *The Wars of Eduard Shevardnadze.* Dulles, VA: Pennsylvania State University Press, 2001.

Elgie, Robert and Sophie Moestrup. *Semi-Presidentialism Outside Europe: A Comparative Study.* New York, NY: Routledge, 2007.

Energy.eu. "Energy Dependency." European Union, http://www.energy.eu/ (accessed January 21, 2009).

EP, "The EU's External Relations." European Parliament, 2008, http://www.europarl.europa.eu/parliament/expert/displayFtu.do?language=en&id=74&ftuId=FTU_6.4.3.html (accessed September 2, 2009).

Ergan, Ugur. "New Approach Reported in Relations Between Turkey, Armenia." *Financial Times,* June 6, 2003.

Eurasianet.org. "Armenia, Azerbaijan Presidents Meet." Eurasianet.net, May 8, 2009, http://eurasianet.net/departments/news/articles/eav050809b.shtml (accessed May 24, 2009).

———. "Azerbaijan Plays Waiting Game Following Cheney Blow Up in Baku." Eurasianet.org, September 9, 2008, http://www.eurasianet.org/departments/insight/articles/rp090908.shtml (accessed May 22, 2009).

Europa Publications Limited, *Eastern Europe and the Commonwealth of Independent States,* vol. 4. New York, NY: Routledge, 1999.

Fairbanks, Charles H. "Georgia's Rose Revolution." *Journal of Democracy* 15, no. 2 (2004): 110–124.

Faradov, Tair. "Religiosity in Post-Soviet Azerbaijan: A Sociological Analysis." *SIM Newsletter* 8 (September 2001), http://www.isim.nl/files/newsl_8.pdf (accessed April 10, 2009).

Farazmand, Ali. *The State, Bureaucracy, and Revolution in Modern Iran.* New York, NY: Praeger 1989.

Fearon, James D. and David Laitin. "Ethnicity, Insurgency, and Civil War." *American Political Science Review* 97, no. 1 (February 2003), 75–90.

Felgenhauer, Pavel. "Russian Railroad Troops Complete Mission in Abkhazia." *Eurasia Daily Monitor* 5, 146 (July 31, 2008), http://www.jamestown.org/single/?no_cache=1&tx_ttnews%5Btt_news%5D=33850 (accessed September 2, 2009).

Financial Times. "Georgia to Maintain Good Relations, Partnership with Iran." *Financial Times,* May 30, 2003.

———. "IMF: Armenia Needs Good Relations with Turkey to Further Boost Its Economy." *Financial Times,* July 21, 2005.

———. "Shevardnadze Says Georgia Intends to Step Up Relations with Iran." *Financial Times,* November 26, 2002.

————. "Turkey to Restore Relations with Armenia, Armenian TV Says." *Financial Times*, June 6, 2003.

————. "Turkey, Georgia, Improve Military Relations." *Financial Times*, June 26, 2000.

Freedom House. "Country Report: Armenia," *Freedom in the World Report*. Washington, D.C.: Freedom House, 2009, http://www.freedomhouse.org/template.cfm?page=22&year=2009 &country=7557 (accessed September 2, 2009).

————. "Country Report: Azerbaijan," *Freedom in the World Report*. Washington, D.C.: Freedom House, 2009, http://www.freedomhouse.org/template.cfm?page=22&country =7560&year=2009 (accessed September 2, 2009).

————. "Country Report: Georgia," *Freedom in the World Report*. Washington, D.C.: Freedom House, 2009, http://www.freedomhouse.org/template.cfm?page=22&year=2009 &country=7612 (accessed September 2, 2009).

————. "Freedom in the World 2009: Azerbaijan." Washington, D.C.: Freedom House, July 16, 2009, http://www.unhcr.org/refworld/docid/4a6452d2c.html (accessed August 19, 2009).

Friedman, Thomas L. *The World is Flat: A Brief History of the Twenty-First Century.* New York, NY: Farrar Straus & Giroux, 2005.

Fuller, Liz. "Nagorno-Karabkh: OSCE to Unveil New Peace Plan." Eurasianet.org, April 9, 2005, http://www.eurasianet.org/departments/insight/articles/pp040905.shtml (accessed May 23, 2009).

Gammer, Moshe, ed. *Ethno-Nationalism, Islam and the State in the Caucasus: Post Soviet Disorder.* New York, NY: Routledge, 2008.

Garsoïan, Nina. "The Emergence of Armenia." In *Armenian People from Ancient to Modern Times*, vol. I. Richard G. Hovannisian, ed. New York, NY: Palgrave Macmillan, 2004.

George, Alexander L. and Richard Smoke. *Deterrence in American Foreign Policy: Theory and Practice.* New York, NY: Columbia University Press, 1974.

George, Alexander L. *Bridging the Gap: Theory and Practice in Foreign Policy.* Washington, D.C.: U.S. Institute of Peace Press, 1998.

Georgia Update. "From Creeping to Sweeping Annexation: Implications of Russia's Establishment of Legal Links with Abkhazian & South Ossetia." Georgia Update, April 17, 2008, http://georgiaupdate.gov.ge/en/doc/10003586/20080417,%20From%20Creeping%20to %20Sweeping%20Annexation.pdf (accessed May 22, 2009).

Georgian Business Week. "Millennium Challenge Corporation Board Approves $295.3 Million Compact with Georgia." *Georgian Business Week*, August 16, 2005.

Gilpin, Robert. *War and Change in World Politics.* Cambridge: Cambridge University Press, 1983.

Glashatov, Oleg. "Azerbaijan Readies for a War for Karabakh. Would it Happen?" *Military Industrial Courier* (in Russian), UN Register of Conventional Arms.

Glassner, Ira Martin, and Chuck Fahrer. *Political Geography,* 3rd ed. Castleton, NY: Hamilton Printing Co., 2004.

GlobalSecurity.org. "The Shevardnadze Era." GlobalSecurity.org, http://www.globalsecurity.org/ military/world/georgia/politics-shevardnadze.htm (accessed July 1, 2009).

Goldman, Milton F. *Russia, the Eurasian Republics, and Central/Eastern Europe,* 11th ed. Dubuge, IA: McGraw-Hill, 2008.

Goltz, Thomas. *Azerbaijan Diary: A Rogue Reporter's Adventures in an Oil-Rich, War-Torn, Post-Soviet Republic.* New York, NY: M. E. Sharpe, 1998.

———. *Georgia Diary: A Chronicle of War and Political Chaos in the Post-Soviet Caucasus.* London: M. E. Sharpe, 2006.

Gorst, Isabel. "Georgia Ends Mutiny at Army Base." *Financial Times,* May 5, 2009, http://www.ft.com/cms/s/0/75c532b4-3951-11de-b82d-00144feabdc0.html (accessed May 29, 2009).

Green, Donald P., and Ian Shapiro. *Pathologies of Rational Choice Theory: A Critique of Applications in Political Science.* New Haven, CT: Yale University Press, 1996.

Grygiel, Jakub J. *Great Powers and Geopolitical Change.* Baltimore, MD: Johns Hopkins University Press, 2006.

Gül, Murat. "Russia and Azerbaijan: Relations after 1989." *Alternatives: Turkish Journal of International Relations* 7, no. 2 and 3 (Summer & Fall 2008): 47–66.

Gularidze, Tea. "Russian Company Seals Controversial Takeover of Tbilisi Electricity Distribution." *Civil Georgia,* August 2, 2003.

Harding, Luke. "Thousands Gather for Street Protests Against Georgia Presidents." *The Guardian,* April 9, 2009, http://www.guardian.co.uk/world/2009/apr/09/georgia-protests-mikheil-saakashvili (accessed September 2, 2009).

Hasanlı, Jamıl. *The Soviet-American Crisis Over Iranian Azerbaijan, 1941–1946.* Lanham, MD: Rowman & Littlefield Publishers, Inc., 2006.

Hill, Fiona, and Omar Taspinar. "Russia and Turkey in the Caucasus: Moving Together to Preserve the Status Quo?" *Russie.Nei.Visions* (January 2006), http://www.brookings.edu/views/papers/fellows/hilltaspinar_20060120.pdf (accessed May 22, 2009).

Høiris, Ole, and Sefa Martin Yurukel. *Contrasts and Solutions in the Caucasus.* Aarhus: Aarhus University Press, 1998.

Holoboff, Elaine M. "Bad Boys or Good Business?: Russia's Use of Oil as a Mechanism of Coercive Diplomacy." In *Strategic Coercion: Concepts and Cases.* Lawrence Freedman, ed. Oxford: Oxford University Press, 1998.

Houghton, David. "Reinvigorating the Study of Foreign Policy Decision-Making: Towards a Constructivist Approach." *Foreign Policy Analysis* 3 (January 2007): 24–45.

Hulse, Carl. "U.S. and Turkey Thwart Armenian Genocide Bill." *The New York Times,* October 26, 2007.

Human Rights Watch. *Azerbaijan: Seven Years of Conflict in Nagorno-Karabakh.* New York, NY: Human Rights Watch, 1994.

Humphreys, Macartan, Jeffrey Sachs, and Joseph E. Stiglitz. *Escaping the Resource Curse.* New York, NY: Columbia University Press, 2007.

ICG. "Nagorno-Karabakh: Risking War," *Europe Report N187.* Brussels, Belgium: International Crisis Group: November 14, 2007.

IMF. *World Economic Outlook, April 2009.* Washington, D.C.: International Monetary Fund, 2009, http://www.imf.org/external/pubs/ft/weo/2009/01/pdf/text.pdf (accessed September 2, 2009).

Info-Prod Research. "Efforts to Expand Georgia-Iran Relations." Info-Prod Research (Middle East) Ltd., May 1, 2001.

Ismail, Alman Mir. "Is the West Losing the Energy Game in the Caspian?" *CA-CI Analyst* (May 6, 2009), http://www.cacianalyst.org/?q=node/5100 (accessed May 12, 2009).

Ismayilov, Rovshan. "Azerbaijan and Iran: Dangerous Liaisons?" Eurasiaet.org, January 19, 2006, http://www.eurasianet.org/departments/insight/articles/eav011906a.shtml (accessed April 10, 2009).

ITAR-TASS. "There is Not Military Aspect in Armenia-Iran Ties: Leader." ITAR-TASS News
    Agency, March 14, 2002.
———. "Turkey-Georgia Relations an Example to Follow: Necdet." ITAR-TASS News
    Agency, November 9, 2001.
Jackson, Alexander. "The Military Balance in Nagorno-Karabakh." *Caucasus Review of
    International Affairs* 18 (January 19, 2009), http://cria-online.org/CU_-_file_-_article
    _-_sid_-_19.html (accessed September 2, 2009).
Jacob, Bercovitch. "A Neglected Relationship: Diasporas and Conflict Resolution." In *Diaspo-
    ras in Conflict: Peace-Makers or Peace-Wreckers?* Hazel Smith and Paul Stares, eds. Tokyo:
    United Nations University Press, 2007.
Jervis, Robert. "Cooperation under the Security Dilemma." *World Politics* 30, no. 4 (Janu-
    ary 1978): 167–214.
———. "From Balance to Concert: A Study in International Security Cooperation." *World
    Politics* 38, no. 1 (October 1985): 58–79.
Joffe, Josef. "Nato: Soldering On." *Time Magazine*, March 19, 2009, http://www.time.com/
    time/magazine/article/0,9171,1886470,00.html (accessed August 8, 2009).
Kandelaki, Giorgi. "Georgia's Rose Revolution: A Participant's Perspective." United States
    Institute of Peace, Special Report No. 167 (July 2006), http://www.usip.org/pubs/special-
    reports/sr167.html (accessed April 2, 2009).
Kasim, Kamer. "The Impact of the Armenian Diaspora in Turkey's Relations with Armenia."
    The Journal of Turkish Weekly (March 9, 2009), http://www.turkishweekly.net/print.asp?
    type=1&id=66480 (accessed April 20, 2009).
Kazanecki, Wojciech. "Géopolitique des Regions: Linkage between French Geopolitics and
    Regional Governance?" (CEEISA 6th Annual Conference, University of Wroclaw,
    May 2007), http://www.ceeisaconf.uni.wroc.pl/wordy/papers%202%20session/Kazanecki
    _CEEISA_Conference.doc (accessed April 10, 2009).
Khachatrian, Haroutiun. "Armenia Concentrates on Balancing Act Between Russia and Georgia."
    Eurasianet.org, November 8, 2006, http://www.eurasianet.org/departments/insight/articles/
    eav110806a.shtml (accessed May 20, 2009).
Kleveman, Lutz. *The New Great Game: Blood and Oil in Central Asia.* New York, NY: Atlantic
    Monthly Press, 2003.
Knight, Amy. "Zviad Gamsakhurdia." *Microsoft Encarta Online Encyclopedia 2009.*
Kramer, Andrew E. "Putin's Grasp of Energy Drives Russian Agenda." *The New York Times*,
    January 28, 2009, http://www.nytimes.com/2009/01/29/world/europe/29putin.html?
    _r=1&scp=2&sq=putin&st=cse (accessed January 28,2009).
Kramnik, IIya. "CSTO—Joining Forces in a Crisis." RIA Novosti, May 2, 2009, http://
    en.rian.ru/analysis/20090205/119991573 (accessed September 2, 2009).
Kucera, Joshua. "NATO: Bush's Support for Georgia, Ukraine is No Pose." Eurasianet.org,
    April 2, 2008, http://www.eurasianet.org/departments/insight/articles/eav040208.shtml
    (accessed May 14, 2009).
Lacoste, Yves. "La géopolitique et les rappprts de l'armée et de la nation." *Hérodote* 116,
    (La Découverte, 1er trimestre, 2005).
Lang, David Marshall. "Independent Georgia (1918–1921)." Excerpt from *A Modern History
    of Soviet Georgia*, David Marshall Lang. London: Weidenfeld and Nicolson, 1962, http://
    www.conflicts.rem33.com/images/Georgia/Lang_9a.htm (accessed May 21, 2009).
Lentz, Harris M. III. *Head of States and Governments: A Worldwide Encyclopedia of Over 2,300
    Leaders, 1945 through 1992.* Jefferson, NC: McFarland and Company, 1994.

Lepgold, Joseph and Miroslav Nincic, eds. *Being Useful: Policy Relevance and International Relations Theory*. Ann Arbor, MI: University of Michigan Press, 2000.

————. *Beyond the Ivory Tower: International Relations Theory and the Issue of Policy Relevance.* New York, NY: Columbia University Press, 2001.

Liberman, Peter. "The Spoils of Conquest." *International Security* 18, no. 2 (Fall 1993): 125–53.

————. *Does Conquest Pay?: The Exploitation of Occupied Industrial Societies.* Princeton, NJ: Princeton University Press, 1996.

Liklikadze, Koba. "Georgia: Funding Cuts May Jeopardise Army Recovery." *Institute for War and Peace Reporting* (February 13, 2009), http://www.unhcr.org/refworld/docid/499a6f22c .html (accessed July 6, 2009).

Lussac, Samuel. "The Baku-Tbilisi-Kars Railroad and Its Geopolitical Implications for the South Caucasus." *Caucasian Review of International Affairs* 2, no. 4 (Autumn 2008), http://cria-online.org/5_5.html (accessed May 20, 2009).

Lynch, Dov. "Shared Neighborhood or New Frontline? The Crossroads in Moldova." In *Russie.Nei.Visions 2006*, Thomas Gomart and Tatiana Kastueva-Jean, eds. Paris: IFRI, 2006.

Lyons, Terrence. "Diasporas and Homeland Conflict." (Workshop on "Contentious Politics," Washington, D.C., March 15, 2004).

MacFarlane, S. Neil. "The 'R' in BRICS: Is Russia an Emerging Power?" *International Affairs* 82, no. 1 (2006): 41–57.

Machiavelli, Niccolò, trans. Julia Conaway Bondanella and Peter Bondanella. *Discourses on Livy*. Oxford: Oxford University Press, 2003.

Mackinder, Halford John. "The Geographical Pivot of History (1904)." *The Geographical Journal* 170, no. 4 (December 1, 2004): 298–322.

Mahan, Alfred Thayer. *Influence of Sea Power Upon History*. Boston, MA: Little, Brown and Company, 1918.

Mahler, Vincent A., and Kunibert Raffer. *Dependency Approaches to International Political Economy: A Cross-National Study*. New York, NY: Columbia University Press, 1980.

Maisaia, Vakhtang. *The Caucasus-Caspian Regional and Energy Security Agendas—Past, Contemporary and Future Geopolitics: Views from Georgia*, 2nd ed. Brussels-Tbilisi, 2007.

Mamedov, Jasur. "Azerbaijan Flexes Military Muscles." *Institute for War and Peace Reporting* (July 19, 2007).

Manaseryan, Tatoul. "Diaspora: the Comparative Advantage for Armenia." Armenian International Policy Research Group (January 2004).

Mccauley, Martin. "Obituary: Zviad Gamsakhurdia." *The Independent*, February 25, 1994, http://www.independent.co.uk/news/people/obituary-zviad-gamsakhurdia-1396384.html (accessed June 30, 2009).

Meloyan, Rueben. "Opposition Leaders Reluctant to Back Ex-President." Radio Free Europe, November 19, 2007, http://www.armenialiberty.org/content/Article/1591618.html (accessed September 2, 2009).

Mendelson, Adam and Peter B. White, eds. "MEJ Author Pinar Ipek on Azerbaijan, Russia, and the World Energy Market." *MEI Bulletin* 60, no. I (March 2009).

Merry, Wayne. "Diplomacy and War in Karabakh: An Unofficial American Perspective," Central Asia—Caucasus Institute (October 25, 2006).

MGIMO. "Doctors Honoris Causa of MGIMO-University." Moscow State Institute of International Relations, http://english.mgimo.ru/index.php?Itemid=276&id=187 &option=com_content&task=view (accessed July 7, 2009).

Microsoft Encarta. "Eduard A. Shevardnadze." Microsoft Encarta Online Encyclopedia 2009.

Minasian, Sergey. "Azerbaijan Against RA and NKR: Military-Political Balance, Estimates of Military Capacities and Prospects of Development of Armed Forces." *Studies on Strategy and Security* (2007).

Minassian, Ter. "Enjeux, Les Armenians au 20e Siecle. Vingtieme Siecle." *Revue d'Histoire* 67 (July–September 2000).

Ministry of Foreign Affairs (Azerbaijan). "Information on Azerbaijan-NATO Cooperation." Ministry of Foreign Affairs, http://www.mfa.gov.az/eng/index.php?option=com_content&task=view&id=263&Itemid=1" (accessed January 31, 2010).

Ministry of Foreign Affairs (Georgia). "Chronology of Basic Events in EU-Georgia Relations." Ministry of Foreign Affairs, http://www.mfa.gov.ge/index.php?lang_id=ENG&sec_id=462 (accessed January 31, 2010).

———. "Information on NATO-Georgia Relations." Ministry of Foreign Affairs, http://www.mfa.gov.ge/index.php?sec_id=455&lang_id=ENG (accessed January 31, 2010).

———. "NATO Freedom Consolidation Act of 2006." Ministry of Foreign Affairs, http://www.mfa.gov.ge/index.php?lang_id=ENG&sec_id=454&info_id=9681 (accessed January 31, 2010).

———. "Relations Between Georgia and the United States of America." Ministry of Foreign Affairs, http://www.mfa.gov.ge/index.php?sec_id=268&lang_id=ENG (accessed January 31, 2010).

Minorities at Risk Project. "Chronology for Azerbaijanis in Iran." *Minorities at Risk Project*, 2004, http://www.unhcr.org/refworld/docid/469f38a21e.html (accessed 14 September 2009).

Mitra, Aaumya, et al., *The Caucasian Tiger: Sustaining Economic Growth in Armenia*. Washington, DC: The World Bank, 2007.

Morales, Waltrude Q. "The Useable Past: Historical Analogy in International Affairs." In *Proceedings, 1998–1999, The Florida Conference of Historians*. Will Benedicks, ed. The Florida Conference of Historians: 2000, http://fch.fiu.edu/FCH-1998/Morales-The%20Useable%20Past1-1998.htm (accessed May 30, 2009).

Morgenthau, Hans Joachim. *Politics Among Nations: The Struggle for Power and Peace*. New York, NY: Knopf, 1967.

Mowchan, John A. "The Militarization of the Collective Security Treaty Organization." *Center for Strategic Leadership* 6-09 (July 2009), http://www.csl.army.mil/usacsl/publications/IP_6_09_Militarization_of_the_CSTO.pdf (accessed September 2, 2009).

Mulvey, Stephen. "Profile: Ilham Aliyev." *British Broadcasting Corporation*, October 16, 2003, http://news.bbc.co.uk/2/hi/europe/3194422.stm (accessed July 7, 2009).

Nahaylo, Bohdan, and Victor Svoboda. *Soviet Disunion: A History of the Nationality Problem in the USSR*. New York, NY: Macmillan, 1990.

Nassibli, Nasib. "Azerbaijan: Oil and Politics in the Country's Future." In *Oil and Geopolitics in the Caspian Sea Region*. Michael P. Croissant and Bulent Aras, eds. Westport, CT: Praeger, 1999.

NATO. "NATO's Relations with Armenia." North Atlantic Treaty Organization, February 24, 2009, http://www.nato.int/issues/nato-armenia/index.html (accessed May 23, 2009).

Nodia, Ghia, and Alvaro Pinto Scholtbach, eds. *The Political Landscape of Georgia*. Delft: Eburon Academic Publishers, 2006.

Olcott, Martha Brill, and Marina Ottaway. "Challenge of Semi-Authoritarianism." *Carnegie Paper*, no. 7 (October 1999), http://www.carnegieendowment.org/PUBLICATIONS/INDEX.CFM?FA=VIEW&ID=142 (accessed May 18, 2009).

Oliker, Olga. *Russia's Chechen Wars 1994–2000: Lessons Learned from Urban Combat* (Santa Monica, CA: Rand, 2001).

Oruc, Saadet. "Armenia Wants Diplomatic Relations with Turkey . . . but What About Ankara?" *Turkish Daily News*, June 30, 2002, http://web.lexis-nexis.com (accessed July 18, 2006).

OSCE. "Facts and Figures." Organization for Security and Cooperation in Europe, http://www.osce.org/ (accessed September 2, 2009).

———. "Overview." OSCE Mission to Georgia, http://www.osce.org/georgia/13199.html (accessed May 22, 2009).

———. *OSCE Handbook.* Organization for Security and Cooperation in Europe, 2007, http://www.osce.org/publications/sg/2007/10/22286_952_en.pdf (accessed September 2, 2009).

Panossian, Razmik. *The Armenians: From Kings and Priests to Merchants and Commissars.* New York, NY: Columbia University Press, 2006.

Papava, Vladimer and Michael Tokmazishvili. "Becoming European: Georgia's Strategy for Joining the EU." *Power, Parties, and Political Development* (January/February 2006): 26–32.

Papava, Vladimir. "On the Essence of Economic Reforms in Georgia, or How European is the European Choice of Post-Revolution Georgia?" *TEPAV* 3, http://www.tepav.org.tr/karadeniz/kei.html (accessed May 23, 2009).

Parsons, Robert. "Caucasus: Georgia, Armenia Consider Options After Russia Pipeline Explosions." *Radio Free Europe*, February 1, 2006, http://www.rferl.org/content/article/1065318.html (accessed May 23, 2009).

Perlo-Freeman, S. and P. Stalenheim, "Military Expenditure in the South Caucasus and Central Asia," in A. J. K. Bailes et al., *Armament and Disarmament in the Caucasus and Central Asia*, SIPRI Policy Paper no. 3. SIPRI: Stockholm, 2003.

PfP. "'Rubezh 2008': The First Large-Scale CSTO Military Exercise." Partnership for Peace Information Management System, http://www.pims.org/news/2008/08/06/rubezh-2008-the-first-large-scale-csto-military-exercise (accessed April 10, 2009).

Pourchet, Georgeta. *Eurasia Rising: Democracy and Independence in the Post-Soviet Space.* Westport, CT: Praeger Security International, 2008.

Preobrazhensky, Konstantin. "South Ossetia: KGB Backyard in the Caucasus." *Central Asia-Caucasus Analyst* (March 11, 2009), http://www.cacianalyst.org/files/090311Analyst.pdf (accessed May 22, 2009).

President of Azerbaijan. "Biography." President of Azerbaijan, http://www.president.az/browse.php?sec_id=25 (accessed July 8, 2009).

President of Georgia. "Biography." President of Georgia, http://www.president.gov.ge/?l=E&m=1&sm=3 (accessed July 1, 2009).

President of the Republic of Armenia. "The First President of Armenia." The Official Site of the President of the Republic of Armenia, http://www.president.am/library/presidents/eng/?president=1 (accessed June 30, 2009)

Priego, Alberto. "NATO Cooperation Towards South Caucasus." *Caucasian Review of International Affairs* 2, no. 1 (Winter 2008), http://www.cria-online.org/2_7.html (accessed May 13, 2009).

PRS Group. "Azerbaijan Country Forecast," in *Political Risk Yearbook*. PRS Group Inc., 2007. http://www.prsgroup.com/

Rashid, Ahmed. *Taliban: Islam, Oil and the New Great Game in Central Asia.* London: I. B. Tarus, 2001.

Rau, Johannes. *The Nagorno-Karabakh Conflict Between Armenia and Azerbaijan: A Brief Historical Outline.* Berlin: Verlag Dr. Köster, 2008.

Redgate, Anne E. *The Armenians.* Oxford: Blackwell, 1998.

Regnum News Agency. "Georgia is Becoming Hostage to Azeri-Turkish Alliance: Interview with Pavel Chobanyan." Regnum News Agency, July 10, 2006, http://www.gab-bn.com/juillet_06/Ge1-%20Georgia%20is%20becoming%20hostage%20to%20Azeri%20Turkish%20alliance.pdf (accessed May 21, 2009).

RFE. "Russian-led CSTO Grouping Adds Military Dimension." Radio Free Europe, February 4, 2009, http://www.rferl.org/Content/Rapid_Reaction_Force_Adds_Military_Dimension%20_To_CSTO/1379324.html (accessed January 31, 2010).

———. "Caucasus: Georgia, Armenia Consider Options After Russia Pipeline Explosions." Radio Free Europe, February 1, 2006, http://www.rferl.org/content/article/1065318.html (accessed May 21, 2009).

———. "Could Russian Pressure Leave Georgia Cold?" Radio Free Europe, September 16, 2008, http://www.rferl.org/content/Russian_Pressure_Georgia_Cold/1200478.html (accessed May 21, 2009).

———. "Nagorno-Karabakh: Timeline Of The Long Road To Peace." Radio Free Europe, February 10, 2006, http://www.rferl.org/content/article/1065626.html (accessed April 10, 2009).

RIA Novosti. "First Stage of Work on Iran-Armenia Gas Pipeline Project to Begin Soon." RIA Novosti, December 26, 2000.

———. "Iran, Armenia Agree to Strengthen Bilateral Cooperation in the Sphere of Regional Security." RIA Novosti, December 26, 2001.

———. "Russia, Armenia to Set Up Joint Air Defense Network." RIA Novosti, February 13, 2009, http://en.rian.ru/russia/20090213/120124464.html (accessed May 24, 2009).

———. "Azerbaijan Votes to Remove Presidential Term Limits." RIA Novosti, March 19, 2009, http://en.rian.ru/world/20090319/120633154.html (accessed September 2, 2009).

Ritter, Laurence. "Getting Ready for a Political Come-Back? Levon Ter Petrosian Breaks His Silence." *Caucaz Europenews*, December 13, 2004, http://www.caucaz.com/home_eng/breve_contenu.php?id=88 (accessed May 24, 2009).

Rosbalt. "Mikhail Saakashvili: Armenia Can Help Georgia Repair Relations with Russia." Eurasia21.com, March 12, 2004, http://www.eurasia21.com/cgi-data/news/files/149.shtml (accessed May 21, 2009).

Sabahi, Farian and Daniel Warner, eds. *The OSCE and the Multiple Challenges of Transition.* Burlington, VT: Ashgate Publishing Co., 2004.

Sadri, Houman A. and Nathan L. Burns. "Geopolitics of Oil and Energy in Central Asia." In Reuel R. Hanks, ed. *Handbook of Central Asian Politics.* Forthcoming from Routledge Press, London and New York, 2010.

———. "The Caspian Region: Arena for Clashing Civilizations?" In D. Katsy, ed. *The Caspian Sea Region: Arena for Clashing Civilizations.* St. Petersburg, Russia: St. Petersburg State University Press, 2008.

Sadri, Houman and Nader Entessar, "Iranian-Azeri Dynamic Relations: Conflict & Cooperation in Southern Caucasus," *Rivista di Studi Politici Internazionali* 76, no. 1 [*Review of International Political Studies*, Rome, Italy], in English (Spring 2009): 59–79.

Sahahi, Farian. "Oil Diplomacy in the Caspian: The Rift Between Iran and Azerbaijan in Summer 2001." In *The OSCE and the Multiple Challenges of Transition.* Farian Sabahi and Daniel Warner, eds. Burlington, VT: Ashgate Publishing Co., 2004.

Sadri, Houman A. *Revolutionary States, Leaders, and Foreign Relations*. Westport, CT: Greenwood Publishing Group, 1997.

Sargsayan, Gevorg, Ani Balabanyan, and Denzel Hankinson. *From Crisis to Stability in the Armenian Power Sector: Lessons Learned from Armenia's Energy Reform Experience*. Washington, DC: The World Bank, 2006.

Schaffer, Brenda. *Borders and Brethren: Iran and the Challenge of Azerbaijani Identity*. Cambridge, MA: MIT Press, 2002.

Schleifer, Yigal. "Turkey: Caucasus Crisis Leaves Ankara Torn Between US and Russia." Eurasianet.org, September 11, 2008, http://www.eurasianet.org/departments/insight/articles/eav091108.shtml (accessed May 22, 2009).

Seely, Robert. *Russo-Chechen Conflict, 1800–2000: A Deadly Embrace*. Portland, OR: Frank Cass, 2001.

Shaffer, Brenda. *Partners in Need: The Strategic Relationship of Russia and Iran*. Washington, DC: The Washington Institute for Near East Policy, 2001.

Shanker, Thom and Mark Landner. "Pentagon Checks Arsenal in Race for Nuclear Treaty." *The New York Times*. September 8, 2009, http://www.nytimes.com/2009/09/09/world/09arms.html (accessed September 13, 2009).

Shain, Yossi. "Ethnic Diasporas and US Foreign Policy." *Political Science Quarterly* 109, no. 1 (January 2005): 811–841.

Singer, Hans Wolfgang. *The Economic North-South Divide: Six Decades of Unequal Development*. Northhampton, MA: Edward Elgar Publishing, 2001.

SIPRI. SIPRI Military Expenditure Database, http://milexdata.sipri.org/result.php4 (accessed August 16, 2009).

———. *SIPRI Yearbook 2008: Armaments, Disarmament and International Security*. Oxford: Oxford University Press, 2008.

Socor, Vladimir. "Gazprom's 'Pure Commerce' in Georgia." *Eurasia Daily Monitor* 3, no. 208 (November 9, 2006), http://www.jamestown.org/single/?no_cache=1&tx_ttnews%5Btt_news%5D=32215 (accessed May 21, 2009).

———. "Moscow Pleased with OSCE's Response to Missile Drop on Georgia." *Eurasian Monitor* 4 (September 11, 2007), http://www.jamestown.org/single/?no_cache=1&tx_ttnews%5Btt_news%5D=32986 (accessed January 31, 2010).

SOFAZ. "Goals and Objectives." State Oil Fund of the Republic of Azerbaijan, http://www.oilfund.az/en/content/3 (accessed September 2, 2009).

Sonn, Tamara. *A Brief History of Islam*. Oxford: Blackwell Publishing, 2004.

Souleimanov, Emil and Ondrej Ditrych. "Iran and Azerbaijan: A Contested Neighborhood." *Middle East Policy* XIV, no. 2 (Summer 2007): 101–116.

Soykok, Jan. "Armenian Tragedy, But Who is Responsible?" *Journal of Turkish Weekly* (January 6, 2005), http://www.turkishweekly.net/comments.php/comments.php?id=107 (accessed April 20, 2009).

Spykman, Nicholas J. *The Geography of Peace*. New York, NY: Harcourt & Brace, 1944.

Stier, Ken. "Study Highlights Inefficiencies and Evils of Armenian Emigration." Eurasianet.org, April 16, 2002, http://www.eurasianet.org/departments/business/articles/eav041602_pr.shtml (accessed April 21, 2009).

Suny, Ronald. "Eastern Armenians Under Tsarist Rule." In *The Armenian People from Ancient to Modern Times*, vol. II. Richard Hovannisian, ed. New York, NY: St. Martin's Press, 1997.

Swietochowski, Tadeusz. *Russia and Azerbaijan: A Borderland in Transition* (New York, NY: Columbia University Press, 1995.

Tcholakian, Lara. "Armenian Diaspora Looks for Presidential Vote to Promote Stable Growth." Eurasianet.org, February 18, 2003, http://www.eurasianet.org/departments/business/articles/eav021803_pr.shtml (accessed May 23, 2009).

The Middle East Journal. "Chronology: Jan. 16, 2008–April 15, 2008." *The Middle East Journal 62*, no. 3 (Summer 2008).

———. "Chronology: October 16, 2007–January 15, 2008." *The Middle East Journal 62* no. 2 (Spring 2008), http://find.galegroup.com/itx/start.do?prodId=ITOF (accessed December 18, 2008).

———. "Chronology: July 16, 2007–October 15, 2007." *The Middle East Journal 62*, no. 1 (Winter 2008), http://find.galegroup.com/itx/start.do?prodId=ITOF (accessed December 18, 2008).

———. "Chronology: Oct 16, 2006–January 15, 2007." *The Middle East Journal 61*, no. 2 (Spring 2007), http://find.galegroup.com/itx/start.do?prodId=ITOF (accessed December 18, 2009).

———. "Chronology: April 16, 2006–July 15, 2006." *The Middle East Journal 60*, no. 4 (Autumn 2006), http://find.galegroup.com/itx/start.do?prodId=ITOF (accessed December 18, 2008).

———. "Chronology: January 16, 2006–April 15, 2006." *The Middle East Journal 60*, no. 3 (Summer 2006), http://find.galegroup.com/itx/start.do?prodId=ITOF (accessed December 18, 2008).

The New York Times. "Europe: Armenia: Fraud Charged After Election." *The New York Times*, March 7, 2003, http://www.nytimes.com/2003/03/07/world/world-briefing-europe-armenia-fraud-charged-after-election.html (accessed September 3, 2009).

Time Magazine. "Southern Corruption." *Time Magazine*, December 3, 1973, http://www.time.com/time/magazine/article/0,9171,908227,00.html (accessed July 6, 2009).

Today.az. "Azerbaijan Shows MIG-29 Fighter Jets." Today.az, March 29, 2007. www.today.az/news/politics/38475.html (accessed September 2, 2009).

Today's Zaman. "An Interview with Mesrob II, the 84th Patriarch of Turkey's Armenian Orthodox Community." *Today's Zaman*, September 17, 2007.

———. "Its up to Turkey, Armenia to Resolve History Row, Says Obama." *Today's Zaman*, April 6, 2009, http://www.todayszaman.com/tz-web/detaylar.do?load=detay&link=171673 (accessed May 24, 2009).

Tölölyan, Khachig. "The Armenian Diaspora as a Transnational Actor and as a Potential Contributor to Conflict Resolution."*Diaspora: Journal of Transnational Studies* (2006).

Trenin, Dmitri. "Russia and Central Asia: Interests, Policies, and Prospects." In *Central Asia: Views from Washington, Moscow, and Beijing*, Eugene Rumer, Dimitri Trenin, and Huasheng Zhao. New York, NY: M. E. Sharpe 2007.

UN News Centre. "Armenia and Azerbaijan of Views on Nagorno-Karabakh During UN Debate." *US News Centre*, October 30, 2007, http://www.un.org/apps/news/story.asp?NewsID=24169 (accessed September 2, 2009).

UN Security Council. "Georgia-Russia Historical Chronology." UN Security Council Report, August 27, 2008, http://www.securitycouncilreport.org/site/c.glKWLeMTIsG/b.2703511/ (accessed November 26, 2008).

UNDP. "Study of Economic Relations Between Georgia and Armenia: The Development of Regional Trade Related Growth in Samtskhe-Javakheti." United Nations Development Programme, May 13, 2008, http://undp.org.ge/new/files/24_248_868263_cbc-eng.pdf (accessed May 21, 2009).

US Department of State. "Georgia: Security Assistance." Bureau of Political-Military Affairs, October 20, 2008, http://www.state.gov/t/pm/64766.htm (accessed January 31, 2010).

Vasquez, John A., ed. *What Do We Know About War?* Lanham, MD: Rowman & Littlefield, 2000.

Vignansky, Mikhail. "Georgia Opposition Vow to Topple Saakashvili." *Institute for War and Peace Reporting* (March 13, 2009), http://www.unhcr.org/refworld/docid/49c0ae622.html (accessed August 24, 2009).

Walker, Christopher. *Armenia: The Survival of a Nation*, 2nd ed. New York, NY: St. Martin's Press, 1990.

Walker, Savannah Waring. "World Briefing." *New York Times*, September 27, 2000.

Walt, Stephen M. "Rigor or Rigor Mortis? Rational Choice and Security Studies." *International Security* 23, no. 4 (Spring 1999): 5–48.

Walt, Stephen M. *The Origins of Alliances*. Ithaca, NY: Cornell University Press, 1990.

Wheatley, Jonathan. *Georgia from National Awakening to Rose Revolution: Delayed Transition in the Former Soviet Union*. Burlington, VT: Ashgate Publishing, 2005.

World Bank. "Country Brief 2008: Azerbaijan." World Bank, http://web.worldbank.org/WBSITE/EXTERNAL/COUNTRIES/ECAEXT/AZERBAIJANEXTN/0,,menuPK:301923-pagePK:141132-piPK:141107-theSitePK:301914,00.html (accessed January 5, 2009).

Zakaria, Fareed. *From Wealth to Power: The Unusual Origins of America's World Role*. Princeton, NJ: Princeton University Press, 1999.

Zürcher, Christoph. *The Post-Soviet Wars: Rebellion, Ethnic Conflict, and the Nationhood in the Caucasus*. New York, NY: New York University Press, 2007.

Index

About the Author

HOUMAN A. SADRI earned a doctorate degree from the University of Virginia in 1993 and completed a postdoctorate fellowship at the Hoover Institute on War, Revolution, and Peace at the Stanford University in 1997. He is a tenured Associate Professor at the Political Science Department of the University of Central Florida. Dr. Sadri is the author of two books, which have received excellent reviews. He also has two more forthcoming books. Moreover, he has published several book chapters and numerous peer-reviewed articles in academic journals, encyclopedias, and periodicals. Sadri's research is supported by a variety of grants and fellowships from both public and private institutions including: the U.S. State Department, Moscow State Institute of International Relation (MGIMO), Fulbright Program, International Research & Exchanges Board (IREX), International Studies Association (ISA), Russian International Studies Program (RISA), Rotary International, and Turkish Ministry of Foreign Affairs, to name a few. Dr. Sadri is a frequent visitor to the Caspian Sea region states from the Caucasus to Central Asia, where he conducts research for his publications.